Conversations with Jonathan Lethem

Literary Conversations Series
Peggy Whitman Prenshaw
General Editor

Conversations with Jonathan Lethem

Edited by Jaime Clarke

University Press of Mississippi   Jackson

www.upress.state.ms.us

The University Press of Mississippi is a member of the Association of American University Presses.

Copyright © 2011 by University Press of Mississippi
All rights reserved
Manufactured in the United States of America

First printing 2011

Library of Congress Cataloging-in-Publication Data

Lethem, Jonathan.
  Conversations with Jonathan Lethem / edited by Jaime Clarke.
      p. cm. — (Literary conversations series)
  Includes index.
  ISBN 978-1-60473-963-3 (cloth : alk. paper) — ISBN 978-1-60473-964-0
(ebk.) — ISBN 978-1-60473-972-5 (pbk.)
1. Lethem, Jonathan—Interviews. 2. Authors, American—20th
century—Interviews. I. Title.
  PS3562.E8544Z46 2011
  813'.54—dc22
  [B]   2010045966

British Library Cataloging-in-Publication Data available

Books by Jonathan Lethem

Gun, with Occasional Music. New York: Harcourt Brace, 1994.

Amnesia Moon. New York: Harcourt Brace, 1995.

The Wall of the Sky, the Wall of the Eye. New York: Harcourt Brace, 1996.

As She Climbed Across the Table. New York: Doubleday, 1997.

Girl in Landscape. New York: Doubleday, 1998.

Motherless Brooklyn. New York: Doubleday, 1999.

ed., with Carter Scholz, *Kafka Americana.* Burton, MI: Subterranean Press, 1999.

This Shape We're In. San Francisco: McSweeney's, 2000.

ed. *The Vintage Book of Amnesia: An Anthology of Writing on the Subject of Memory Loss.* New York: Vintage, 2000.

ed. *Da Capo Best Music Writing 2002: The Year's Finest Writing on Rock, Pop, Jazz, Country & More.* Boston: Da Capo, 2002.

The Fortress of Solitude. New York: Doubleday, 2003.

Men and Cartoons. New York: Doubleday, 2004.

The Disappointment Artist. New York: Doubleday, 2005.

Believenicks!: The Year We Wrote a Book About the Mets, with Christopher Sorrentino, as by Ivan Felt and Harris Conklin. New York: Doubleday, 2005.

How We Got Insipid. Burton, MI: Subterranean Press, 2006.

You Don't Love Me Yet. New York: Doubleday, 2007.

Omega: The Unknown. New York: Marvel Comics, 2008.

Chronic City. New York: Doubleday, 2009.

Deep Focus #1: They Live. New York: Soft Skull Press, 2010.

Talking Heads' Fear of Music. New York: Continuum, 2011.

Contents

Introduction

My first memory of Jonathan Lethem is from a literary event at Joe's Pub in New York City, circa the late 1990s: in being introduced to the stage, the speaker, who had known Lethem from his days living in Berkeley, told an amusing story about picking Lethem up for some sort of doings, only to be made to wait while Lethem finished up a piece of writing he was working on. As applause brought Lethem to the stage, he shuffled some paper and remarked, "Sorry, I didn't catch most of that, I was just working on the ending of a new story." That Lethem's prolificacy was at the heart of this joke was lost on me until I undertook interviewing him for *Post Road*, a literary magazine I cofounded that same year with some friends from Bennington College. I simply thought it was a jest about the writer as Preoccupied Citizen, always dreaming up fictional landscapes and peopling them with characters that represented the best and worst of humanity. I mention this memory not to draw attention away from the subject and reposition the footlights in my direction, as only the worst introductions do, but to intimate that the work of Jonathan Lethem is experiential at its root, not just the old saw about how the writer's life informs his work—a trope that in Lethem's case is the not-so-secret decoder ring to a further understanding of his work; his experiences don't just inform, the very themes at the core of his work are burnished by his personal experiences—but also how we the reader encounter the works both as individual, encapsulated narratives and as an emerging body of work.

After my initiation at Joe's Pub, I was soon to discover what Lethem's strident fan base already knew: that he was by the late 1990s the author of five novels and a collection of short stories, no mean feat for someone just south of forty. Lethem's bibliography, when I first encountered him, was comprised of *Gun, with Occasional Music* (Harcourt Brace, 1994), *Amnesia Moon* (Harcourt Brace, 1995), *The Wall of the Sky, the Wall of the Eye* (Harcourt Brace, 1996), *As She Climbed Across the Table* (Harcourt Brace, 1997), *Girl in Landscape* (Doubleday, 1998), and *Motherless Brooklyn* (Doubleday, 1998). I aimed to experience the texts in the order they were written (or at least published) in order to divine their meaning and to follow the assumed arc to prep for my interview, an assumption and course of study so wide of the mark as to border on criminal foolishness as I quickly learned as I began to turn the pages of Lethem's work. (It was with some amusement that Lethem revealed the same strategy in his essay collection-cum-memoir *The Disappointment Artist* for reading the entire works of Philip K. Dick.)

The arc was a cosmic zigzag: *Gun, with Occasional Music* propels the reader down the rabbit hole and into the dystopian world of Conrad Metcalf, Delia Limetree, Theodore Twostrand, and other characters with Pynchonian names. Did I mention the highly evolved, gun-toting kangaroo (you read that right) named Joey Castle? Lethem's ambition to marry the crime novel with science fiction tripped the sanctimonious alarm bells my newly-minted MFA had hard-wired into my aesthetic sense, and I read *Gun* without feeling like I understood it and made for *Amnesia Moon*, another dystopia that plainly read to me like science fiction (even though I'd never read any science fiction). More alarm bells, precipitating an inherent loathing for genre. An impulse to jump forward to *Motherless Brooklyn*, the novel that had brought Lethem recent raves and a wider audience (including my attendance at Joe's Pub) is quashed. I would stay the course. The main character in *Amnesia Moon* is called Chaos, but sometimes Everett Moon, depending. There's apocalypse, messiahs, green fogs, and a luck-based social system, among other ingenuities. I begin to cotton to Lethem's sense of irony, and to pick up the theme of loneliness that seems to pervade his work. The short story collection, *The Wall of the Sky, the Wall of the Eye* is unlike the Raymond Carver and Alice Munro stories I'd been reading, though the wild experimentation is dazzling. The premise of the stories are so outlandish they beg you not to take them seriously (basketball players who are assigned exosuits that grant them the powers of historical basketball legends; a prison built out of bricks made from the hardened criminals sent for incarceration, etc.), but upon closer examination the reader senses a thematic thread, that of human suffering, a theme my Fitzeraldian and Hemingwayesque sensibility (which begins to feel quotidian) can grasp. By the time I crack the spine of *As She Climbed Across the Table*, the fact that one of the main characters is a black hole named Lack—and that the novel is a love story between Lack and a particle physicist named Alice Coombs (love triangle, really, when you include the narrator)—is simply par for the Lethem-designed course. As are the hermaphroditic Archbuilders in *Girl in Landscape*, Lethem's paean to the Western. *Motherless Brooklyn*, a noirish detective story featuring a Tourettec narrator, Lionel Essrog, feels like realism in comparison.

Still, as I contemplate the *Post Road* interview, I'm stuck on genre. I can't get over it, can't see past it. I'm too sophisticated a reader to take Lethem's work seriously. I want to be more than entertained, as impressed with the author's imagination as I am. I conduct the interview, ask some pertinent questions that mostly don't miss the mark, learn in the process that Lethem is a tremendously patient and good person and an engaging conversationalist.

That my prejudice toward genre had closed me off to a fuller understanding of Jonathan's early work occurs to me only as I begin to collect the interviews for this volume, by which time I'd read *The Fortress of Solitude*, *You Don't Love Me Yet*, and *Chronic City*, which reviewers sometimes condescendingly refer to as his more realist novels, conveniently overlooking the fact that the novels are full of magic rings and space-orbiting girlfriends and hotels for dogs, etc. And it quickly becomes apparent that he's been fighting the fight against being labeled a genre writer from the very beginning. In fact, the very first question of the very first interview in this volume, conducted by Fiona Kelleghan for *Science Fiction Studies* in 1997, is the question Jonathan will spend his life answering:

FK: Your books don't appear to be marketed specifically as science fiction. So what I want you to do is to reassure me that you're not going to abandon science fiction, that you do love it, you're based in sf, your roots and influences are sf.

JL: I don't think I'm going to give you the blanket reassurance that you're asking for, because for me the question isn't as simple as that. I don't think I'll ever abandon sf to the extent that I ever was in a position to abandon it, if that reply makes sense. To me sf's a description that doesn't completely work. As I experience it, I've always been a writer who was absorbed in and obsessed with science fiction, and I will continue to be that kind of a writer. I have projects in mind that are more and less like science fiction than some of the projects I've already written. What I can promise is that I won't ever betray my own sense of the complexity of that question and suddenly pretend to have nothing to do with science fiction. It wouldn't make any sense. The work wouldn't be coherent if I insisted that it be read in ignorance of that context or if I tried to reduce the degree to which the work was engaged with that tradition. But it's also engaged with other sources and other realms and other traditions. It's also frustrating for me to accept the conditions and deprivations associated with a career exclusively in science fiction. I've been very adamant that I not allow myself to be pigeonholed in the larger operations of the publishing industry and the bookselling industry.

Over the course of these interviews, Jonathan dispenses with this question repeatedly and we hear how his thinking about genre and its influence on his writing evolves:

JL: I think that I have a propensity or weakness for writing meta-fictionally about genre. All of my stories tend to be, at one level, interrogations of the genre they inhabit. Since most of my work is fantastic in some sense, I'm usually asking questions at some level, often subconsciously or automatically, about what happens to a given story when a fantastic element intrudes into it, and this becomes a parallel interrogation into the question of what happens to a human existence when fantastic elements intrude. (*Science Fiction Studies*, 1998)

JL: [G]enres are sweetly pathetic confessions of adolescent longings. I mean, the only really obedient mystery novels or science fiction novels that don't somehow write themselves out of the genre, but instead fulfill it completely, are diagnosable as, you know, adolescent yearnings cloaked in various forms. And I mean, I've often argued that science fiction isn't a genre. There isn't a genre there. When you look at it closely it disappears. But it's sort of a nest of impulses and tendencies and borrowings from other, from literary genres that I think do have that deep generic structure. (Silverblatt, 1999)

JL: My writing is only just beginning to grow beyond the obsessive need to reach for those [genre] touchstones. I'll probably never outgrow it completely. Which is probably about the time to point out that I'm almost always (half-consciously) hiding one apparent "genre" under another, or under several. (*Paradoxa*, 2001)

JL: Things get really confusing when you bring in the word *genre* as if everyone understands what it means. In my view, the words which name bookstore sections (and reviewing and publishing categories) describe clusters of genres—and that includes the bookstore section called "fiction" or "literature." Novels obedient and disobedient to the conventions of various definable and specific genres like "the campus novel," "the bildungsroman," "the hard-boiled detective novel," "the family romance," "the epic quest," "the dystopian social novel," "the paranoid noir," "the gothic tale," "the epistolary romance," "the ghost story," and many others nestle within those big, broad, and nearly meaningless (meaningless, anyway, within any really interesting critical or "literary" conversation) categories like mystery or fiction or science fiction or literature or romance. But I'm pontificating. But your question invited me to pontificate. But I'm not really liking hearing myself pontificate. So I'll take the easy out: I'm personally not much interested in these dissections anymore. Taxonomy thrives on dead subjects. I'm always more thrilled by fiction which is disobedient to the genre conventions with which it engages, and by fiction which engages simultaneously with more than one genre or mode or set of expectations. And for me the material always dictates form. Ever more so as I've grown as a writer. (*Post Road*, 2002)

JL: I've always been uninterested in boundaries or quarantines between tastes and types, between mediums and genres. It's a form of autism, perhaps. I've never felt I had to pick from among *these* things and renounce *those others*. Good stuff's found across the spectrum . . . I don't try to cultivate any genre of writing in myself. I write what I urgently need to write at the time. What I try to cultivate in myself is the permission to do anything I can think of. (*The Paris Review*, 2003)

JL: What becomes exasperating is the routine assertion that when, for instance, George Orwell produces *1984* or Don DeLillo produces *Ratner's Star*—or any one of hundreds of other examples—they were doing something categorically different from the activities of the [genre] writers under quarantine. Oh, no, the cry arises: That's real writing! Please don't sully it with this déclassé association. Well, if every admirable result from setting a story in the future, or from using images of the fantastic, or extrapolative concepts, isn't science fiction—because it's too good—then all that's left to represent the label are the failed attempts to use those motifs. So, of course, the genre is contemptible. In my opinion there's no meaningful critical borderline at all, and I don't think there has been for a terribly long time. (*The Missouri Review*, 2006)

Jonathan's genre burden is best explained away, for those who want to hear it, by a simple statement he gave in our *Post Road* interview: "I'm responding to individual writers always, whole genres never." One writer in particular, as we'll see as we trip through the experiences that form the spine of the body of his work, is as important to Jonathan's work as the experiences that led to creating it.

Growing Up on Dean Street

As identified as Jonathan is to one particular landscape, Brooklyn generally and Dean Street in Boerum Hill specifically, he has led an uncharacteristically nomadic life. The characters in his work are often outsiders, or made to feel that way, and one comes to learn from these interviews that Jonathan himself, almost from the start, was imbued with an outsider's perspective. He was the rare white kid in his neighborhood, and in his school, made to negotiate his immediate circumstances daily; his parents were bohemians whose creative lifestyle lent Jonathan's childhood a protective nimbus, but also enmeshed him early into the world of adults so that he toed the water of childhood and adulthood simultaneously.

JL: I inherited a skepticism. My parents were war-resisters, and I grew up, I came to consciousness in the early seventies, during Watergate, essentially, so as with my relativism, it's a ground I stand on, that powerful skepticism. (*Science Fiction Studies*, 1998)

JL: The first third of my life was spent at political demonstrations, shouting my lungs hoarse. It was as much a part of my existence as having a holiday off from school. Those were my holidays. That's how I visited different cities, that's how I met adults besides my parents. I was a protester by birthright. I put in my time before I could conceive that the world wasn't being transformed by the people around me, my parents' generation. When you're in the center of demonstrations, you believe. My life *was* a demonstration. I was sent to public school in impoverished neighborhoods on principle. The day-care center on the corner of Nevins and Atlantic, in Brooklyn; I was there on its opening day, and I understood it as something that our protests at City Hall, the years before, had produced. I stood at the feet of police horses, holding a sign for day care, and then was there the first day it opened. I lived the belief that private school was anti-American. Can you possibly understand? It's personal. It's there in my work. (*The Paris Review*, 2003)

JL: [I came] of age in the Watergate era, when our society was explicitly broken. My parents were political radicals. The Vietnam War and Watergate obsessed them. I felt that I lived in a broken land. New York City was itself a broken place, where loss was manifest. Everything about this world I grew up in evoked the idea that there had been a great and complete and glorified past and now there was a ruined present and we were living in the shambles of something formerly great. (Sarah Anne Johnson, 2005)

JL: I had an unusual head start as an artist, generally, which is that I grew up in a painter's household. My father was and still is a painter and a lot of my parents' friends were his students or colleagues, and so this activity—specifically, going into the studio every day and trying to make paintings—seemed normal to me. It was just everyday, and something that I could aspire to, but it wasn't esoteric; it wasn't a remote possibility, it was something very everyday and available. I can't remember a time when I didn't think I was going to be an artist of some kind. Specifically, at the beginning, I thought I would paint too, and this was different, I learned, from the way most writers or artists grow up. They're usually in families where even if making art is regarded as an interesting possibility, it's somewhat esoteric, seen as impractical or unlikely. For me, it was inevitable. In fact, it would have been very strange, I think, for my parents if I hadn't been creative in some way. My brother grew up to be a graphic designer and my sister's a photographer, so I fell the furthest from the tree by switching to writing. But even that was in the ballpark, because my parents were very literate. My father's painting itself is very narratively based, full of symbols and at times even language—some of his styles include words on the canvas.

My mother was a big reader and a great talker, very dynamic. You've mentioned my talent for recall—well, she was famous for her memory, and memory is a real novelist's gift. I think it's the most important natural gift I inherited, her capacity for recall—not in a photographic sense, not a pure, scientifically accurate recall, but a recall that centers on an interest in emotional situations, conversations, language, affect, people's styles. She was socially brilliant; a great talker, raconteur, and joke-teller. I grew up in a house full of anecdotes and descriptions of friends—everyone had a nickname. We'd savor how different friends of the family, or relatives, were great characters. We shared an instinctive narrative curiosity. I think if my mother had lived, she might have turned out a writer. Certainly a lot of her friends thought of her as a kind of proto-writer, even though she didn't write anything. But she was so verbal, and so interested in stories, that people expected she would do that. Too, her books were available to me, and her love of reading was imparted to me very early on. I grew up in a house where writing was a very accessible ambition to latch onto. (*The Missouri Review*, 2006)

Loss of Mother

The loss of a parent, especially during one's formative years, is an obvious influence not only on personality, but also shapes to some degree the course of the lives of those left living. The death of Jonathan's mother at age fourteen had a sudden and lasting impact on him, and while he told Michael Silverblatt in a 1999 interview for *Motherless Brooklyn* that "I've written about fathers and sons obsessively," this can be seen as another not contradictory manifestation of Jonathan's simple and poignant admission in an essay in *The Disappointment Artist*: "I find myself speaking about my mother's death everywhere I go in this world."

JL: My mother died when I was fourteen. She began to be ill when I was eleven, in and out of hospitals and having brain surgery. It was a loss that occurred in slow motion, so that I got to think about as it was going on. I don't know if that's easier or harder for a kid to go through, but whichever it was, it was definitely not a sudden, sharp loss that could be isolated and denied to then be contemplated later. It was something to dwell on as it was unfolding. I had to participate in losing my mother over a period of years. That's a big experience. In my early work there are metaphorical versions of incomplete families, incomplete tribes, and incomplete worlds, even before I start writing directly about motherless-ness. (Sarah Anne Johnson, 2005)

JL: [F]or my fourteenth birthday, the last birthday while she was alive, my mother gave me a manual typewriter. She sensed my desire to write and gave me this gift. Within a year she was dead, and I had begun, at fifteen, during summer vacation, a novel, a 125-page manuscript that I typed on torn-out notebook pages with blue lines and hanging chads along the edge. I wasn't concerned with quality—I was just impressed with myself for typing 125 pages of anything at fifteen. By then, writing was the only thing I seriously wanted to do. Yet I was still playing the role of the art student, because it was such an appealing role, and because that same year, the year I'd turned fourteen and my mother died, I'd gotten in to the High School of Music and Art in New York, which is the official school for little art prodigies to attend. I was still painting by the time I got to college four years later. It was only then, at eighteen or nineteen, at school in Vermont, that I threw over the painting completely, and said, "Okay, I'm a writer." I came out of hiding. Up to then I'd been furtive about that identity, though I had a typewriter and my room was lined with books. (*The Missouri Review*, 2006)

Bennington College

Jonathan left Bennington short after enrolling, for reasons he enumerates in these interviews. His brief tenure at Bennington, as well as his subsequent flight to the shores of California, as far west continentally as one can flee from the Green Mountain State, helped him to define himself at an early age, and forced him to recognize some personal truths not readily evident living on Dean Street.

JL: My experience there was overwhelming, mostly having to do with a collision with the realities of class—my parents' bohemian milieu had kept me from understanding, even a little, that we were poor . . . It's an endlessly fascinating subject for me—the oddity of being raised in a hipster fog where intellectualism and cultural access obscured poverty so completely it became a kind of privilege.

Partly a New York experience, and partly a sixties-seventies thing. I thought I was one of the chosen ones. But at Bennington that was all demolished by an encounter with the fact of real privilege. I couldn't have articulated this at the time, but within a year there my sunny sense of boho destiny was transformed into surly outsider-underclass resentment, an artist's identity which was simultaneously self-loathing and arrogant. I was shocked, shocked, to discover that a large number of artistic careers are essentially purchased, and Bennington was implicated in this awakening. I spun out, unable to continue there, to make use of what was, in fact, being offered. Even so, the year-and-a-half I spent was hugely influential, and some of my teachers and fellow students made me aware of standards I still measure myself against. Paradoxical, how much influence could be imparted by a place I seemed to be rejecting almost as soon as I set foot in it. Like a family experience, I guess. (*Post Road*, 2002)

JL: It's impossible to talk about my going to Bennington without talking about the fact that I began dropping out of Bennington—rejecting it in a "you can't fire me, I quit" sort of way—immediately upon arrival. It's absolutely true that I was trying to prove something by running away to a world of privilege. I meant to prove I wasn't deprived, and my reward was a violent confrontation with the realities of class. A confrontation I'd then spend ten years recovering from. I was frightened by my father's bohemian idealism, and I was equally frightened by what I saw as the corruption of art by money and connections at Bennington... When I got to Bennington, and I found that Richard Brautigan and Thomas Berger and Kurt Vonnegut and Donald Barthelme were not "the contemporary," but were in fact awkward and embarrassing and had been overthrown by something else, I was as disconcerted as a time traveler. The world I'd dwelled in was now apocryphal. No one read Henry Miller and Lawrence Durrell, the Beats were regarded with embarrassment. When all that was swept away, I stopped knowing what contemporary literature was. I didn't replace it; I just stopped knowing. (*The Paris Review*, 2003)

JL: I loved Bennington, but I was also freaked out by it. I'd never been to private school. I was a public school kid. I had this bohemian ethos that I'd absorbed from my parents' world, which was misleadingly classless. I was kidding myself about the fact of privilege. It was a very jarring confrontation for me with that fact. I'd existed in a bohemian demimonde where the circumstance that my parents were lower-middle class would never have registered on me. The cultural advantages, the richness of their lives and their friends' lives, and the richness of our existence in New York City, disguised for me the fact that we were poor.

So, I didn't completely identify with Bennington, but I was excited by it in other ways. It was a school that had attracted a lot of self-defined future bohemians like myself. In that sense it was a perfect setting for me, but I couldn't resolve my discomfort . . . Part of dropping out of Bennington to go off to California to write consisted of arrogance or bravery: "I can do this on my own." The rest was ego failure, from encountering the level of accomplishment of the writers at Bennington. I couldn't fully confront it. I'd already been working at used bookstores when I was a teenager, and I had something in my temperament of the autodidact. I enjoyed training myself as an outsider. I'd never been a very good student. Yet I always read more than the people who were doing well in school. I read eccentrically, the things I wanted to read. So, for better and worse, I decided to train myself. (Sarah Anne Johnson, 2005)

Moving to California, or, Philip K. Dick

In *The Disappointment Artist*, Jonathan ascribes his longing for the American West, California in particular, as a simple equation: "All through my high-school years I'd planned to visit California and plant myself at the feet of my hero [Philip K. Dick], but before I managed it, he died. So I clipped obituaries and went to college instead. When one of the clippings announced the formation of a Philip K. Dick Society, dedicated to propagating his works and furthering his posthumous career, my flame of pilgrimage was relit. I dropped out and hitchhiked west." While Jonathan's well-recorded lust for All Things Philip K. Dick rescues this story from apocryphy, causes can sometimes have unintended effects and his move west came to inform his work in an unanticipated way:

> **JL:** I didn't set out ten years ago to write a series of stories, spread out over a number of years, examining my own resistance to . . . technology. But living in San Francisco during the years of an intense kind of utopian ideological boom in virtual reality and computer technologies, I felt an instinctive need to represent my own skepticism about claims that were being made that seemed to me naive, founded in a lack of awareness of the corruption inherent in most technological opportunities, and a search for zipless transcendence which seems to me usually a mistake. Virtual reality's reception was a combination of some of the utopian, consciousness-revolutionizing claims that had been made for radio and film when they appeared, and the utopian nuttiness that surrounded the first experiments with LSD. "We finally have a mechanism by which we can take human conscious-

ness to another level and abandon tired, earthly concerns." And so I found these resistance stories coming out of me. (*Science Fiction Studies*, 1998)

JL: I'd thought it was very obvious that I'd been writing insistently about the Golden State until *Girl in Landscape.* Writing about it in a series of metaphorical or allegorical cartoons, because that was how I experienced California—as an ahistorical (*Gun*), simulated ("Forever, said the Duck"), postulated ("How We Got in Town and Out Again") space, a "faked" environment in many ways, where projection (*As She Climbed Across the Table*) and illusion (*Amnesia Moon*) flourished, an intrinsically experimental place where utopias and dystopias could be set up and knocked down quickly by Teamsters with sledgehammers. A set of props that exposed how human society is a consensual fiction. And, as a kind of adjacent subject, I'd written about the desert states, which made such an impression on me on my visits to Arizona and Utah and through the Westerns I'd begun to obsess on: this was the real, vacant, pre-human landscape upon which the bluff of California was so recently set up. (*Paradoxa*, 2001)

JL: There were moments in my twenties when I did feel lonely for precisely those things I'd been so cavalier in tossing aside. I scratched around for some people in the Bay area who I could swap manuscripts with, in order to alleviate that typical writer's loneliness. I had some colleagues and a writer's group and that was very important at the time. When you aren't good enough to have editors focusing hard on your work, you need amateur editors who can give you feedback, so I sought that out informally . . . The other thing that was going on was that I was rediscovering my connection with Brooklyn, and I realized I wanted to move back. I experienced a sentimental urgency to proclaim that Brooklyn was where I was from. The way people talk there, the way they're louder and more sarcastic, the way they're more impetuous in their talk: that's what I'm like. That's why I'd been uncomfortable in California, I decided, because everyone was so careful and damped and gentle in the way they spoke. I was constantly being responded to as if I was out of control when I just thought I was being emphatic. People would take a step back and act like I was always a bit too much . . . Estrangement is the deeper truth. It's the long estrangement of being away from New York City and rejecting it for a decade, that enabled me to get to [writing about Brooklyn]. If I'd been there continuously, I'd never have been able to write about it. It was the objectifying estrangement that allowed me to write about it. (Sarah Anne Johnson, 2005)

By trade, writers are chameleons, channeling something from the actor's trade as they assume voices and modes and roles in their work, shifting perspective, beguiling their readers one moment, foot on their throat the next, but just as rare as actors who can so completely disguise themselves from role to role, so too is it rare to contemplate the work of a writer whose gift for invention is so natural as to surprise from book to book. Jonathan Lethem is in this exclusive class and, as noted in the interview excerpts above, while the invention may vary, the engine on which it runs is fuelled by themes that have visited Jonathan over the course of his life, informing his work with a seriousness of purpose and illumination his legion of fans embrace, a notion that was unavailable to me in the days after my first Jonathan Lethem experience in Joe's Pub back in 1999. I had no idea an education was in store for me about the reductive thinking involved in ascribing genre to a piece of fiction that wanted only the chance to challenge me by juxtaposition, an effect Jonathan describes in these interviews and elsewhere. (His insatiable desire for juxtaposition once led him to obtain a vanity plate from the California DMV that said SQUALOR or, in total, California Squalor, a tale he relates to *Stop Smiling* magazine.) Another enlightenment along the path of Jonathan's work, underscored over and over in the interviews that follow, is the idea that nothing is off limits when it comes to creating a fictional world and fictional characters. The notion that high culture and low culture can be blended together in fiction is a late twentieth-century invention (witnessed by the vestiges of holdouts who decry low culture's seat at the table), and while it would be easy to point to Jonathan Lethem as a pioneer, a notion he would undoubtedly demur—he spends a fair amount of each of these interviews acknowledging his debt to the writers who came before him, writers he discovered plying his trade in used bookstores, an experience equally important as those named above to his development—it's more accurate to say that he couldn't have turned out to be any other kind of writer.

In following the standard procedure of the Literary Conversations series, the interviews collected in this volume are reprinted without any significant editing. Therefore questions, or variants, are often repeated throughout the course of the volume, though this effect is desirable not just for scholarly integrity, but for an examination of the evolution of the given answers.

My thanks to Leila Salisbury and Walter Biggins for their infinite wisdom and invaluable aid along the way, and to Mary Cotton, my secret weapon.

JC

Chronology

<table>
<tr><td>1964</td><td>Born February 19 in Manhattan, the eldest of three children to Richard Brown Lethem, a painter and teacher, and Judith Lethem, a social worker and political activist.</td></tr>
<tr><td>1978</td><td>Lethem's mother dies from a malignant brain tumor. Lethem gets job at Brazen Head Books; attends the High School of Music and Art, where he produces a zine, The Literary Exchange, and writes an unpublished novel, Heroes.</td></tr>
<tr><td>1980</td><td>Gets job at Clinton Street Books.</td></tr>
<tr><td>1982</td><td>Enters Bennington College as a prospective art student.</td></tr>
<tr><td>1983</td><td>Gets job at Avery Books; begins an unpublished novel, Apes in the Plan.</td></tr>
<tr><td>1984</td><td>Leaves Bennington and hitchhikes from Denver to Berkeley; gets job at Gryphon Books.</td></tr>
<tr><td>1986</td><td>Gets job at Pegasus/Pendragon Books.</td></tr>
<tr><td>1987</td><td>Marries writer and artist Shelley Jackson.</td></tr>
<tr><td>1988</td><td>Publishes the zine Idiot Tooth with Shelley Jackson.</td></tr>
<tr><td>1989</td><td>First published short story: "The Cave Beneath the Falls" in Aboriginal SF, January/February 1989.</td></tr>
<tr><td>1992</td><td>Gets job at Moe's Bookstore.</td></tr>
<tr><td>1994</td><td>Gun, with Occasional Music is published by Harcourt Brace.</td></tr>
<tr><td>1995</td><td>Amnesia Moon is published by Harcourt Brace.</td></tr>
<tr><td>1996</td><td>Moves back to Brooklyn.</td></tr>
<tr><td>1996</td><td>The Wall of the Sky, the Wall of the Eye is published by Harcourt Brace.</td></tr>
<tr><td>1997</td><td>As She Climbed Across the Table is published by Doubleday; is divorced from Shelley Jackson.</td></tr>
<tr><td>1998</td><td>Girl in Landscape is published by Doubleday.</td></tr>
<tr><td>1999</td><td>Motherless Brooklyn is published by Doubleday and wins the National Book Critics Circle Award; Kafka Americana, with Carter Scholz, is published by Subterranean Press.</td></tr>
<tr><td>2000</td><td>Moves to Toronto, marries Julia Rosenberg, a Canadian film executive; This Shape We're In is published by McSweeney's; edits</td></tr>
</table>

<table>
<tr><td></td><td>The Vintage Book of Amnesia: An Anthology of Writing on the Subject of Memory Loss.</td></tr>
<tr><td>2001</td><td>Writes introduction to Poor George by Paula Fox, published by W. W. Norton; writes introduction to The Man Who Was Thursday by G. K. Chesterton, published by Modern Library Classics.</td></tr>
<tr><td>2002</td><td>Divorced from Julia Rosenberg; edits Da Capo Best Music Writing 2002: The Year's Finest Writing on Rock, Pop, Jazz, Country & More; writes introduction to On the Yard by Malcolm Braly, published by New York Review of Books Classics; moves back to Brooklyn.</td></tr>
<tr><td>2003</td><td>The Fortress of Solitude is published by Doubleday; writes introduction to Dombey and Son by Charles Dickens; writes introduction to Meeting Evil by Thomas Berger, published by Simon & Schuster; writes introduction to It Happened in Boston? by Russell Greenan, published by Modern Library Classics.</td></tr>
<tr><td>2004</td><td>Marries Amy Barrett; Men and Cartoons is published by Doubleday; writes introduction to A New Life by Bernard Malamud, published by Farrar, Straus & Giroux.</td></tr>
<tr><td>2005</td><td>The Disappointment Artist is published by Doubleday; writes introduction to Fierce Attachments by Vivian Gornick, published by Farrar, Straus & Giroux; awarded a MacArthur Fellowship.</td></tr>
<tr><td>2006</td><td>How We Got Insipid is published by Subterranean Press; writes introduction to We Have Always Lived in the Castle by Shirley Jackson, published by Penguin Classics; in June, publishes "Being James Brown" in Rolling Stone; in September, publishes "The Genius of Bob Dylan" in Rolling Stone. Believenicks!: 2005: The Year We Wrote a Book About the Mets, with Christopher Sorrentino, as by Ivan Felt and Harris Conklin, published by Doubleday.</td></tr>
<tr><td>2007</td><td>In February, "The Ecstasy of Influence" is published in Harper's Magazine. In May, son Everett Barrett Lethem is born. You Don't Love Me Yet is published by Doubleday. Lethem edits Philip K. Dick: Four Novels of the 1960s, published by the Library of America.</td></tr>
<tr><td>2008</td><td>Issues 1 through 10 of Omega: The Unknown is published by Marvel Comics. Lethem edits Philip K. Dick: Five Novels of the 1960s and 1970s, published by the Library of America.</td></tr>
<tr><td>2009</td><td>Chronic City is published by Doubleday. Lethem edits Philip K. Dick: Valis and Other Late Novels, published by the Library of America, and writes introduction to Miss Lonelyhearts & The Day</td></tr>
</table>

of the Locust by Nathanael West, published by New Directions. He opens Red Gap Books in Blue Hill, Maine, with Marge Kernan and Andre Strong.

2010   In February, son Desmond Brown Lethem is born. In April, appointed the Roy Edward Disney Chair in Creative Writing at Pomona College.

Conversations with Jonathan Lethem

Private Hells and Radical Doubts:
An Interview with Jonathan Lethem

Fiona Kelleghan/1997

From *Science Fiction Studies* 25:2, no. 75 (July 1998): 225–40. Copyright © 1998 Science Fiction Studies. Reprinted by permission.

Jonathan Lethem began publishing short fiction in 1989 with "The Cave Beneath the Falls," which *Locus* magazine promoted in its list of recommended stories. Since then, he has received Nebula nominations for the stories "The Happy Man" (1991) and "Five Fucks" (1996). His first novel, *Gun, with Occasional Music* (1994), a near-future murder mystery, won the 1995 Locus Award for Best First Novel and Crawford Award for Best First Fantasy Novel, and was another Nebula nominee. *Gun* was followed by the novels *Amnesia Moon* (1995), *As She Climbed Across the Table* (1997), and *Girl in Landscape* (1998), and by the 1997 World Fantasy Award–winning short-story collection *The Wall of the Sky, the Wall of the Eye* (1996). It is not hard to see why *Newsweek* proclaimed Jonathan Lethem one of "100 people to watch in the next century."

Born in Manhattan in 1964, Lethem was a voracious and precocious reader in his childhood; he wrote a novel in 1979 about which he says, "I learned to type, at least." He attended Bennington College in Vermont sporadically in 1982 and 1983, and in 1984 decided to hitchhike alone from Denver to Berkeley, "a thousand miles of desert and mountains through Wyoming, Utah, and Nevada, with about forty dollars in my pocket, one of the stupidest and most memorable things I've ever done. Those experiences became the seed of *Amnesia Moon*." In 1986 he took up residence in Berkeley, where he learned the sales side of the literary industry by working in bookstores. There, he wrote and sold around forty short stories and his first three books; in 1996, he moved back to New York to settle in Brooklyn.

Lethem is widely praised as a brilliant pasticheur—among other influences, *Gun, with Occasional Music* pays homage to Raymond Chandler, the unsettling road novel *Amnesia Moon* to Philip K. Dick, the unearthly love-triangle novel *As She Climbed Across the Table* to the work of Don DeLillo, and *Girl in Landscape* to various Westerns—but as any knowledgeable sf reader can attest, that powerful narrative voice is ultimately his own. Stories such as "Walking the Moons" (1990), a vicious satire of the extravagant claims for virtual reality; the title-says-it-all comment on the entertainment biz, "The Elvis National Theater of Okinawa" (1992, written with Lukas Jaeger); "Receding Horizon" (1995, written with Carter Scholz), which conflates Franz Kafka with Frank Capra; and "The Insipid Profession of Jonathan Hornebom" (1995), a parody of Heinlein's "The Unpleasant Profession of Jonathan Hoag," show that Lethem thinks seriously and profoundly about science fiction and other phenomena of late twentieth-century popular culture.

Despite Lethem's fondness for pastiche and allusion, his fiction displays a harsh skepticism toward received wisdom. His stories reveal a modernist concern with questions of identity, though he is comfortable with postmodern techniques of dramatizing them. He has been listening seriously to the delirious cries of the world, and his work often partakes of that helplessness amid powerful images characteristic of nightmare. His settings can be surreal—they often plunge the reader into an experience of a hellish, artificial, or alien world—but his landscapes smell and feel grittily real, and they are rarely decadent.

Most of Lethem's stories privilege metaphors of time and sequentiality over metaphors of space and synchrony, thereby revealing a cunning for narrative and a suspicion of the conventions of myth. Even stories which feel like myths leave us without certitude: such as "Holidays" (1996), a calendar of religious holidays as described by . . . an alien? a far-future anthropologist? a madman?; or "The Happy Prince" (1993), a pseudo-fable of operatic love between a migrating swallow and a golden robot which pays homage to Oscar Wilde's fairy tale of the same name and which may be about self-sacrifice (or may not). The Lethem theory of information flow through the world describes a proliferation of noise and an increasingly rapid distortion of perspective, as if to say that the present is dark enough, but the future is an abyss. His stories are disturbing and disorienting; they are also wickedly funny. Above all, and what is perhaps surprising for a clever young satirist who prefers observation to proselytism, Lethem's stories can be deeply poignant, as they image countless inescapable minor invasions into our daily lives, and render the stark irrevocability of seeing those ways of life change forever.

This interview was held at Readercon, Westborough, Massachusetts, in July 1997.

FK: Your books don't appear to be marketed specifically as science fiction. So what I want you to do is to reassure me that you're not going to abandon science fiction, that you do love it, you're based in sf, your roots and influences are sf.

JL: I don't think I'm going to give you the blanket reassurance that you're asking for, because for me the question isn't as simple as that.

I don't think I'll ever abandon sf to the extent that I ever was in a position to abandon it, if that reply makes sense. To me sf's a description that doesn't completely work. As I experience it, I've always been a writer who was absorbed in and obsessed with science fiction, and I will continue to be that kind of a writer. I have projects in mind that are more and less like science fiction than some of the projects I've already written. What I can promise is that I won't ever betray my own sense of the complexity of that question and suddenly pretend to have nothing to do with science fiction. It wouldn't make any sense. The work wouldn't be coherent if I insisted that it be read in ignorance of that context or if I tried to reduce the degree to which the work was engaged with that tradition. But it's also engaged with other sources and other realms and other traditions. It's also frustrating for me to accept the conditions and deprivations associated with a career exclusively in science fiction. I've been very adamant that I not allow myself to be pigeonholed in the larger operations of the publishing industry and the bookselling industry.

FK: We need not only to congratulate you but to thank you for being a crossover writer. It makes the whole field look good.

JL: That's a nice way to put it. On the one hand, I try not to worry about these issues at all. If I'm talking to someone who I think can be moved on to other topics that seem to me more crucial, I do my damnedest to brush these questions aside, in a way that's almost disingenuous. I'll pretend to be oblivious, in the classic American tradition of artists pretending merely to tell their tales. If you asked John Ford or Howard Hawks to analyze their own films, you got this disgruntled, "Oh, come on, you intellectuals can do that. I just make this stuff." The advantage in that is that it throws off the yoke of certain kinds of questions. Sometimes it seems oppressive even to acknowledge my own awareness, which is in fact a hyperconsciousness, of category and genre issues, both on the practical level of marketing my books and on the deep level of the sources and inspirations and even the writing process.

In fact, my own sense of it is extremely complicated. It never makes sense to me to simply say, "I am writing a science fiction novel," let alone to say, "I am simply a science fiction writer," any more than it would make sense for me to say that I'm not, or that I'm a mystery writer, or a magical realist. But I promise you here and now, Fiona, I will never betray my powerful sense of origin in and indebtedness to and involvement with science fiction.

FK: Okay, fairly put. Stories such as "Light and the Sufferer" [1995] and "Walking the Moons" contain a cautionary note about the sf elements. In the first one, the visit to Earth of the aliens appears to be as aimless and meaningless as the life of the crack addicts they follow around, and the glamour of virtual reality is viciously undermined by the squalor of the young explorer's reality in "Walking the Moons." Do you want to comment on this pessimism?

JL: It doesn't always feel to me explicitly like pessimism. Interesting, because I haven't seen those two stories yoked together in the way your question yokes them. But it makes sense to me, and I can think of other examples of my tendency to problematize the science fiction, the futuristic tropes in my stories—the *fantastic* tropes, because often they're not particularly science-fictional.

FK: Often they're displaced from the center in your fiction. I thought of those two as stories in which the sf tropes are central—

JL: —Are central, but are subjected to radical doubt. I think you're right, although I think that "Light and the Sufferer" is a story where the question of the centrality of the fantastic element is a point that is being argued in the story. The aliens don't appear until six or seven pages in. The narrator is explicitly worrying about their relevance, or lack of relevance, to the human story that he's so helplessly involved in.

I think that I have a propensity or weakness for writing meta-fictionally about genre. All of my stories tend to be, at one level, interrogations of the genre they inhabit. Since most of my work is fantastic in some sense, I'm usually asking questions at some level, often subconsciously or automatically, about what happens to a given story when a fantastic element intrudes into it, and this becomes a parallel interrogation into the question of what happens to a human existence when fantastic elements intrude. So the text and the characters are disrupted in a similar way.

But I'm still evading the question of the pessimism that you raised. I guess I feel it's a traditional pessimism. I don't identify with any kind of simplistic Luddite position, but I think there's a strain of exciting and healthy and vibrant skepticism about technology in some sf . . . Here's where I'll take your question and divide the two stories.

"Walking the Moons" I would class with "'Forever,' Said the Duck" [1993] and a recent story called "How We Got in Town and Out Again" [1996] as a sequence where I'm specifically skeptical about claims being made for virtual reality technologies. That was not a conscious choice; I didn't set out ten years ago to write a series of stories, spread out over a number of years, examining my own resistance to that technology. But living in San Francisco during the years of an intense kind of utopian ideological boom in virtual reality and computer technologies, I felt an instinctive need to represent my own skepticism about claims that were being made that seemed to me naive, founded in a lack of awareness of the corruption inherent in most technological opportunities, and a search for zipless transcendence which seems to me usually a mistake. Virtual reality's reception was a combination of some of the utopian, consciousness-revolutionizing claims that had been made for radio and film when they appeared, and the utopian nuttiness that surrounded the first experiments with LSD. "We finally have a mechanism by which we can take human consciousness to another level and abandon tired, earthly concerns." And so I found these resistance stories coming out of me.

Those stories come out of the *Galaxy*–Frederik Pohl–C. M. Kornbluth–*New Maps of Hell* tradition where the skeptical 1950s-style science fiction writer takes a debunking position on his society's infatuation with technological development, usually in light of some instinctively Marxist sense of how capitalism corrupts the reception of radical technology. Whereas "Light and the Sufferer" can't be said to participate in that tradition at all. It's a skeptical story about the—I'm working off the cuff here, because I've never analyzed this story from this perspective; I haven't analyzed it much at all—but I guess the skepticism in that story is about the ability of external forces to provide any relevant assistance to, or even to focus any competent awareness on, the family and personal dramas that always threaten to overwhelm us. It's a story about interventions. There are two possible interventions in the story. The narrator fails in his intervention into his brother's life, and he considers a possible intervention on the part of the aliens into his brother's life and eventually his own, and discovers that's also hopeless. It's a codependency story. But there's zero cultural critique going on there.

Again, I'll use the word "traditional": I grew up reading dystopian and skeptical science fiction passionately, and I write that way by default. Most of my stories work from a ground assumption that dystopian realities are plausible ones, that we're probably living in a dystopia ourselves at the moment. That's my vocabulary. So any specific skepticisms that arise are against that ground.

FK: Do you outline?

JL: No. I sometimes boast about writing improvisationally, and behind that boast lies a variety of different techniques, none of which involves outlines. Sometimes I know a lot about where I'm going, and sometimes I know very little. I'm not sure the results are evident, but I'll give you a couple of examples and you can tell me. "Light and the Sufferer" is a short story where I knew nothing about where I was going, as is "Sleepy People." "Five Fucks" was a story that appeared to me as a single revelation. There was a flash of lightning that illuminated the landscape. All I had to do was then go back into the studio and represent the landscape that had been illuminated to me.

FK: That looks like a carefully plotted story!

JL: "Carefully plotted" is a funny phrase, but it's a very deliberate story, it's a very self-aware story. I knew what I was doing all the way through it. There's improvisation only in the language, in the treatment. There's always stuff I discover as I go along, but sometimes I'm discovering everything, and sometimes I really know where I'm headed. But I never outline. I jot notes when specific bits of dialogue or language insist themselves upon me before they're needed. I'll just jot down a phrase to keep it. But to the extent that I can, I prefer to hold everything, the impending sense of the story, in my head, because it's that pressure of holding it all in my head that makes me work hard to get it on the page, and also, I think, keeps interesting connections happening. If I took more notes, I would have discharged some of that tension. The story would already be told, in a sense. I wouldn't still be at full boil when I'm writing.

FK: "The Happy Man" is a curious piece of meta-fiction about a man who travels to Hell. At first we think it's a literal Hell, then we think it's metaphorical. Then the narrator insists it's literal; but then it proves to be a metaphorical construct of Freudian concepts. "The Hardened Criminals" [1995], "The One About the Green Detective" [1996], and "Sleepy People" also seem to me to be generated by literalizing a metaphor. Was the genesis of each of those stories the result of thinking about a phrase and then making it literal?

JL: No. Certainly I work by the method of concretizing metaphor frequently. But rarely do I generate a story as long and complicated as any of the ones you've just listed out of what is essentially a pun. There always has to be a stronger impulse, and then sometimes I work backwards to something as apparently specific as the title of "The Hardened Criminals." But the image of that prison was quite fully developed in my conscious-slash-subconscious before I noticed that in effect what I was talking about was a pun on the phrase "hardened criminals." The richness of that prison I doubt would have arisen for me if I'd merely noticed that "hardened" is a funny word to put in front of a noun that describes human beings. I may sound a bit defensive on behalf of that story in particular, because I've seen in print and heard aloud on panels a couple of times the criticism that in "Hardened Criminals" I've piled an enormously serious attempt on the precarious foundation of a pun. The story may very well collapse under its own weight, but it's not resting initially on a pun. I made a mistake in titling the story so glibly, because it's misleading.

"Happy Man" even less so. The story came from strange places and insisted itself upon me in a way that's still unusual for me in my writing process, but I was not conscious of it being a story where I was literalizing metaphors. Often I'm very conscious of it. There's a story called "Mood Bender" [1994] where I'm plainly and openly and happily making an enterprise of concretizing metaphor. "Happy Man" was not like that. "Happy Man" arose out of a barrage of dream imagery that I wanted to write about and which gradually found a home in this premise of the man who dies and goes to his own private hell. But it certainly didn't arise because I was meditating on what the meaning of "private hell" would be if there really was such a thing. In that case, it's more pleasing to me that it has that appearance. It seems so tidy. But there was so much to the story before the phrase "private hell."

"The One About the Green Detective" is an odd story in that it's almost a discussion of concretization of metaphor. It's as though I set up a little detective agency to explain to my readership how I operate and I'm saying, "For this writer, these things that to others are jokes or metaphors exist in a real landscape and, here, we'll take you to a few of them." So it's a very meta-generic or meta-fictional story within my own shelf of work. It's also a very light story, not tremendously weighty, and the emotional material in it is nil. It's a jaunt.

"Sleepy People" is a very important story to me, and one that's hard for me to talk about because I don't understand it completely, but I think I would argue that that story has even less to do with concretization of metaphor than any of the others that we're talking about and than the majority of my fiction, including the novels. In fact, I'm not even sure what metaphor we'd be talking about, because it doesn't seem to me that there is one. Perhaps there is, since it's such a reflexive form of operation for me—

FK: People who sleepwalk through their lives.
JL: People who sleepwalk through their lives. Fair enough. I can honestly claim that it never crossed my mind at any point in the composition or even subsequent to the publication of that story that at some level I'd played my usual game—which is essentially like calling a metaphor's bluff. "All right, what if people really sleepwalked through their lives." Except the answer is "no, not, never," in the case of "Sleepy People." I was working in a deeply intuitive way in that story and it seems to me, in fact, a reply story to "The Happy Man." Essentially "Sleepy People" is an attempt to compensate for the plights of the female characters in some of my stories—more than anyone, Maureen in "The Happy Man" is the prime example—who are treated unfairly by the texts. They're made to be the witness and the buffer in a story of a man's tortured relationship to his own psychic/emotional/symbolic/et cetera agenda. Which takes him out of the real world and poisons his potential relationship with the woman in question. I wanted to write from the point of view of a woman trying to love a man who's caught up in some remote world of strife, some symbolic, cataclysmic terrain. The character, the sleepy man in "Sleepy People," in a sense he's off in his own private hell. And for once we're made to see how pathetic a retreat that is, from the perspective of the female character.

What "The Happy Man" and "Sleepy People" have in common that's even simpler is that they're both, at some level, descriptions of the plight of someone living with an artist.

FK: Have you lived with an artist?
JL: Yeah. And I've been the artist lived with, of course. Anyway, "Sleepy People" is very much a lucid dream among my fictions.

FK: It's very Kafkaesque, very dreamlike.

JL: I wrote it by a process of discovery that still feels to me unique and very desirable, and I'd like to write from that position again. I haven't gone as deeply into that state again since writing it, but it seems a very important story to me, because it feels one hundred percent felt and intuited and, as I say, written by means of a completely open exploration into my own themes. There is very little mental ideological armature insisting itself upon that story. The opposite is a story like "Five Fucks," which is *all* intellectual armature. It's a series of brilliant games, completely propositional, completely intentional, completely a work of cleverness, where "Sleepy People" is completely a work of intuition and reception. I sat and I let that story feel its way through my fingertips onto the page. That may be a mystical description. I don't usually describe my processes in very mystical terms, but I'll risk it in this case.

FK: It was nominated for the Tiptree?

JL: It's been completely ignored, as far as I know. You're thinking of "Five Fucks."

FK: No, I just read this in the *New York Review of Science Fiction.* "Sleepy People" was short-listed for the Tiptree.

JL: I'd love to be wrong, because I'm very fond of "Sleepy People." But I debuted two stories in the collection *The Wall of the Sky, the Wall of the Eye,* "Five Fucks" and "Sleepy People," and again and again people will tell me that "Five Fucks" is their favorite story in the book. And it was nominated for the Nebula. Whereas "Sleepy People" has been very quietly received.

FK: I'll send you the page where I saw it. The comment by the Tiptree jury was that it was a very sympathetic portrait of a woman who has to care for this guy who's just this passive sleeping figure.

JL: Well, I'm delighted. Actually, that's what those two stories have in common: my sympathy with the female character. "Five Fucks" is one kind of method of getting closer to the women in my fiction. "Sleepy People" is a very different way of making that contact.

Otherwise, the stories are unrelated.

On the other hand, if you get me started on resonances between the stories in the collection I may never stop. Some of it is deliberate, of course: I picked the five stories from among the dozens I'd published, and I wrote the two originals to fill out the book. But there are also accidental relationships that now seem very exciting to me. I think the collection turned out to be almost as thematically unified as a novel.

"The Happy Man" became my calling card in the sf field, and it was a very strange, uncharacteristic, and in some ways unpleasant way to announce myself. Of course, some people still think I've never equalled that story. But one organizing principle visible to me in the book is that the stories that follow "The Happy Man"—and they were all written afterwards, almost exactly in the order they appear—each attempts to compensate for that story in some way. To correct for the impression it makes. A series of antidotes. "Vanilla Dunk" [1992] is my normative story, my attempt to show I can keep you just as enthralled with completely innocuous, uncontroversial material. "Light and the Sufferer" is an attempt to reach the same level of emotional intensity without the mechanistic, over-determined plotting. The polymorphous sexuality in "'Forever,' Said the Duck" is an apology for the homophobic reading "The Happy Man" allows—it's *Philadelphia* to my *Silence of the Lambs*. Sort of. "Hardened Criminals" is a self-conscious attempt to displace "The Happy Man" with a family nightmare that's even grimmer. I think it fails. And the other two, as I just said, are critiques of the men in my fiction, and rescue attempts for the women.

I also noticed that every story in the book contains some version of a finite artificial world, a potted world, a cartoon world, a prison or arena, carved out of the real world. So the collection taught me something about my own motifs and themes.

FK: Stories such as "The One About the Green Detective" and "Vanilla Dunk" have a fabulistic structure, but they conclude that there can be no moral drawn from the story. *Amnesia Moon* likewise reveals a deeply relativistic disinclination to privilege one interpretation over another. Is this a comment on the nature of storytelling, or is relativism your philosophical stance?

JL: By deep instinct that provokes the John Ford or Howard Hawks in me again, and I want to say [growling]: "What philosophical stance?" But I'm helplessly of my age and milieu in being, by intuition, by training, by context, a relativist, yes. I'm sure I am one; I've never even looked twice at it. I'm probably so deeply a relativist that the question is confusing to me, because I've never wavered long enough to *glimpse* any other position. It doesn't even seem to me to be something I'm debating in my work. Just a ground I work from. The relativist dilemmas of my characters are just reflections of the underlying stance.

At the same time, I tend to write about the nature of storytelling. Certainly the temptation to resolve our ideological dilemmas in fiction reverberates in the real world, where we're tempted—and frustrated always, I think—by those attempts. The questions of an ending, in *Amnesia Moon*—the book refuses to end, essentially, because it would be a betrayal of the premises. That book is powerfully influenced by Dick, and also by Cornell Woolrich, the mystery writer who specialized in amnesiac, paranoiac plots. Both of those writers are characterized by their disappointing endings. It seemed to me that to write a perfect Cornell Woolrich novel, you had to find a way not to write a bad last Cornell Woolrich chapter, and that at some level, that paranoiac, identity-shattering reality those writers draw you into is in some ways intrinsically betrayed, fundamentally betrayed, by any kind of ending at all.

So I wanted to write a book about that problem, among other things. The protagonist, Chaos, is desperately yearning for a coherent explanation, and most of the trouble he gets into is because he's stumbled into situations where people have made a tradeoff. They've exchanged freedom and awareness for some kind of organizing principle or explanation. And it's usually a bad deal. He considers various bad deals himself and then wanders off to a career of rejecting them forever. I hope. He may make another very bad turn right at the end, right after the last page of the book. I did my best to genuinely be unsure about the realities behind some of the illusions in that book, so when people ask me questions, I'm not playing my I'm-only-a-storyteller-don't-ask-me-questions-I-can't-answer role; I'm genuinely as puzzled as my readers about some of the turns in that book.

FK: A related question takes note of the fact that what organizing principles or explanations there are in your stories do tend to be handed down from above, so my next question was whether you consider yourself a political writer.

JL: Well, I'm very uncomfortable with the idea that I'm a political writer, because I'm very confused about politics.

FK: I mean political in the anthropological sense of power structures, not in the specific sense of the modern American political system.

JL: I inherited a skepticism. My parents were war-resisters, and I grew up, I came to consciousness in the early seventies, during Watergate, essentially, so as with my relativism, it's a ground I stand on, that powerful skepticism. But I'm equally resistant—and this is something I find myself bumping against as I've entered into a dialogue with people who respond to my work—there's a tremendous susceptibility to conspiracy theories out there. Those always seem to me as naive about the way the world works as utopian fantasies. They're equally attempts to understand the world according to one vast, organizing principle, which is a betrayal of the complex and ambiguous and, most importantly, the uncontrolled nature of our experiences. Conspiracy theorists believe that things feel chaotic and out-of-control only because someone bad is controlling them, which is one fiction among many fictions that people use to feel less out of control.

When you ask me if I'm political, what you're really saying is, "Do you identify your critique of everyday life as a political one?" It seems to me a politics of consciousness and a politics of awareness are so lacking in most of what are considered to be political viewpoints, that I'm not sure I want to call it politics. Before I can begin to discuss the kinds of questions that people normally call "politics," I would have to solve perceptual and mental and emotional confusions that seem to me to so surround every discourse that I certainly haven't gotten anywhere close to "politics" yet.

FK: I was thinking of politics in that more general sense, just because you are so keenly aware of rhetoric. I thought that you might be interested in the linguistic aspect of politics.
JL: I'm very interested in the linguistic aspect of our struggle to control or understand our experience of everyday life. That's a kind of politics, a root kind. It's a politics of everyday life and a politics of perceptual coping that underlie what seem to me to be the falsely dichotomized arguments that are carried on instead of these deeper interrogations. That stratum of falsely dichotomized arguments seems to me to be "politics."

FK: Well put. Okay, we don't have to beat that one to death.
JL: (laughs)

FK: Oh no, the next one is a political question.
JL: No, go for it!

FK: The ecology of many of your stories seems almost naturalistic. Characters are divided into predator and prey.
JL: I'm interested because I've never thought about my . . . I often sort out my characters and I make distinctions, probably oversimple, like parents and children, and there are characters who I think are secretly children, like

Chaos in *Amnesia Moon*. But predators and prey wouldn't have occurred to me, and I want you to give me some examples to help me.

FK: "Light and the Sufferer," it seems to me, describes the urban life of the junkies as a series of choices about whether to behave as predator or as prey. *Gun, with Occasional Music* describes what is tantamount to a police state, where the civilians are victimized by the Inquisitor's Office. "The Happy Man," again.

JL: Well, yeah, "Happy Man" has a predator in it, and that's one of the reasons that story doesn't feel to me as characteristic of my fiction. I've always felt that that story stood a little bit apart, and I think it's the presence of the predator. The uncomplicated villain. Even some of the bad guys in *Gun, with Occasional Music*, who are pretty stock heavies, have their sympathetic moments and their frailties and occasionally have, if not a moral, at least an intellectual upper hand on the main character. [The villain Danny] Phoneblum is to [the protagonist] Conrad Metcalf as Kellogg is to Chaos, at the beginning of *Amnesia Moon*, in that they're both sort of corrupt fathers whose lesson is "Don't trust me. And grow up." That doesn't seem to me to be a predator profile. Both of those characters have discovered a willingness in themselves to manipulate others and play villainous roles in the world, but because the bad guys in most of my work seem to me conscious of their role-playing, they don't strike me as predators, and that's why the uncle in "The Happy Man" is the exception. And even he, in his human incarnation, in the mundane scenes, has some of that droll, role-playing aspect. It turns out his appetites make him a real predator, and that the role-playing is a lie. But most of my characters that pass for villains or predators are too self-conscious and ironic about it to seem really predational to me.

FK: Well, you're right, and in fact now that I think about it there aren't that many *predators*, but I feel as though a lot of your characters feel that they're *victims*.

JL: They do. A lot of my characters feel that they're victims, and I hope it's not a weakness in my work. If it isn't, it's *only* because I usually end up complicating it, and, demonstrating the "victim's" complicity with the "oppressing" apparatus or personalities, whether it's a family or a society. Their complicity with the structure that makes them feel victimized. And I know I'm thinking about that better and harder in recent works.

I would say there's also another typology of character in my work, and that's the character who imagines that he is in command of something and is a victim instead. Delusions of control. Cale in *Amnesia Moon* imagines that he's sort of a master webspinner of virtual realities, and he's a serum in a bottle in a refrigerator. Philip in *As She Climbed Across the Table* imagines that he's mastering Alice and mastering his world, and he's not. He's not in mortal danger, but he's a helpless character. So I flip it both ways, I think. My victims who feel sorry for themselves are forced to learn how they've oppressed others or conspired in their own oppression, and my bluff and confident characters are exposed as really not controlling their own circumstances.

FK: You frequently deal with the theme of evolution: not showing us a grand Stapledonian sweep, but snapshots of evolution in progress, as in *Gun, with Occasional Music*, or characters who reinvent themselves, as in "Using It and Losing It" [1990], which I find a very interesting story, one that is concerned with speech and meaning.

JL: You have to read deep in my shelf to find "Using It and Losing It," but I'm tickled that you've done that, because it was a major turning-point story for me. I'm not sure that I'd collect it, because the language seems to me precious. I was just discovering my tools, and I was infatuated with what I could carry off. Also, it's in some ways a dangerously derivative story. But it was a real turning point for me in discovering my own methods and my own obsessions and finding a way to give them free play.

It's a classic deflationary science fiction story. The character thinks he's making a breakthrough into a next level of consciousness, and in fact he's diminished his ability to participate in consensual reality so radically that it doesn't matter, that he's immediately caught up in pathetic practical issues instead of enjoying his breakthrough. In that sense, "Walking the Moons" is a rewrite of "Using It and Losing It." "Using It and Losing It" is directly indebted to a story which is a powerful influence on *As She Climbed Across the Table* as well, called "Stanley Toothbrush," by Terry Carr. I name-check Stanley Toothbrush in *As She Climbed Across the Table*, probably the most obscure reference in the book. The narrator, Philip, calls Lack his own personal *Stanley Toothbrush*. My editor circled it and said, "What the hell is this?" And I said, "That's for me. Just leave it there."

"Stanley Toothbrush" is a Terry Carr story where the main character is a hapless lover who has a girlfriend and an office job. One morning he wakes up saying the word "shelf" to himself again and again and again until the word loses its meaning, and he hears a clatter in the back of his apartment and all the shelves have disappeared. It turns out that, for him, when he wears words out, which is exactly what my character in "Using It and Losing It" does, they disappear from the world. In a funny way, "Using It and Losing It" is a reverse of my normal method, because I usually take metaphors and concretize them. In fact what I did was re-metaphorize Terry Carr's short story. I made it a mental story instead of a physical story. In my story, when you wear words out, you lose them from your vocabulary. And in Terry's, when you wear words out, the objects disappear from the world. So it's exactly the opposite of the process that I normally apply to other writers' work.

The result, in "Stanley Toothbrush," is that he's removing items from the world, and glorying in this funny new talent he has, and then his girlfriend jokes that she's busy, she can't do anything with him that night because she's got a date with a guy named Stanley Toothbrush. And she's made him up. But our hero begins reciting that name, over and over again, and it just seems realer and realer and realer, until, what do you know, Stanley Tooth brush walks in and he's this brilliant rival. The whole story, in a sense, is a real germ of inspiration for *As She Climbed Across the Table*, because Philip does participate in creating Lack. The speech he gives at the press conference humanizes Lack. He's the one who really draws Lack out of the world of physics and out of the realm of scientific metaphors and starts talking about his desires and tastes in human terms, so he's done the Stanley Toothbrush trip there. He's made his imaginary rival into a real thing.

If you asked me to list the things that I write about, I don't know how many I'd have to go through before I said "evolution." But your perception is interesting me now. "Five Fucks" is also an evolutionary or de-evolutionary story. And that snapshot effect is a method I use, skipping the transitions. That description in your question, of the snapshot trick, in a sense is a description of a method that I employ at the mechanical level of my writing. I had a breakthrough at some point, figuring out that I didn't need to show transitions, and that, at many levels of the text, the proper thing to do is just skip to the next thing that interests me. That was one of the most important technical lessons for me.

FK: How do you invent character names?
JL: Actually, it's a hobby. It's my only writerly activity that's radically inefficient. I create character names when I'm stuck or bored, or just to amuse myself. I have thousands of them. A big fat manila folder full, more than I could ever invent characters for. I plunder those lists. Of course, a lot of them are bad and silly and wouldn't work. But sometimes there'll be one that

seems silly and wrong until I've invented a story or got a notion for a story, and suddenly it jumps off the list and fits that character. There are instances in my fiction when you see me playfully using up some of those names, like in "'Forever,' Said the Duck," where I thought, "Let's see how many of my *most* ludicrous names I can get into one story." Of course, the most important character names tend not to come from those lists, tend to come from some slightly deeper, less arbitrary place. My naming has changed. In the book I'm just finishing, the names are more realistic—I wouldn't call them realistic—but they're more realistic.

FK: Names like Phoneblum and Teleprompter [in *Gun, with Occasional Music*] are a little hard to believe, but not only is it the future, it's possibly not even our world.

JL: Right. Well, that's it. And it's a way to point at the artificial nature of fiction, and not one that I invented. Certainly Donald Barthelme and Thomas Pynchon beat me to that, easily. Sometimes it's a way of making an ironic point, although that's really dangerous if names are too meaningful. But Phoneblum and Teleprompter are both in a book about a world of radically diminished communication, and they're both named for communication devices. Also, communication has been decanted out of the natural into the . . . it's been technologized, in that world, so they were both named for technological means of communication. That was an intuitive move.

Other names are just to make me laugh, or just to make the characters seem special and to help create the atmosphere of oddity. Unrealistically strange character names are an easy way to make sure the reader feels, at the deepest level, they're entering a propositional space where they have to suspend some of their reading protocols and suspend disbelief and make leaps. It makes people ready for leaps.

FK: It can also, as you hinted, make the fiction seem allegorical, but sometimes the allegory seems to work at cross purposes. You do run the danger of having the reader stall for a moment, trying to puzzle it out.

JL: Yeah. I'm not sure I'm always as careful about that danger as I could be. Sometimes I'll use a name that suggests a lot, and it means zero. I think that at some level I cue the degree of artificialness of the world that you're in by the degree of artificialness of the names. The book I've just written [*Girl in Landscape*] wants to feel more like the real world, and the names cue that. The story I've written that takes place the least in the world as we know it, of course, is "'Forever,' said the Duck," and that's cued by the consummately artificial names. They're the first clue that we're not even in a spatial reality, that we're just listening to voices babble. Then there are other qualities in the worlds that I'm creating that can be cued by the kinds of names, not just whether they're strange or not, but in what way they're strange. If they feel more allegorical, they may point more towards an allegorical space. If they feel more droll, then it can help people lighten up and start to play with the language. The names in "Five Fucks," for example, help establish it as a story that exists in the realm of game-playing.

FK: For example, the policeman's name, that changes scene to scene from "Pupkiss" to "McPupkiss" to "Pupkinstein."
JL: The mutations of the policeman's name, even if you just pulled those out of the story, you'd say, "This is a story that's a meta-fictional game."

FK: Your fiction is very playful and, as I'm not the first to notice, is also very funny. I thought that *As She Climbed* was laugh-out-loud funny. Things like when Professor Soft, after hearing the deconstructionist speak, just throws up, or bringing in a blind man to help with the problem of the observer in physics, are really funny. Do you laugh at your own writing?
JL: Oh, definitely. I try to make myself laugh. That's probably not surprising, in a book like *As She Climbed Across the Table*, but I'm also writing to make myself laugh in stories where the effect is much less humorous. I'm thinking about the new novel that I've just written, which is probably the least profitable thing for me to be bringing up, since you haven't read it yet. It's a grave book, in many ways. Full of tortured emotions. But there's a lot of that book that was conceived at some level to amuse me. A way to keep yourself in the game, and excited, is to make yourself laugh. A way to make the writing process less precious and less solemn and more fluid is to make sure you're enjoying yourself.

FK: Did you sit down and read all of DeLillo before you wrote *As She Climbed Across the Table*?
JL: Yes, DeLillo is a huge influence. It's interesting, the history of my reading of DeLillo. I wasn't sure I liked him when I first read him. I heard the name, I don't know why, and I checked out *End Zone* when I was in college. I was the first person to check it out of the Bennington Library in, like, seven years. His reputation was as a real writer's writer at that point, and I don't know why I got interested. I read about half of *End Zone* and wasn't sure I liked it. It seemed chilly to me. The formal and chilly qualities of his sentences and

his scene construction at first turned me off. Then, a couple of years later, I came across a paperback of *Ratner's Star*, and read that with enormous interest, and I did read it all the way through. But I still wasn't sold on DeLillo. I could tell he was an awesome writer in some ways, I was intimidated by him, but I wasn't relating to everything in that book.

Then another two years go by, and just after conceiving the notion of *As She Climbed Across the Table*, I read *White Noise*, and it all came together for me. Suddenly he was a crucial writer for me, an unavoidable writer, one whom I was going to have to digest and incorporate. Then I read everything else. I read the rest of his works as well as some criticism, some secondary sources, during the year and a half of the first composition of *As She Climbed Across the Table*.

Having said all that, there are other really strong influences, on that book. Lem, and Lewis Carroll, and John Barth, and Malcolm Bradbury, and Terry Carr [laughs], and even Philip K. Dick are all influences. The voice is an amalgam of the voice Barth used in *End of the Road*, and *White Noise*. No one ever spots the Barth, partly because he's out of fashion, and even when he's read, it doesn't tend to be that book but the later, bigger books; and DeLillo is very much in fashion. But *End of the Road* is as strong an influence as anything, and the love triangle comes very directly out of that book. Philip's frustrations at having a rival who is elusive are exactly the problems of, not the narrator, but the other man in the love triangle. *End of the Road* is essentially a book written from the perspective of the Lack character, a formless, teasing, unstable, and elusive lover who breaks up an established couple. So I wrote from another leg of that triangle. And, you guessed it, I concretized Barth's metaphor!

FK: The ending, in which Philip climbs through Lack and finds alternate universes, reminded me of the ending of *White Noise*, when Jack Gladney rehearses in his mind various different behaviors he can act out, although I thought that the dialogue throughout was very *Ratner's Star*. I assume that Professor Soft is a nod to DeLillo's scientist character named Softly.

JL: Yes, it's a nod to Softly, absolutely. The science comes out of *Ratner's Star*, and the campus comes out of *White Noise* and other campus novels. Malcolm Bradbury's *The History Man* was a very strong influence on the party scenes and the social atmosphere of the campus.

FK: Since we're talking about influential voices, *As She Climbed* and other stories like, again, "Using It and Losing It," are concerned with problems of meaning, and understanding the world, and silence. I thought that, not only do you mention Beckett in *As She Climbed*, but it seemed to me very Beckettian, and I'm wondering what you think about Absurdism.

JL: Well, I like Beckett. He's one of those writers who seems almost too obvious to me. When I talk about ground I stand on—encountering Beckett, which I think for people a generation before was very destabilizing and very challenging, for me was very confirming. It was a very direct and confirming encounter for me. I saw what Beckett was up to, and I thought, "Yup. This makes sense." I didn't happen to get as deeply involved with Beckett as I did with, say, Kafka or Borges, to take people who are sort of in the same ballpark as icons of alienation and modernity, in that way. But I appreciated everything I understood about Beckett. There were particular works that I liked a lot. A play called *Krapp's Last Tape*. I didn't ever read the novels, the trilogy, and I know to a lot of people that's the great work. I really probably ought to read those. I read a short science fiction novel, about disembodied voices lying in storage and talking to each other through the coffins, called *The Lost Ones*. It's like Beckett's *Ubik*. I think there are things in Beckett that await my discovery, but everything I know, I like and respond to. But what I suspect are the essential ingredients in Beckett I happened to come to by means of Dick, or Lewis Carroll, or Borges, or Kafka first, and so when I got to Beckett I just nodded and said, "Yup, that's fine, that's good. It fits right in there." He didn't happen to be the transforming experience for me. Other people were.

FK: That's true. Those other writers are also concerned with problems of meaning and meaninglessness.

JL: Yeah. The funny thing is, I read Sartre's novels when I was very young. God knows why. It's almost as though I surrounded Beckett before I got to him. I was very well prepared, with one thing and another.

FK: None of that surprises me. Moving from absurdist silence to noise: What music do you listen to? Do you listen to music when you write?

JL: I do, constantly, yeah. I listen to a lot of different music. A lot of what I guess is called alternative rock, or the precursors to alternative rock. And jazz and funk and R&B and doo-wop and singer-songwriters. Lots and lots and lots of popular music. It's easier to list the things I don't listen to. I don't listen to heavy metal and I don't listen to fusion and I don't listen to classical music. I'm only just beginning to dabble in some world musics, some Third World musics. But in American popular music I listen to more forms and to more musicians than not.

FK: For the record, do you want to mention what you've contributed to music? You used to be a lyricist.
JL: Oh, yeah. Well, no.

FK: You don't want to get into that?
JL: I don't. It's silly. I've written lyrics for a few friends' rock bands, and I still do, every once in a while, and they're quietly being played, and in a couple of places recorded, but it doesn't seem to me a part of my—

FK: Oh, but it's cool.
JL: It's cool, yeah. But I'll tell you what's more interesting, what's more germane to this discussion: there's music that becomes very, very important, thematically loaded and resonant with things I write. *Amnesia Moon* has a soundtrack. It's an album by a band called My Dad Is Dead, called *The Taller You Are, The Shorter You Get.* Every song on that record has a chapter. It's the soundtrack to the book. The book I'm finishing now has a theme song, a song by John Cale called "Dying on the Vine." I can enunciate to some extent why that's the theme song of the book, and also some of it's just mysterious in that emotional way that musical connections can be. I get to a point where the relationship can be so strong that I'll use the song to help get back into the space of the book when I'm revising. All of this is simply to say that music is very, very important to me. I love film and I love painting and I love the arts. I'm passionate about the arts, but music is particularly—really reaches me very deeply, and if I was a talented musician I might not be a writer at all. I would be very grateful just to be able to sing like Al Green. I would just do that for people and be very, very fulfilled.

FK: I'll give you one last question, and this is one you can interpret any way you like, personally or universally. Where do you think the narrative impulse comes from?
JL: Well, I'm about to go sit on a panel about dreams, and if it goes in the direction I'd like it to, I'll talk about that. Because I think the narrative impulse comes out of the most fundamental functions of consciousness. Which is to say, the dreaming brain attempting to make sense of the dream—the dream in this case being the waking dream. Everything is so much more overwhelming and chaotic and discombobulated and paradoxical than anyone can cope with, and the brain is frantically, as I see it, sorting and organizing and narrativizing, just to be able to cross the room, just to be able to carry on this interview, and that is the narrative process. We're living, writing, the

novels of our lives all the time, and the novels of our relationships, and the novels of our family lives, and the novels of our friendships, and the novels of our own relation to objects and architecture and capitalism. That *is* narration. We're all helplessly narrating in order to proceed.

An Interview with Jonathan Lethem

Michael Silverblatt/1999

From *Bookworm*, KCRW-FM, November 18, 1999. Copyright © 1999 by KCRW-FM. Reprinted by permission.

Silverblatt: Hello, and welcome to *Bookworm*. This is Michael Silverblatt and today my guest is Jonathan Lethem. He's the author most recently of *Motherless Brooklyn*, a book from Doubleday, and in, well, the first book was called *Gun, with Occasional Music*, followed by *Amnesia Moon*, then a book of short stories, *The Wall of the Sky, the Wall of the Eye, As She Climbed Across the Table*, and *Girl in Landscape*. Now, he writes my favorite kind of book, which is a sort of fantasy containing elements of science fiction, mystery, but not locatable in any genre, almost as if smearing or bringing into hyperspace the best effects in all of these books without much caring about their simplified morals or their easy solutions. And so *Motherless Brooklyn* is, like his previous book, a book it seems to me about parents, although it takes the form of a detective novel in a way with a detective with Tourette's syndrome, and I wanted to start by asking you about orphans and parenting.

Lethem: Well, I feel that you've sort of nailed me. I think I've written about fathers and sons obsessively. And it's taken various forms . . . and there are generic echoes for me. I think Orson Welles's films are some sort of deep structural analogue where there's always the sort of the Kane figure and the reporter chasing him, the sort of remote father or mysterious father or grandiose father, sometimes an evil father, and a son who's trying to define himself in opposition or just struggle to separate the useful or pleasant parts of his inheritance from the odious ones. And sometimes I think I push into a larger family structure and talk about siblinghood a bit or motherhood a bit. But this new book is certainly absolutely a fathers-and-sons book, again. And I come to this material helplessly. It's not something I understood that

I was getting at until I'd already committed three books that had that theme in common.

Silverblatt: It's fascinating to me because Freud talked about the family romance and the family fantasy. And it has interested me that the books I've been caring about in this fantastic arena that are not genre bound are often ways of presenting an elaborate, beautiful, mesmerizing surface in order to explore a fantasy having to do with re-parenting or ghostly, ghastly figures of parents in a gallery who appear in this inexplicable pattern, almost as if the books were the result of a free association that occurs in narrative.

Lethem: You're making me think of the book previous to this one, *Girl in Landscape*, which I wrote partly with the phrase, just the two words, family romance as a kind of mantra for the feeling I wanted to get into it. And there's an underlying thinking about Henry James ghost stories where there's that uncertainty about characters who are transubstantiating out of the ghost realm into the psychological realm. And the intensity of projection onto a remaining parent when one parent is missing, the extrapolation of the ghost limb of a missing parent. And I do think that there are truisms that can be fertile—the old one that I'm always hearing and agreeing with and disagreeing with is that all novels are mysteries. But I also think all novels are Bildungsromans. They're all sagas of adolescence disguised in various ways. The second novel I wrote, *Amnesia Moon*, is about a man ostensibly in his thirties, but it's absolutely an x-ray of a kind of teenage search for self among the tattered remnants of adult identities. And I think that in some ways the new book is a confession or an uncloaking of that theme. I go back to the adolescence as the kind of key to the story.

Silverblatt: Well, let me restructure this then. What we have here in these last two books, the newest book is *Motherless Brooklyn*, the earlier one is *Girl in Landscape*. One book is a science fiction Western. The other is a putative detective novel whose hero is an orphan with Tourette's syndrome who is discovering in fact that his tic, his vocal tic, is a way of looking at the world, the way of scrambling the world out of its difficult and unknowable hierarchies so that he can gain some kind of control over it, while most people see this as loss of control. It would seem, in fact they have a nickname for him, Freakshow, but his actual name is—

Lethem: Lionel Essrog.

Silverblatt: [laughter] And interestingly, the Essrog, which is used in [unintelligible], never comes up as a reference in this book.

Lethem: Yeah, well, the secret heart of this book is Jewish, but Lionel isn't permitted to know that. And there are those couple of moments where he calls his relatives, his likely relatives, and they're named Essrog and they're in the Brooklyn phone book. And to my ear, just around the corner is the discovery that he's a Jewish kid, which is never discussed. And his faint double in the orphanage, the one who is left behind when the others are taken, is Stephen Grossman, who's obviously an overweight Jewish kid who's despised by the Italian and black kids there.

Silverblatt: At the orphanage. Now why in the course of scrambling the famous Oedipal romance do genres like science fiction, Westerns, mystery novels become useful to you?

Lethem: Well, I think, and I haven't ever formulated this thought before so it's going to come out and then I'll have to look at it, but that genres are sweetly pathetic confessions of adolescent longings. I mean, the only really obedient mystery novels or science fiction novels that don't somehow write themselves out of the genre, but instead fulfill it completely, are diagnosable as adolescent yearnings cloaked in various forms. And I mean, I've often argued that science fiction isn't a genre. There isn't a genre there. When you look at it closely it disappears. But it's sort of a nest of impulses and tendencies and borrowings from other, from literary genres that I think do have that deep generic structure. But if there's an exception to that, if there's one archetypal story that's been written in science fiction again and again, it's the sort of A. E. van Vogt slam narrative, the despised geeky kid in some form discovering that he's really the secret master of the universe and is needed to save the universe. And that comes up again and again in various forms. And so once you've identified that you can't write one honestly anymore. You have to look as much at the impulse to write something that stirs those feelings as allow yourself to stir them.

Silverblatt: I noticed that in each of the books as well there is the impulse to deform and restructure language. In *Motherless Brooklyn*, it takes the form of the Tourette's utterances, which in this case are not curses and obscenities. They're wild improvisations, homologues, Finnegan's Wake–like assemblages that nest together many of the elements that Lionel is facing and trying to articulate at the same time. In *Girl in Landscape*, there are creatures, Archbuilders, who regard English as only a language of naming things without meaning them. And so the books begin to take on this funny secondary language; almost as if in order to move forward in their dilemmas, your heroes have to work in a language different from the one spoken that obscures rather than reveals meaning.

Lethem: I'm absolutely in agreement that this is an arrow moving through my work and I think finding its target in the new one, in *Motherless Brooklyn.* I'd created a series of excuses, essentially, for Joycean wordplay, and it was always a marginalized character or characters who were allowed to thrive as a subculture in my earlier novels. In *Motherless Brooklyn,* I challenged myself to take this marginalized impulse for wordplay and free association and let it drive the book. Let it stand front and center and not quarantine it the way I had in the past, and let that become structure. But I think my impulse towards control also dictated that I symptomatize it, that I find Tourette's as my means so that it's bounded conceptually in some way. I mean, it would be a strange challenge which I hadn't ever considered until now to write a book with a character whose language resembles Lionel's but never explain or justify it any way. But I didn't take it to quite that degree. And there's a division in my work which is something you're getting at there, which is that growing up the two streams of my reading roughly broke into the beats and related influences, reading Whitman, reading Kerouac, reading Ginsberg, Henry Miller, and in the same camp I'd put my fascination as a teenager with Dada and surrealist writings. Where what's valorized is free linguistic play and a kind of unreconstructed, often unrevised ocean of language, torrents of language in all those writers. And at the same time I was reading voraciously in the crime genre, in science fiction, and I was also reading terribly influential novelists for me, like Graham Greene, for whom a tidy structure, organizing plot—that's what makes a book.

Silverblatt: For many of my friends who share your interest in science fiction and detective novels, the person who exploded it, who opened the door for them was William Burroughs, that mixture of the tough, hardboiled dick talk, meeting science fiction and all of it in a collage structure that's a metaphor for some kind of apocalypse that has torn everything apart. Leaving only elusive shards. Yeah?

Lethem: Right. He's a crucial writer for this notion of the tension between fiction making the allowances for modernist, linguistic play and yet retaining its ground in form and narrative plot.

Silverblatt: You're listening to *Bookworm.* My guest is Jonathan Lethem.

He's the author most recently of *Motherless Brooklyn.* Now I want to start and give a little bit of background here. Suddenly I was noticing your name everywhere. And in a period, very brief period, you went from publishers that specialize in genre fiction like Tor to publishers like Harcourt Brace Jovanovich, Doubleday, the majors, and your name has been appearing everywhere now. And I wondered, you know, it's a very rapid rise. Could you describe it?

Lethem: Well, first one quick correction. I started at Harcourt Brace, which in a strange sense was the key to the place I find myself now because I was published in a very undirected way by Harcourt Brace. They have no genre fiction per se as a tradition at that house. And so though they understood themselves to be acquiring a science fiction novel, their—what you might call the folkways of their in-house publishing—meant that it was published in a kind of genre-neutral way where it became a Rorschach blot. In fact *Gun, with Occasional Music* was largely received as a mystery novel when it was first published and when I'd done nothing else. And initially I had to explain again and again that I wasn't starting a series and you'd never see this character again.

Silverblatt: [laughter]

Lethem: Because I wasn't really that sort of writer. Fortunately I had another novel coming very quickly, and so I sort of shattered those, disappointed those expectations very quickly and took care of that bit of business. But, so it was always Harcourt Brace in hardcover and Tor in paperback, and then when I switched to Doubleday it became Doubleday in hardcover and Vintage in paperback. And what I've struggled for, I've sort of struggled in the cause of confusion in my career. On behalf of books unwritten, I've tried to make sure that my career didn't harden or settle into any one definition because I was adamant that I was going to do something different the next time. It wasn't that I wasn't excited to discuss *Gun, with Occasional Music* as a mystery, say, but that I had to keep clearing space for the fact that I knew I wasn't going to write anything that would satisfy a mystery, a strict mystery readership or strict expectations in a reader of a mystery again, at least for a long time.

And again I, then when *Amnesia Moon* made me a science fiction writer, I was thrilled to talk about that book in that context, but I had to keep sort of arguing for a proliferation of identities. And I was nudging book sellers to put the book in more than one section. And I got away with it. And I got away with it for a number of reasons, mostly luck of timing. That I wasn't in

Phil Dick's or J. G. Ballard's or Patricia Highsmith's situation, because they'd preceded me and set a context for doing this sort of thing. Whereas they had struggled unsuccessfully for the most part, for the majorities of their careers to be understood to be doing more than one thing at once or to be doing sort of none of the traditional things completely. And so that was just luck. I was standing on the shoulders of giants in that way. But then I simply began to be published more aggressively when I moved to Doubleday. And the aggressiveness was in the direction of asking reviewers to take the books seriously. And I guess it's mostly worked. I've been very fortunate in the reception of the last few.

Silverblatt: Well, it seemed to me that a good deal of what's grown through your work is adumbrated or, you know, referred to by the epigraph from Raymond Chandler in your very first book, *Gun, with Occasional Music.* It's there was nothing to it. The super chief was on time, as it almost always is, and the subject was as easy to spot as a kangaroo in a dinner jacket. Now there we've got—there's no real reason for Chandler to have written that way. And often it's not that little style as obvious as a tarantula on a slice of angel food cake, has become the key signature for hardboiled writing now. And it seems so irrelevant and passé that you wonder why people are still drawn to it. In your work there seems to be a recognition that almost unconsciously Chandler was being a surrealist and was referring while writing detective stories, it might be profitably thought of as a parallel universe being referred to in which kangaroos in dinner jackets or tarantulas and angel's food cake consorted with one another. Your work becomes a step further. Let's write solely about that alternate universe. Let's create a world in which these unlikely conjunctions, in which—what did they say about surrealism? That it was the meeting of an umbrella and a sewing machine on an operating table. Let's make a world which will have all the trappings of the Chandler world or of the Western world or of the sci-fi world, but let's see the umbrella and the sewing machine talk to one another.

Lethem: The idea of literalizing metaphors or calling metaphors' bluffs is . . . it almost becomes a mechanical process. If you look at my work from that angle, I again and again take sometimes things as apparently limited as an embedded or invisible pun in an everyday phrase, like a hardened criminal, and I take it autistically. I take it as though it were a non-metaphorical phrase. And I build a fictional world. Often every subsequent tool, every subsequent addition I make is pushing it closer and closer to realism. But it's founded on this misunderstood or autistically grasped metaphor, this literalized metaphor that is so powerfully absurd that the world is surrealist and becomes all the more surreal for being taken with deadly seriousness. The more I try to entrench a kangaroo in a suit or a criminal hardened into a brick-like form or whatever it is—

Silverblatt: [laughter]
Lethem: —the deeper I try to entrench them in realism, the more surreal the result.

Silverblatt: Which leads us to the new book where, for the first time in your fiction, the geek that Leslie Fiedler described as the man, the geeky guy who invented Superman, and the greater the impotence of the writer, the greater the virility of the superhero by the Fiedler formula. Here for the first time we have a geek who knows he's a geek, and the surrealist world is also a function of a psychological slippage.
Lethem: Um-hm.

Silverblatt: And so oddly enough this narrator, Lionel Essrog, who's constantly permuting phrases, Tourette's style, is oddly as well a stand-in for the author because when he narrates the book, the narration doesn't have any Tourette's slippages. It's only in dialogue that these occur, although this is a first-person novel. So it's as if the book is being written in collaboration with Jonathan Lethem and the two, the reporter and the criminal, are finding homes in one another, that this is a place where you have inter-penetrated the freak life.
Lethem: I love the description. And certainly I feel it's a book about denial in many ways or it's a book with masks always on the verge of being ripped off. And certainly it's always about to confess itself a book about the writing process and it never quite does. And the Tourettec compulsive generation of imagery and language, the compulsive reversals, the almost mechanical inversion of simple ideas or phrases or word forms, is a deep confession of my own writerly process. And also the grooming and organizing and currying is a confession of my experience of revision, which I think is about as Tourettec as—

Silverblatt: Your new book, *Motherless Brooklyn*, announces in its title the condition that *Girl in Landscape* ends with, the death of the mother. And I wanted to end by returning to our first subject, that subject of parentage. Can you draw this full circle?

Lethem: The simplest thing to add to the conversation is that I'm writing around, circling the death of my own mother when I was fourteen. And in fact that is treated fairly directly in the opening chapters of *Girl in Landscape*, which then hurtles into a John Wayne Western on another planet, as though in recoil from the direct address of the autobiographical material. I've snuck up on it in a very different way in the new one where I've omitted real parentage or known parentage completely and set these characters rather romantically in a Dickensian way in this unlikely orphanage in downtown Brooklyn. But I then proceed from more or less exactly the point where *Girl in Landscape* flinched to go on to talk about adolescence, parentless adolescence in the neighborhood I grew up in. So if you connect the two parts, you get a kind of autobiographical whole.

Silverblatt: I've been speaking to Jonathan Lethem, the author most recently of *Motherless Brooklyn*, from Doubleday. Thank you very much for joining me.
Lethem: Thanks for having me.

"Involuntary Deconstructionism": *Paradoxa* Interview with Jonathan Lethem

Shelley Jackson/2001

From *Paradoxa* no. 16, "Dark Alleys of Noir," edited by Jack O'Connell, 2002, ISBN: 1-929512-10-4. More information about this and other *Paradoxa* titles can be found at www.para doxa.com. Reprinted with permission.

Jonathan Lethem has snuck up on the literary establishment from the underside. His first novel, *Gun, with Occasional Music*, was part science fiction, part hardboiled detective novel; later books have paid due to other reaches of what is called genre writing, while dodging easy labels themselves. This shifty behavior could be a publicist's nightmare, but Jonathan has made a name for himself. Apparently he is easy to spot behind his masks. He earned his mainstream stripes with last year's *Motherless Brooklyn*, a crime novel (but also, as he points out below, "a Bildungsroman, a family romance, a coming-of-age story . . . a 'geek' novel") about a detective with Tourette's syndrome, which won the National Book Critic's Circle Award.

It would be underhanded to pretend the ordinary interviewer-subject relations obtain here. Jonathan and I have known each other for a long time, and our writerly beginnings are all snarled up together. Consequently, this is an interview straining to become a conversation, and partly succeeding, though perhaps at the cost of some of the traditional virtues of interviews. Maybe it would be best to think of this interview on noir as a particularly noir interview: an interrogation in which it is not always clear who is under examination.

Shelley Jackson: Do you think there is something particularly "noir" about *Motherless Brooklyn*? Offhand, I don't find the genre an especially useful reference, probably because I mostly think of noir in literal terms of black and white. The way those movies look—the plotless drama of light on objects. And I don't think about your writing in visual terms. But I suppose the noir connection has more to do with a sense of "degraded world" and faulty morals on all sides . . . and a "hero" with a problem?

Jonathan Lethem: There are many answers to that. First, impulsively, the visual stuff—you're absolutely right that I'm a less visual writer than you, a less visual writer than most, and a less visual writer than I'm often taken to be. Early on it was a constant surprise to be taken that way. The percentage of actual visual description in my work is unusually low—especially taken literally, as a sort of word-count per page of how I spend my writerly capital. Instead I tell stories in dialogue and reaction, in emotional descriptions and actions—stage plays or screenplays filled out everywhere with subjective response and counter-response, and speculation and concept, almost anything but visual information. And in fact what visual description—faces, rooms, clothing, landscape—is actually present in the published work has often been wrenched out of me by frustrated editors who say, "I can't see anything!"—a recurring passage in my editorial relationships. But I've come to see that the unusual environments my characters are forced to move through and their powerfully confused responses to those environments create an implicit visual level. I force visualization on the reader, and he then credits me with the work that he's done himself. Even in *Girl in Landscape*, which is openly a book about the desert, I don't so much describe the place as name it and its features again and again, until I've stacked up a big self-contradicting pile of nouns: pillars, rusty pipes, ruins, wreckage, pylons, monoliths, spires, smashed furniture. People get angry at me because I can't confirm their impressions of what an Archbuilder looks like! I ought to say "if I knew I'd tell you," but a more honest response would be "if I knew I wouldn't have been interested in writing about them," or "if either you or I knew I would have failed"—because keeping you in an irritated state of unreality is the point.

SJ: Wait a minute. Before you go on, tell me what you mean by "keeping the reader in an irritated state of unreality."

JL: Nothing more original or elaborate than that I'm just fond enough of metafictional moves to want to tease at them constantly, without quite committing overt metafiction. And of unreliable narration to tease at that without commitment as well. And that in a very Rod Serling sense I prefer—in an age of the "literal-fantastic"—to tease at the possibility of allegory or psychological metaphor every time I use fantastic motifs. Without ever doing Dorothy waking up and realizing that Oz was a dream. The ambiguity of an image woven of words is very dear to me—it distinguishes fiction from the literal, photographic quality of film, and film is otherwise intrusive on nearly every other special characteristic formerly reserved for the novel. So, however corny it may seem by now, I'm quite dedicated to bringing the "maybe it's all a dream or a metaphor or an allegory" level into view. Keeping it unresolvable. All my realist moves contain some back door of surrealism, if I get them right. And vice versa.

SJ: So you keep the visual information minimal to leave room for doubt.

JL: But, but, but—*Motherless Brooklyn* is somewhat an exception. There is more visual information on the page, in some places. It's true, though, that what information is there is quite colorful, not particularly noirish—the sepia seventies of gentrification-struck Brooklyn, the brownstones, the hues of tee-shirts and Italian ices and basketballs. Where my visual imagination clicked in, in that book—in some ways for the first time—it probably came out looking a lot like the colors of Spike Lee's *Crooklyn* or Scorsese's *Goodfellas.*

Switching rails completely: what you may have overlooked as influences out of traditional film noir in my work—and they're strong—have nothing to do with visuals. First, the great noirs of the forties and fifties are full of talk—vibrant, hostile, punning, impossible language—which, taken at its best and to its furthest in films like Hawks's *To Have and Have Not* and *The Big Sleep*, both of which were worked on by Faulkner, and most especially in *Force of Evil*, written by Abraham Polonsky, has a quality almost like Beckett crossed with Damon Runyon. Noir is one of the great fountains of American language. It sometimes—but perhaps not actually quite as often—reaches that same level of compression and vividness in the novels which are rightly associated with the films: Horace McCoy, Kenneth Fearing, Hammett, Chandler, and so on.

Second, filmed noir is full of tremendous narrative disjunctions—bizarre shifts of narrative perspective, flashback stunts which verge on unreliable narration, and a digressiveness which is anything but writerly or plot-defeating in the way digressiveness usually is in the novel. Instead imagine plots made up of all digressions or non-sequitur! Films like *Phantom Lady* and *Dark Passage* and *D.O.A.* are surrealist masterpieces. Don't take my word for it, ask the French.

Okay, now to your suggestion, the "degraded world." Yup, I'd say. I find it difficult to speak of this intelligibly anymore, because in many ways it's the ground against which the figure of my writing exists: the world is fucked: yes. Paranoia is frequently justified: yes. As a young reader I found confirmation for these intuitions in dystopian science fiction and in noir crime fiction and films.

SJ: Want to be specific?

JL: I read what felt to me then—1975 through 1980—like the entire backlist of science fiction. I read science fiction like a machine: Poul Anderson and Clifford Simak and Michael Moorcock and Perry Rhodan stories and Terry Carr anthologies and Robert Heinlein as though he were Shakespeare and Joanna Russ and Harlan Ellison and John Brunner and Vonda MacIntyre and C. M. Kornbluth and Olaf Stapledon and Robert Silverberg—everything. What stuck is what you'll find me sometimes talking about in interviews as an influence: Delany, Disch, some LeGuin, some Walter Tevis, one book each by George R. Stewart, George Orwell, D. G. Compton—and Philip K. Dick, who became at age fifteen simply and absolutely my favorite writer (in a way that's impossible now, when I've got a hundred favorites). Almost uniformly near-future dystopian settings and prose which pined for the "mainstream." Those are the only ones I really think about now. But it's worth confessing that all that other stuff soaked into my brain on a daily basis for a while. I was much more selective—snobbish, even—about crime fiction. I discovered Hammett, Chandler, and Stanley Ellin, and decided nothing else was good enough. So I reread those guys obsessively. Later, when I was twenty-one and just setting out to write *Gun*, I read the entire shelf of Ross MacDonald's books—those became very important to me for a while. And later the Black Lizard–type pulp rediscovery guys mattered to me enormously: Goodis, Woolrich, and Willeford especially. But that wasn't childhood reading, or formative influence.

SJ: What's your relationship to that stuff now?

JL: My writing is only just beginning to grow beyond the obsessive need to reach for those touchstones. I'll probably never outgrow it completely. Which is probably about the time to point out that I'm almost always (half-consciously) hiding one apparent "genre" under another, or under several. For instance, I just don't think *Motherless Brooklyn* is a noir novel in any important sense. It's just a crime novel: people carry guns and threaten one another with them constantly, and the secret that's revealed at the end involves money. But it's really a Bildungsroman, a family romance, a coming-of-age story, whatever. It's also a "geek" novel, in the tradition of *Catcher in the Rye* and *A Confederacy of Dunces*, maybe even *Flowers for Algernon*: the guy everybody thinks is an idiot or a jerk is really the most sensitive soul imaginable. And, if I'm right that it's a coming-of-age story, or a jerk story, it's in some ways a very sunny one. Whereas *Girl in Landscape*—which is apparently, but unimportantly, a science fiction novel, which fairly quickly peels away to reveal a Western underneath, and then perhaps also wants to be called a coming-of-age story—by the time you reach the finish is also more noir than any of my novels (I'll leave out the question of stories, some of which are quite noir) except possibly *Gun, with Occasional Music*. That's a degraded world, all right. And the morals are corrupted on all sides, you bet. Which curls back around to the way in which every dystopia is a noir and also a sentimental Paradise Lost and also a Western—a vision I'm probably a little suspicious of by now. The Planet of the Archbuilders was heaven before the bad people came, just as Chandler and James Fenimore Cooper know that southern California and the American West were paradise before the bad people came. Whereas Brooklyn is merrily corrupt forever, and nobody's claiming that humanity is a pox and a poison. You just shouldn't kill your own brother—that's low shit, man.

SJ: You said earlier that the colors of your Brooklyn are not very noir, but there is also that California vein in the noir tradition, which colorizes the noir—because even when the movies are black and white, California is always in color. (There's a statement for you, in the French tradition of dubious assertion delivered with bombast.) Noir California is bleached blond (dust, hills, hair), bleached blue (sea, sky), neon lights in the not-quite night, and that particular sordid feeling of lazy corruption in vacationland. The corruption in your Brooklyn feels more like that—kind of cheerfully, carelessly deadly—than like cold, practiced big city big business crime. Even though your bad guys are big business, they're also goofy; it's the contrast between their dorkiness and ineffectuality and the fact that they still might really hurt you that makes them sinister. Now it seems to me you often pull this kind of trick in your writing—you create almost cartoonishly goofy characters and situations, then give them mortal consequences for your main characters. I see something like this in noir too, in that good and evil are both in the hands of bozos—the good guys have dirty secrets, the hero isn't one, the bad guys are mean without being evil in a swirling black cloak, Forces of Darkness way; they're just small-time entrepreneurs with particularly forceful business practices. Nonetheless there's a feeling of high tragedy hanging around these clowns.

JL: Well, there's a buried skepticism in *Motherless* about the likelihood of sophisticated evil. I guess I was feeling that the real literary lie contained in so much crime fiction and so many crime films is the Machiavellian authority and charisma credited to the villains—and though I failed to completely avoid that fallacy in the book, I did manage to get my uneasiness with it onto the page.

SJ: You mentioned that you like to leave the back door open to surrealism, and in fact I've always noticed the absurd and the surreal sort of burbling up through the loopholes you leave for them, a kind of outbreak of pointless gay mayhem. (I can't help thinking of Tourette's here.) But because your sensibility is plotty, or to put it more politely, you are interested in truth and consequences, you make those blips part of the motor of the plot, instead of either editing them out or turning them into scenery. Like if the drunken porter suddenly pulled a gun on Macbeth. I think of this as a way for someone dedicated to a traditional model of novel as plot machine to let linguistic and visionary excess into your writing. What do you say?

JL: Well, I actually think you're simply naming one of the purest fiction virtues: surprise. Startling turns and digressions in fiction are lifelike and exciting in traditional ways. The freshness of a good surprise isn't really intrinsically surrealistic, only absurd in the way life can be. What's surrealistic and disjunctive isn't the turn, I think, but the rationalizing mind's attempt to knit it into a reasonable plot. It's the explanations which claim to justify the outbreaks which are truly surrealistic.

SJ: Which brings us back to Philip Dick, and the way he upsets the logic of his novels over and over again, creating these disjunctive moments that leave you as disoriented as if you were reading, say, Robbe-Grillet, but then rescues you (barely) with a new level of plotting. (Not that your writing is discombobulating in the same way—I just mean that, similarly, it's indulging a taste for chaos while giving it an alibi within the logic of the fictional world.) So one might say you're following a tradition of genre fiction that is not really good at being genre fiction, that fucks up its own project out of restlessness and excess of imagination, but becomes more complex and interesting in the attempt to rescue it. But, paying attention to what you said about noir as disjunctive and surrealist, maybe that is not "fucking up its own project," maybe it's what makes the project work. And maybe I shouldn't be trying to place you in relation to Philip Dick, anyway, since *Motherless Brooklyn* is not science fiction, although as science fiction goes, Dick's books seem very noir to me (in the California vein): the world is crumbling, there is no innocence, the surface will not hold your weight and underneath things are very different . . .

JL: Disjunction as noir's method: yes. Dick as noir: yes. California noir: yes. Nothing I need to add to those thoughts. But I will go on about California a bit, and let that lead me back to Brooklyn.

I'd thought it was very obvious that I'd been writing insistently about the Golden State until *Girl in Landscape.* Writing about it in a series of metaphorical or allegorical cartoons, because that was how I experienced California—as an ahistorical (*Gun*), simulated ("Forever, said the Duck"), postulated ("How We Got in Town and Out Again") space, a "faked" environment in many ways, where projection (*As She Climbed Across the Table*) and illusion (*Amnesia Moon*) flourished, an intrinsically experimental place where utopias and dystopias could be set up and knocked down quickly by Teamsters with sledgehammers. A set of props that exposed how human society is a consensual fiction. And, as a kind of adjacent subject, I'd written about the desert states, which made such an impression on me on my visits to Arizona and Utah and through the Westerns I'd begun to obsess on: this was the real, vacant, pre-human landscape upon which the bluff of California was so recently set up . . .

In *Girl in Landscape* I'd dared myself to set something in Brooklyn again, and wrote those opening chapters, which were so unexpectedly autobiographical and sad, then set the characters in flight from the troubling realistic ground of Brooklyn to another desert fantasy—a California or Arizona of forgetting disguised as a Burroughsian Mars. (Actually, there is one very early precursor to *Girl*: the only other time I'd written about New York City before that was a story called "Light and the Sufferer," a darkly autobiographical piece which contains in it the yearning for flight to—surprise—California). So in *Girl* I'd recapitulated the terms of my own migration west and exposed the need to address Brooklyn in order to transcend my own exhausted, detached, and cynical take on "home" and "place."

SJ: So Brooklyn is a place you can't take lightly, and that's why in *Motherless Brooklyn* your setting has more solidity than in earlier books. But so, I think, does your main character. What's most striking to me about *Motherless Brooklyn* is what you're calling the "geek" thing: this book has much more of a still center than your others (though *Girl* is getting there); everything wheels around the figure of Lionel. And the genre stuff—the action, the machinery of plot—is more important for how it makes him move than for its own sake. It even seems like you're staging a little confrontation between two motives in your writing, like: what happens if plot meets this character? It's like you're doing the plot *to* the character and there's some reluctance and resistance; the character would like to just *be*, but you won't let him.

JL: Well, that's partly just to say that there is an unreliable narration aspect to *Motherless*—Lionel wants to believe he's already an important hardboiled detective at the start of the book, but he's forced to know he's just a stooge. The illusion that he's a Chandler character is only sustainable in the theatrical set of his own apartment. He's also motivated to distract himself from his own Tourette's, and so he's awfully complicit with the plot which comes and "does itself" to him. But I'll agree you're onto something in a larger sense— I'm pushing towards a more meditative and character-based writing in this book—paradoxically so, since the surface is mostly boiling with distractions and action. The whole book, apart from the long flashback to boyhood, is one "guy walking through the door with a gun."

SJ: But to me there's an illusive quality about some of his trials: are they really real? Is he going to let them make him do things or is he going to resist? His character doesn't dissolve into the plot, it stays slightly separate from it and more real. So it feels a bit like the author is fucking with this poor guy, and his real life is getting contorted by these silly events, because he's stuck in this novel!

JL: In *Motherless Brooklyn* I set up a dialogue between my new "earnest" exploration of landscape and culture and my old, cartoonish methodology. That's the noir plot calling me back to California, and Lionel Essrog's personal history and yearning for home and for an understanding of the "real" Brooklyn working in opposition to it. I suppose it will seem predetermined when I explain that in the book I'm writing now I think—I hope—I'm tackling Brooklyn as Brooklyn at last. But, in response to your comments on Lionel's seeming somewhat trapped in his own book—a real character plagued by cartoons (from within and without, perhaps?): I'm with you. I've just myself noticed the tendency of thriller plots to have a moment where a plot-bound man has to persuade a skeptical, innocent woman of the reality of his preposterous dilemma—just this week I've seen it in *Three Days of the Condor* and *The 39 Steps*. I've unconsciously recapitulated that in *Motherless*, and it reminds me of how I'd felt intuitively, without even being certain what I meant by it, that Kimmery is the only other "real" character in the book besides Lionel. She encounters his realness and briefly tempts him out of his thriller plot, into a calmer world. And when he refuses to leave the cartoon she slips away.

There's something else we've been implicitly discussing here: the "uses" of noir for fiction, and there's one I probably should have mentioned already but forgot. Noir has effortlessly made a tradition or motif out of doing something that fiction struggles elsewhere to do easily (or fails to even try) which is move through class boundaries. Detectives plop in and out of ghettos and the homes of the wealthy . . . somehow that rather simple value has been slighted in our talk. It sort of fits here where we're going on about milieu, I think.

SJ: You could also look at this as another way noir creates disjunction. This is part of the feeling of world broken down: the detective, as an outsider, exposes the fragility of normality, which relies on its internal consistency to maintain its cred. Noir is less about the one humdrum crime that triggers the investigation than it is about the broad disintegration of normality, a sort of chain reaction of collapse which is also just a revelation of the way things already are. The introduction of the detective into the normal world, even though he's there to preserve it, is also itself already the collapse of that normalcy. It doesn't really matter whether his motives are good or bad, he's trouble. He's trouble for the criminal element, too, for the same reason—he's kind of the pure agent of discombobulation—a sort of Coyote figure. But, tragically, he's sentimental, he adores the normal world he ruptures, and he's prepared to take extraordinary risks to save it, though the rewards for him are minimal at best. Lionel is sentimental like that: he longs for a sense of belonging, but it's frail and provisional (he's an orphan, what he "belongs" to is a group of other displaced people). In other words there's nothing there— which is also the dark noir truth, what is revealed at the end: that what he's saving doesn't exist, the dame is rotten, the nice home is supported by dirty money, his own code of ethics, which might be something to hang onto in a degraded world, turns out to create its own horrors, etc. etc.—that is, that the breakdown isn't a breakdown but a revelation of the way things are.
JL: All of the above: it's exhausting to be understood so thoroughly. It does provide a service, however: for all that some reviewers and readers might have seemed to want to persuade me that *Motherless Brooklyn* was a "new" kind of book, a breakthrough into new realms, I always suspected that it

was instead a consolidation, a crystallization, at best a culmination of the narrative-political-Weltanschauung material I'd been obsessively reworking in all three of the dystopian books and of the linguistic material I'd begun chewing on in *Table* and *Girl*—that it was in some ways much less a breakthrough than a finishing, a clearing the decks for work that would strike (at least me) as more persuasively new. Your analysis seems to me an effective and undeniable demonstration that my suspicions are true. A part of me never wants to have to think about this stuff again.

SJ: Oh, but you must. Let's talk about Tourette's for a minute: if the detective is a device to create disjunction, then you've amped that in *Motherless Brooklyn* by giving your detective Tourette's. His affliction (or gift) also makes him an agent of discord, linguistically and socially. That's an interesting point of connection: the noir detective is professionally what the Tourette's victim is personally, someone who breaks code. But both are actively trying to preserve the code they're breaking.

JL: One of the unfulfilled ideas I plopped into the first chapter of the book was that the other guys at the Minna agency appreciate Lionel because he doesn't mind sitting and listening to wiretaps all day—the presumption that the flood of banal talk is overwhelming and stultifying to anyone else, but that he's comfortable listening to monologues, interior or otherwise. What the detective and the Tourettic have in common is that they try to isolate meaning in a flood of nonsense—code, in this case, consisting of that buried meaning. And if you've ever looked at long transcriptions of spoken language (Andy Warhol's ostensible novel, called "A," is what I have in mind) you'll understand when I say that the novel's relationship to spoken language is something like the difference between traditionally mediated and edited sentences and Tourette's ludicrous flood (except I should stress here that, as always, this is my literary fantasia of Tourette's, not anything realistic or medical!)

SJ: Lionel's Tourette's isn't purely chaotic, though. In fact it's a sort of temptation to create alternate codes that seduce him away from the standard grammar—of language, of behavior. The revelation of the criminal plot is seductive to Lionel, in the same way Tourette's is seductive: it's an alternate patterning of reality, which has a gathering force over his imagination. For some time, if I remember correctly, he's not completely convinced that it's the real world, just that it has an attractive consistency as a pattern. (I think of *The Crying of Lot 49*: reality as just the most persuasive pattern.) Conspiracy theories work this way too: eventually an alternate pattern acquires enough density and internal consistency that it can snap free of its mooring in the "reality pattern" that has our group vote and compete with it. At a certain point it doesn't matter whether it's true or not: what matters is it works. In fact it's pretty senseless, as any pattern is senseless: it exists because it has a formal strength. This is how Lionel's Tourette's works, his outbursts are like fractals generated off the material of everyday; they have a logic, certain permutations are possible and not others. Like crystals proliferating in a solution (as in Ballard's *Crystal World*): the runaway patterning of stuff. Even though it looks chaotic, its power is its formal, even mathematical necessity. Tourette's exposes the autonomous, recombinant, impersonal side of language, it exposes that an active patterned chaos lies very close under the surface of what we think of as transparent self-expression and meaningful communication. You could think of Tourette's as an involuntary deconstructionism. You could also think of Tourette's as the noir of speech.

JL: I'm paralyzed by the flood of analytical relevance here—your interviewer's Tourette's is rather overwhelmingly covering this interview in a flood of language, and I come to see that excessive sympathy between interviewer and subject can be a disadvantage. As in certain love affairs, which compel attention because of the difficulty of pushing meaning across some psychological or emotional or cognitive (or foreign language) "gulf between"—or the case of a novelist pursuing his own themes blindly, energized precisely by his ignorance and the necessity of groping towards glints of light—the unsympathetic interviewer might actually elicit more interesting responses than someone who's been for me a sort of simultaneous writing-teacher and writing-student. You, say. Excessive sympathy can be a disadvantage. Or did I say that already?

SJ: So it's the communication gap that keeps you going: you feel a compulsion to fill the void. And you're talking about *my* Tourette's? I can't help pointing out that in talking about floods of language, codes and patterns, sense and nonsense, we're also inevitably talking about the writer here, the writer as someone helplessly, almost pathologically drawn to creating patterns, someone bound to follow the logic of the pattern even when it takes him off to one side of the "real" world, but who tries to serve the real world through this peculiar activity, though in a sense his activity actually threatens the patterning of the real (partly by providing alternatives, partly by exposing the extent to which it is a pattern). Now from the noir point of view the "thriller plot" is the real world, and the stable everyday is a sweet delusion. True for Philip Dick too. But despite all the points of similarity here, I think in *Motherless Brooklyn* you are drawn away from that template. Like you say, the thriller world is a little cartoonish, and there is a more stable place where slower and more unclear things go on, as embodied in Kimmery. I get the feeling that for you in this book, reality might be the place where you can't find a pattern. Resisting the temptation to follow the plot might be the only way to have a real life. Lionel kind of screws this up. So where does that leave him?

JL: Okay, okay, I'm "drawn" away—yes. There's that glimmer of breakthrough. In the mood I'm in today I wish it were more substantial, but you're right, I'm afraid: I smothered reality with cartoonish motifs and plot from underneath—a ground of cartoon—and then dropped a low sky of cartoonish Tourette's language on top, so that you can barely stand up straight for lack of room!

Well, you'll see that in lieu of any other method for interestingly screwing this interview up I've allowed a certain irritability to enter my tone—my answers are shorter by far than your "questions" now, and that's because you're so right you not only leave me nothing to say, but cause me to find my own work dull and pedantic.

SJ: So this is the interview where the interviewer drowns out the interviewee like some sort of (more amicable) Kinbote. The commentator has the last word, and most of the other words too. Perhaps by the end of the "interview" I will allow only the occasional "um" or "well . . ." from you. Hey, I can't help it if you keep agreeing with me! I guess if I said something markedly dumb or wrong you could at least put me straight. But would that be interesting?

JL: No.

SJ: I think the real problem is that I'm more interested in your book than you are, for the obvious reason that, unlike you, I've only read it once.

JL: Yes.

SJ: I will mention that I don't agree with *you* about a few things: I don't think the Tourette's language is a cartoonish aspect of the book, or a "low sky"—if anything it opens outward, it unravels thing. And it comes from a completely different part of the writer-you than the "cartoonish" genre stuff does, and one you've never given such free rein. But how have I suddenly persuaded you that your work is "dull and pedantic"? Is there something wrong with returning over and over to the themes that obsess you? (That was a rhetorical question, not an interviewer's question. I'll answer it: no.) And what's all this about smothering reality with cartoons? Reality is a literary construction. It's a cartoon too! But perhaps you disagree? No, really, I'm asking: what's going on—what's this "reality" business?

JL: How could I disagree? Of course you're right, reality is a literary construction and a cartoon. You've brought me back to my senses. But my tantrum perhaps points out how I'm leaning away from certain kinds of reality-as-cartoon in my work, and towards others. What I began to get at with Lionel and his language—and from this view the book seems so terribly at war with itself!—is the way reality is a cartoon inflated from within language and the psyche. I began to want to put a naturalistic skin over the top of this balloon of the imaginary that is of course always expanding. So when I reached for the reality-sandwich metaphor I guess I meant it was this stretched veneer of the naturalistic over Lionel's sensibility that itself became pressed against the cartoonish-noirish exoskeleton of plot—and that's what I'm sick of. The exoskeleton of genre plot. I'm done with noir in that sense, at least for the time being.

Reality. Sigh. I'm at odds over whether to talk about the book I'm working on next—but whatever amount I do talk about it, it surely feels like the end of this exchange to me. I've been reading things like Henry Roth's *Call It Sleep*, Kazuo Ishiguro's *The Unconsoled*, and James Baldwin's *Another Country*, and Anthony Powell's twelve-volume *Dance to the Music of Time*, and Paula Fox's *Desperate Characters*, and Samuel Delany's *Dhalgren*—mostly very long books, or long books made of many short books, but in every case, even the Paula Fox novella, books absolutely structured by a "naturalistic" sprawling shaggy life-likeness. They spill and swell and stagger and do anything but move forward from within a working machine of plot. They're shaped like bags, which take the form of what's contained—not like things with skeletons at all. And I'm adamantly writing one like that myself, which in that regard will be adamantly unlike any of the previous novels. But also— more complicated to admit—I've become much more interested in mimetic textures like David Gates's, and Ann Beattie's, and Richard Yates's, and Philip Roth's. All that stuff. I know this isn't supposed to be my strength! But I'm headed towards a fantastic which is grained like realism, which everywhere makes feints of realism. Which is all "realism" can ever do, right? So I'm be-coming a realist. Right? Right. I said it. There. Except there are going to be superheroes. And that's all I can say about it at the moment.

SJ: Maybe we should end it there.
JL: Right, excellent. Let's be done.

The Art of Fiction No. 177:
Jonathan Lethem

Lorin Stein/2003

From *The Paris Review*, Issue 166, Summer 2003. Copyright © 2003 by *The Paris Review*, reprinted with permission of The Wylie Agency LLC.

Jonathan Lethem was born in 1964, the son of the painter Richard Lethem and the late political activist Judith Lethem. His first three novels earned him a following among readers of crime novels and science fiction, and a reputation among readers of experimental novels as a pasticheur whose parodies had an uncanny beauty and depth of their own: *Gun, with Occasional Music* (1994) is the first and only volume in a notional series of Chandleresque whodunits. *Amnesia Moon* (1995) is a post-apocalyptic road novel. *As She Climbed Across the Table* (1997) is an academic novel, a Don DeLillo spoof, about a professor whose girlfriend falls in love with her physics experiment. Lethem's stories, many of which first appeared in the purist pages of *Asimov's Science Fiction* magazine, were collected in *The Wall of the Sky, the Wall of the Eye* (1996).

Each of these books brought Lethem new readers, but it was *Girl in Landscape* (1998), a short novel about a Brooklyn girl's sexual awakening on a distant planet, that first showed his mettle as a psychologist and won converts among readers who hadn't cut their teeth on Philip K. Dick or Robert Coover. Although *Girl in Landscape* is set in the future, in space, it wasn't just dreamlike and learned and funny, it was moving. Its voice was intimate. It was a novel for common readers. Lethem now calls it the first novel of his maturity.

Girl in Landscape was also the first of Lethem's novels to return, obliquely, to his Brooklyn childhood. Lethem grew up in Gowanus, the racially mixed neighborhood of brownstones, tenements, and housing projects that surrounds the Gowanus Canal (an area now gentrified and rechristened Boerum Hill). This makes Lethem the only inner-city kid in the generation of novelists with whom he is usually associated: Jonathan Franzen, David Foster Wallace, Jeffrey Eugenides, Michael Chabon, Colson Whitehead, and Rick Moody. His memories of the city life of children provided raw material for the fantastical Carroll Gardens of *Motherless Brooklyn* (1999); they are the heart of *Fortress of Solitude* (2003).

As a teenager Lethem studied painting at the High School of Music and Art in Manhattan. After high school he attended Bennington College, briefly—making him the one novelist of that group named above never to get a college degree—then eventually moved to the Bay Area, where he lived until 1998. During these years he supplemented his income as a writer by working in used bookstores. It's the only job he's ever had, and it has given him an erudition peculiar to antiquarians, a knowledge of books that is precise, catholic, and bibliographical, with particular concentrations in the underdog and outsider. A conversation with Lethem usually renews the cheerful conviction that some of the best books you will ever read are books you haven't heard of yet.

Around the time that *Girl in Landscape* appeared, Lethem moved back to Brooklyn, took an apartment in his old neighborhood (as many writers were doing), and began to hold impromptu get-togethers every few months at his local bar, the Brooklyn Inn. This interview—or, rehearsals for this interview—began late one of those evenings, about three years ago, when I asked Lethem why the Brooklyn House of Detention—the big, glow-in-the-dark brutalist jail down the street from the bar—never shows up in *Motherless Brooklyn*. This question led to a very friendly and intense discussion of the various imaginary jails in Lethem's science fiction, the relationship between novels and their real-life settings, and the book that Lethem was then writing. Which, he said, was partly about the jail.

That novel, *Fortress of Solitude,* is Lethem's first novel of wide-angle social realism. It is indeed about the jail, and the place of jails in American life. It is also about superheroes, soul music, science fiction, community empowerment, Spaldeens, graffiti, gentrification, and headlocks. The novel follows two friends, Dylan Ebdus and Mingus Rude—one white, the son of an experimental filmmaker, the other black, the son of an R&B singer, both motherless, both obsessed with comic books—from the 1970s through the 1990s. Along the way it captures a big swath of what used to be called, reverently, the inner city, and of boyhood and manhood in America.

To this day Lethem remains his own best, most curious biographical critic: all an interviewer needs to do is sit down, press record, and try to keep up. And that is exactly what happened last fall, during three sessions in Lethem's third-floor walkup—in a study neatly lined with mass-market paperbacks—over the bottle of old scotch that came with Lethem's Gold Dagger Award for crime fiction, and next to it, an ever-growing, generously proffered stack of recommendations for further reading.

Lori Stein: You don't strike me as an especially paranoia-prone guy, but there is paranoia all over your writing. Is that just a literary device?

Jonathan Lethem: My parents were Vietnam War protesters; I grew up in the era of Watergate; the first president I remember is Nixon. I remember being instructed as a child that I shouldn't go to school and blurt that Nixon was evil. Not that we didn't *know* he was evil at home, it just might not be such a good idea for me to say it. I felt he was evil like Dracula. It was like being taught not to curse when you go to your grandmother's. So when I found that Rod Serling and Philip K. Dick and Thomas Pynchon also agreed with me that the president was probably an evil robot programmed by a computer, it was merely a matter of pleasurable recognition that someone was naming the world.

In that sense, I'm a native. When you say I don't appear paranoiac to you, I figure you mean I don't traffic in the thin membrane of social paranoia. Why bother? We live in a fallen universe. We can at least be kind to one another and not jump on one another's slightest errors or moods. In a desperate situation, pick your battles.

Stein: My sense of you, compared to people we know in common, is that you don't care much about politics.

Lethem: Listen: I'm thirty-eight. The first third of my life was spent at political demonstrations, shouting my lungs hoarse. It was as much a part of my existence as having a holiday off from school. Those were my holidays. That's how I visited different cities, that's how I met adults besides my parents. I was a protester by birthright. I put in my time before I could conceive that the world wasn't being transformed by the people around me, my parents' generation. When you're in the center of demonstrations, you believe. My life *was* a demonstration. I was sent to public school in impoverished neighborhoods on principle. The day-care center on the corner of Nevins and Atlantic, in Brooklyn; I was there on its opening day, and I understood it as something that our protests at City Hall, the years before, had produced. I stood at the feet of police horses, holding a sign for day care, and then was there the first day it opened. I lived the belief that private school was anti-American. Can you possibly understand? It's personal. It's there in my work.

Stein: In the form? In the imagination?

Lethem: In the hope that some fourteen-year-old kid in Milwaukee reads *Amnesia Moon* and is ratified in his suspicion that the government is television, that George Bush is the star of a rotten soap opera. That's all I have to offer, what Philip K. Dick had to offer me, solidarity. My politics are everywhere.

Stein: You've said elsewhere that by going to Bennington College you'd rejected your family's political dedication to the idea of public school. But Bennington was an art school.

Lethem: It's impossible to talk about my going to Bennington without talking about the fact that I began dropping out of Bennington—rejecting it in a "you can't fire me, I quit" sort of way—immediately upon arrival. It's absolutely true that I was trying to prove something by running away to a world of privilege. I meant to prove I wasn't deprived, and my reward was a violent confrontation with the realities of class. A confrontation I'd then spend ten years recovering from. I was frightened by my father's bohemian idealism, and I was equally frightened by what I saw as the corruption of art by money and connections at Bennington.

Stein: You don't seem to have bothered to rebel against your parents' milieu—their bohemianism, their leftism.

Lethem: I tried. It's very hard to rebel against parents whose lives are so full and creative and brilliant—the option is my generation's joke: the rebel stockbroker. That wasn't for me. I wanted what my parents had, but I needed to rebel by picking a déclassé art career. My father came from the great modernist tradition, and so I found a way, briefly, to disappoint him, to dodge his sense of esteem. *Very* briefly. He caught on soon enough that what I was doing was still an art practice more or less in his vein.

I felt I ought to thrive on my fate as an outsider. Being a paperback writer was meant to be part of that. I really, genuinely wanted to be published in shabby pocket-sized editions and be neglected—and then discovered and vindicated when I was fifty. To honor, by doing so, Charles Willeford and Philip K. Dick and Patricia Highsmith and Thomas Disch, these exiles within their own culture. I felt that was the only honorable path.

Stein: But elsewhere you've described the sustenance you were taking, around this time, from international writers like Calvino, Cortázar, and Borges.

Lethem: Yes. As a teenager I read those writers voraciously in a rich collision—or should I say conflation?—with the American crime and science fiction writers I was equally obsessed with. And I devoured literary writing in English as well, but only the kind that had been fashionable in the sixties. Once I began to understand the contemporary atmosphere of the eighties—the Ann Beattie, Richard Ford, Raymond Carver attitude, which I've admired in retrospect, but which was an absolute shock to me at the time— I felt only more deeply confirmed as an outsider. Between disreputable or out-of-fashion American writers and those "International Fabulists," neither of which camp seemed relevant to the writers at Bennington, I stitched together a notion: I'd be the American Calvino, but nourished by scruffy genre roots. As though this would comprise a movement or school of writing to contextualize lonely me. It just didn't exist, that was the only problem. There was nothing there. I could declare it, and a few people would be gulled and say, Oh, you're going to be that thing!—but only because I'd just described it with such energy and affection. But there's no such thing.

Stein: So you'd say things to your friends like, There's nothing going on at the big houses, Knopf hasn't published anything in years.

Lethem: I had no idea what Knopf had published in years. Listen, you can't imagine what a freak I was. I worked in used bookstores as a teenager. I grew up with hippie parents. I lived in a ten-year cultural lag. At *all* times. I had not the faintest idea what was contemporary. When I got to Bennington, and I found that Richard Brautigan and Thomas Berger and Kurt Vonnegut and Donald Barthelme were not "the contemporary," but were in fact awkward and embarrassing and had been overthrown by something else, I was as disconcerted as a time traveler. The world I'd dwelled in was now apocryphal. No one read Henry Miller and Lawrence Durrell, the Beats were regarded with embarrassment. When all that was swept away, I stopped knowing what contemporary literature was. I didn't replace it; I just stopped knowing.

Stein: Were kids actually talking about writers in college?
Lethem: Bret Ellis was. Bret, Donna Tartt, Jill Eisenstadt, others.

Stein: How quickly did you and Bret Easton Ellis get to know each other?
Lethem: Quickly, but not well. I could probably count our conversations. They were always wary, glancing, and extremely interesting. We discussed film. I talked about Hitchcock, and Bret about Altman. I realized that I actually didn't know *anything* about what was going on. That there was such a thing as *going* on—the last time I checked in with it was when my mother died when I was thirteen. There was no weather vane for me. Bret and a few others dragged me, halfway, into the present.

Stein: Before you dropped out.
Lethem: I'd begun a first novel, and I told myself I was dropping out to write it. The school cost a then astronomical fourteen thousand dollars a year. I only wanted to work in bookstores and write fiction. I explained it to myself very logically at the time—I liked hanging out with my new friends and I hated going to class. Since I was paying to go to class, I dropped out. I was one of those creepy dropouts who moves into his girlfriend's dorm room. She stole meals from the dining hall in a Tupperware container hidden in a hollowed-out textbook, and I sat in her room and wrote an unpublishably bad first novel.

Stein: You could have gone to a state school.
Lethem: I could have done a lot of things.

Stein: It's a funny decision for a kid to make.
Lethem: I needed to make it. I was in another educational system, anyhow—antiquarian bookstores. I'd worked in three of them already before going to Bennington, and I resumed that career as soon as I dropped out. I worked my way up to one of the best in the country, Moe's in Berkeley. An old-fashioned apprenticeship for a writer. It's still the only job I've ever held, besides authoring.

Stein: I'd like to ask if you can remember something about the actual writing of each book.
Lethem: Sure. *Gun, with Occasional Music* is a piece of carpentry. I wanted to locate the exact midpoint between Dick and Chandler. William Gibson had published *Neuromancer* and people called it "hardboiled science fiction."

I was like, Dude, that's just well-written science fiction. It's not hardboiled. Those saying it had never read Pynchon, who Gibson was really doing. It's Pynchon in spades, very nicely done. I thought, "You want hardboiled? The California tradition is quite exacting. I've actually read those books. Let me show you. And I fused the Chandler/Ross MacDonald voice with those rote dystopia moves that I knew backwards and forwards from my study of Ballard, Dick, Orwell, Huxley, and the Brothers Strugatsky.

Stein: Who?
Lethem: You've neglected your research. The Strugatskys were Soviet SF writers. Tarkovsky based *Stalker* on one of their novellas. Their *The Ugly Swans* depicts people trudging through their lives in a very Orwellian way, and raising a generation of dronelike, eerie children who hate them and constantly rat them out to the authorities. Basically, a thinly disguised depiction of what it was like to be a pre-Soviet parent raising a Soviet-educated child. I lifted this allegory and stripped the political meaning from it. Hence the babyheads in *Gun*.

Stein: I was recently rereading *Amnesia Moon*, the only book of yours that no one has stolen from me. I liked it much better this time. It's risky for a novel to posit different "levels" of reality because once you start doing that the reader doesn't know . . .
Lethem: What matters.

Stein: It seems that you were free-associating, from the very beginning of the novel, and the voice you heard happened to be outrageously *funny*.
Lethem: I like that description. That's the best I can hope for *Amnesia Moon*. It was meant to be honestly dreamlike. Humbly so. That book's an anthology of my apprentice work. It was made out of failed short stories. It actually contains my earliest published writing. But it also consists of an analysis of the reasons for the failure of my earliest work. Those shameless, earnest early stories that now seem to me to be written by an obnoxious child. In them I'm compulsively imitating J. G. Ballard and Philip K. Dick. But also getting curious about Italo Calvino and Steve Erickson. And making the discovery that I really couldn't possibly be a science fiction writer.

Stein: What did that mean to know that you weren't going to be a science fiction writer?
Lethem: Well, I'd romanticized something that didn't exist.

Stein: What did you romanticize?

Lethem: An exile identity, that seemed to me heroic in Dick. I thought everyone understood he was more interesting than what was in fact the genre's main center of operation. I thought once there had been Dick or Ballard or Thomas Disch that you couldn't ever glance back at that other stuff. I projected my own feeling about it onto the world, as I was doing relentlessly then. Of course, that became part of the subject matter of *Amnesia Moon.*

Stein: Can you talk about what kinds of problems you thought were getting definitively solved, by Dick or the others?

Lethem: Pulp SF of the 1930s magazine type is folk art. Then Dick comes along and isolates those tropes that connect it to literature, surrealism, film, comic books, rock and roll. He's George Herriman, he's Buster Keaton, he's Bob Dylan. Dick discards the uninteresting stuff, the pedantic explanations, and preserves precisely the dreamlike, surrealist, evocative, paranoiac reverberations that were all I ever cared for, when I found them scattered elsewhere. I couldn't imagine that someone else would think Dick had thrown out the wrong stuff, which is exactly what many who exalt the genre think.

That's what *Amnesia Moon* is about. Getting over the illusory affiliations and the chimerical causes and locating your heart's real concerns. And recognizing what interference is coming from you, your own projections. Another reason I couldn't go on wanting to be J. G. Ballard for very long is that the personality that contentedly destroys the world at the outset of every story, just in order to feel at home, ought to spend at least *some* amount of his energy wondering why. I've come to understand that it had to do with Watergate, with Abe Beame, with New York City in 1971—the crumbling infrastructure, the Paula Fox *Desperate Characters* backdrop. That's where I came of age. My appetite for reading tales set in dystopian cities, my pleasure in Orwell, my pleasure in Ballard, was a pleasure of recognition. Of consolation. So *Amnesia Moon* was a diagnosis of my own morose complicity. It's too easy for Chaos to think, Oh, poor me, I live in a movie theater because everything's fucked up. The book is a diagnosis of my own complicity with alienation, paranoia, dystopia. Why do I feel at home there?

At fifteen I thought I'd spend my whole life writing books like *Amnesia Moon.* Hipster science fiction. By the time I was halfway through I knew it was a farewell to the kid who has to destroy the world in order to begin writing. I glanced at the early stories and they were all the same tissue-thin material, more alike than dissimilar. Wish-fulfillment over-running the insights. The limit you often run into reading Dick, or for that matter William

Burroughs or Vollmann or any number of other nightmarish social satirists, is that you feel that their own fantasies intervene just at the moment where they're about to say something.

But again, more recent influences began to invest in the book. I was thinking of Italo Calvino's *If on a Winter's Night a Traveler*, which is a book of first chapters. I thought, Let me do *If on a Winter's Night a Traveler* as pulp. I was also thrilled by Steve Erickson at the time. Erickson's prose shifts easily from concrete and tangible and sensory images to extremely abstract language. I have difficulty with abstract language. I'd read Erickson and find pages I couldn't parse. So I proposed an Erickson novel with the abstract stuff left out. A Dick novel with the clumsy stuff left out. A Calvino novel with the high mandarin stuff left out. And the novel that I'd have written at fifteen, but couldn't. I attacked it with great passion. The result was messy. It took a lot of editing to smooth it out. There are still rotten sentences in that book. It breaks my heart. *Amnesia Moon* is an emotional book for me. But now I'm overselling it, because you've gotten me so interested in these questions.

Stein: What about *As She Climbed Across the Table*?
Lethem: *As She Climbed Across the Table* was another conscious pastiche, this time of Don DeLillo and John Barth, as well as a handful of other campus novels—Malcolm Bradbury's *History Man* in particular.

Stein: Where's the Barth?
Lethem: Just *End of the Road*, actually. I was obsessed with *End of the Road* at that time.

Stein: What about *End of the Road*?
Lethem: Before I began publishing, I'd imagined that pointing out my thefts would be the occupation of my enemies. I had no idea I'd be so routinely called to take up that work myself! *End of the Road* is a love triangle set on a college campus: an established couple, both tenured academics, and a newcomer, the narrator of the book, the interloper who specifically describes himself as being the ultimate blank slate, a man without properties. So where Barth has a character who metaphorically believes himself to be "without properties," I made the third wheel in my love triangle the cosmic void—a literal rival without properties. And I reassigned the narration to the jilted lover. Oddly, and I just thought of this, both books end with a nude

woman on a cold steel table—though Barth's is an ugly scene of a botched abortion.

Stein: What attracted you so much to that novel?
Lethem: The voice. Its knowingness. By imitating it, I learned to instill my own knowingness into my voice. In the earlier books, knowingness was all implicit between reader and writer, but the characters were left in the dark. Metcalf in *Gun* and Chaos in *Amnesia Moon* are both explicitly mocked by minor characters for the narrowness of their vision, of their field of reference. By *As She Climbed* I'd worn out that strategy. Though I still had a ways to go. It took Lionel Essrog, in *Motherless*, to show me that I could actually let a narrator tell you why he likes a pop song or a sandwich. I was always in a terrible hurry. At some level I must have thought it was illegal for an "inventive" writer to dally over real information. It took Essrog, with his obsessiveness, to stop and talk about Prince or a turkey sandwich with Russian dressing for a full page.

Stein: How did you get the idea to write *Girl in Landscape*?
Lethem: I was reading Carson McCullers and Shirley Jackson and I was thinking about the teenage girl as an archetype. The tomboy. Also Charles Portis's *True Grit*. And I was falling in love with John Ford westerns, *The Searchers* especially. There's a generic postmodern move, an assault upon a classic work by taking the neglected or minority viewpoint and retelling the tale—think of Jean Rhys rewriting *Jane Eyre* as *Wide Sargasso Sea*. Given my interests at the time, it wasn't much of a leap to watch *The Searchers* and wonder about Natalie Wood's version of events. What might it be like to see John Wayne through her eyes? You can see how the idea fell to me very naturally.

Then I made two large, unconscious thefts. One was from a Philip Dick novel, *Time-Slip*, which depicts immigrants on Mars and contains extremely vivid images of lonely children digging in the Martian desert. Digging in the ground off in the distance; they're viewed like figures in Bosch. It turned out I wanted to know what those children were saying when they played and ran and fought. So the idea drifted from being a literal Western—I wasn't at all interested in factually historical fiction, anyway, nor with the pitfalls of depicting Native American culture—to a tale of interplanetary migration. That way I could have my desert, I could have John Ford's Monument Valley, without all the necessary clutter of history.

And I ransacked chunks of E. M. Forster's *A Passage to India.* When I was creating the Archbuilders—the odd, gnomic humanoids who happen to populate this place where my settlers have come—I knew they couldn't be threatening or evil, as in the manner of the Comanches in a John Ford film. Instead I wanted them to be harmless, thoughtful, befuddled types, who stand to one side and comment on the action. What I reached for, unconsciously, were the *Indian* Indians in Forster. And this unconscious choice shaped the plot to a large degree.

The Archbuilders, like Forster's Indians, spend the first half of the book puzzling over the behavior of the colonists, seemingly safe, to one side of the action. Then in *Girl*, as in *Passage*, there comes a crisis in the middle of the book—in Forster, a possible rape or an imagined rape in a hidden cave. That Marabar Caves incident became, in *Girl*, Efram fondling or not fondling Pella. And the natives are the ones who fall under suspicion. One among them is martyred to the hysteria that comes over the settlers. And so on.

Stein: How odd to see Forster hijack a Western.
Lethem: It's finally quite dull to consider the book on its initial premise, as a reply to *The Searchers.* The Ford film, like any great art, has mysteries that cannot be excavated, and the effort is tendentious—wearisome. So when I meet readers who speak passionately of *Girl in Landscape* and have never seen the Ford, never considered the relationship between Efram and John Wayne, I feel great relief.

Stein: When I came in you were listening to Ethiopiques as you were working. You listen to music even as you write novels?
Lethem: Always.

Stein: What were you listening to when you wrote *Girl*?
Lethem: A ton of Dylan. I was obsessing on Dylan in that period. But *Girl*, like several others, had a musical keynote, a song or album I kept returning to. In this case, a John Cale song called "Dying on the Vine." Just as *Amnesia Moon* was a Neil Young book, but the skeleton key was an album by My Dad is Dead, called *The Taller You Are, The Shorter You Get.*

Stein: When did you start going to movies?
Lethem: My mother had the schedule for the Thalia pinned to our kitchen wall. I remember pretending to understand when she'd make distinc-

tions: This is good and this is bad, just looking at that calendar. She loved Hitchcock—*The 39 Steps, Notorious.* Films that may not hold up as well, *A Thousand Clowns* and *King of Hearts.* She loved early Polanski. She adored Truffaut. *Shoot the Piano Player. Beat the Devil.* She loved Bogart. As typical a sophisticated film taste as you can have in her generation. But she had it. So I was an imaginary cinephile before I'd seen more than *Mary Poppins* and *Yellow Submarine.* And then I was old enough to go. I followed my parents to *The Harder They Come, Black Orpheus, The Red Shoes, Small Change, Sabotage, Barry Lyndon.* Big moments for my little mind. And my first encounter with Freud and Sherlock Holmes was Alan Arkin and Nicol Williamson. *The Seven-Per-Cent Solution* terrified me. You can see me rewriting it in my early story "The Happy Man."

Stein: You couldn't have known the demographic when you were a kid, so how did you understand your mother's taste? What did you think those films had in common?

Lethem: It wasn't a matter of them needing to have anything in common. It was the sense there were good things out there. I've always been uninterested in boundaries or quarantines between tastes and types, between mediums and genres. It's a form of autism, perhaps. I've never felt I had to pick from among *these* things and renounce *those others.* Good stuff's found across the spectrum. Boundaries aren't going to tell you where the good ones are; your interest, your Spidey-sense going off, is going to tell you. That describes my mother's appetite for books and film, and it describes my father's approach to painting, his own, and the work we'd see in galleries and museums. When I say I'm lucky in my inheritances, in what dropped into my lap, I mean this attitude above all.

Of course, my film taste had to develop backwards. I loved Godard and Kubrick and Truffaut first—I'd seen dozens of French films indebted to Howard Hawks and John Ford before I'd ever seen an American Western or screwball comedy, before I'd ever understood that the Europeans rested on the shoulders of the early Hollywood giants. This is also akin to growing up inside the music of the post–*Sgt. Pepper* Beatles before discovering their early music, let alone Elvis Presley. Those backwards trails of discovery created in me a rage for authenticity and origins, which perhaps cuts against the postmodern grain of my category-autism. I'm fascinated by *influence,* which is why I discuss it so much, perhaps awkwardly much. And you're no help.

Stein: What TV shows have mattered most to you?
Lethem: Thanks. *Twilight Zone.* I mean, Orson Welles was asked his influences and said, "John Ford, John Ford, John Ford." Television? *Twilight Zone, Twilight Zone, Twilight Zone.* That and Ernie Kovacs.

Stein: Who is Ernie Kovacs?
Lethem: You must find out! Put it this way, if the famous innovators of the early days of television were the French New Wave, Ernie Kovacs would be Godard. In that no one followed him. Milton Berle and Henny Youngman and Steve Allen all created television that we now watch. Ernie Kovacs created television that no one could ever follow. There was no successor. Channel Thirteen replayed his entire archive for one brief, beautiful moment in the seventies. My mother sat me down to watch, as though it were school.

Those experiences are as mysterious and deep to me as any childhood reading. They connect absolutely to my mother's handing me Lewis Carroll or Ray Bradbury or Kurt Vonnegut. And it's an ordinary boast, but it needs be said, that the majority of my childhood was spent entranced—mummified—in the pages of a book.

Stein: Do you remember what you were doing when you were reading like that?
Lethem: I don't know. I'm still doing it. You're interrogating a fish on the nature of water.

Stein: Is it still like that?
Lethem: Well, that's the ideal. I get there less frequently, for so many reasons. In many ways, my immersion-hours have moved from reading to writing.

Stein: Do you ever feel envy of other writers who are near your age? Deep envy about their writing, about what they can do?
Lethem: There are people who can do amazing things. But I never take it personally. Any more than I would take it personally if Christina Stead could do things that I can't imagine doing, as she does, or Philip Roth, as he does. The generational thing just doesn't really come into it. That sounds like a real wussy answer, but writing is a private discipline, in a field of companions. You're not fighting the other writers—that Mailer boxing stuff seems silly to me. It's more like golf. You're not playing against the other people on the course. You're playing against yourself. The question is, What's in

you that you can free up? How to say everything you know? Then there's nothing to envy. The reason Tiger Woods has that eerie calm, the reason he drives everyone insane, is his implacable sense that his game has *nothing* to do with the others on the course. The others all talk about what Tiger is up to. Tiger only says, I had a pretty good day, I did what I wanted to do. Or, I could have a better day tomorrow. He never misunderstands. The game is against yourself. That same thousand-yard Tiger Woods stare is what makes someone like Murakami or Roth or DeLillo or Thomas Berger so eerie and inspiring. They've grasped that there's nothing to one side of you. Just you and the course.

From that perspective, the fact of others carrying on the struggle beside you is no more threatening than the fact that libraries are full of great books. It makes the context for what you do. You'd never want to be the only writer, would you? How meaningless. Writers lose their temper sometimes and express a self-destructive wish in the form of a pronouncement that the novel is dead, that it's a terrible time for fiction, etcetera. In fact there are thrilling novelists everywhere. It's an amazing time.

Stein: OK, that's the pure relationship between the writer and his work, sure. What about envying other writers?

Lethem: Every human life includes moments of rage at unrecognition. We're all injustice collectors. But that's not the truth of *any* situation. I don't mean to pretend that those bad feelings don't exist. I know them intimately; they're daily friends. But once you give them their name and shape, they're like a set of really lousy cats living in your house. You kick them out of the way to get to where you're going. In truth, it's only dazzling when, say, Colson Whitehead puts out *John Henry Days* and there are sequences where I just don't know how he did it. God what a great feeling! To have him over there in Fort Greene, living a few blocks away, as opposed to Christina Stead, dead and in Australia. Holy shit, right over there in Fort Greene and I don't know how he did it. What a fantastic sensation. Would I want to be the only writer? No. Would I want to be the best? Well, that's a lie, there's no best. So there's nothing to want.

Stein: You can't imagine experiencing a crisis of faith.

Lethem: Crisis of faith? But that's not where the writer lives. He lives in sentences, in fictional architecture. Look, anyone seeking ontological meltdown can easily find it in the attempt to write. Many have. The need to fall apart is well indulged in this line of work.

Stein: I'd like to talk about *Motherless Brooklyn.* Why did it take you so long to write straight novels?

Lethem: I'm not writing straight novels. What's straight? I understand your assumptions, but you know that I have to point out how silly they are. There's no important sense in which I ever began or resumed or stopped writing straight novels.

Stein: Is there a kind of writing that you're trying to cultivate in yourself?

Lethem: I don't try to cultivate any genre of writing in myself. I write what I urgently need to write at the time. What I try to cultivate in myself is the permission to do anything I can think of. I've cultivated a *lot* more freedom in myself. For instance, there are elements of the first three books that are hidebound, not by disinterest or external concerns of publication; they're hidebound by fear of saying what I knew, of being fully myself.

Stein: What were you afraid to do?

Lethem: I'd be afraid to not be funny, afraid to not be charming. You can only do so many things. This is something I've come to understand: there's a strict ecology on a given page. Those things that people feel are missing from books are missing because they are crowded out by other things. Not because the person wouldn't have liked to also do them. Once you've devoted a lot of energy and attention to accomplishing certain things, that's where your energy has gone. It's a zero-sum game.

It's delightful that readers will look at someone who's accomplished in some areas and say, Wouldn't it be great if their women were great too, or, Too bad they can't do really good landscape description. It's sweet that people always want that little more. But the extent that *As She Climbed* and *Gun* are full of one-liners—this desperate juggling, come on, love me, love me, love me—does, on a simple, technical basis, mean that other things are not present.

Most recently I've let go of a certain kind of lean efficiency, a devotion to structure. To plot. The fact is, almost every writer I ultimately find most important to me is hugely digressive, and largely uninterested in any plot that can be admired for its exoskeletal integrity. Yet I thought I had to provide one each time out.

Stein: Sometimes with pretty bizarre results, frankly.

Lethem: Sure. I'd say, You want plot, you want causality, you want a system undergirding the book? Well, I'll give you one you've never seen before. Or one only I understand. But they're always there. Until *Girl in Landscape*. In *Girl* I learned to write out of character and language, without the safety net. Then *Motherless Brooklyn* is a funny case. There, I relaxed with pleasure into some of the oldest ones in the book, just by borrowing the hardboiled methodology again. But I also really threw them all out the window. Call that book my farewell to plot.

Stein: Do you find that it's hard to forgive anything about those early books?

Lethem: Answering that question suggests I read them. When I was a kid I read a Graham Greene interview. Greene's another important influence. In the interview he said, in that dry, don't-ask-me-that-a-second-time way, I don't read my books. Not only did my jaw drop, I was certain he was a liar. I felt it was inconceivable to write books and not read them. Now I find I've never read my books. Never. I'm not interested. It's not reading. So when we do this, you're hearing me talk about what I *hope* is there, what I infer might be there from your questions.

Stein: *The Fortress of Solitude* is like nothing you've ever written before.

Lethem: Actually, it's a lot like *Girl in Landscape* and *Motherless Brooklyn* crushed together. Perhaps I hadn't demonstrated this breadth of ambition before, but the ingredients are present, in the second chapter of *Motherless Brooklyn*, in the psychic entirety of *Girl in Landscape*.

Stein: The plot seems more intricate than the plots of your previous novels, with old-fashioned realist commitments. Was the plot hard to figure out?

Lethem: You prepare by rereading books with architecture you sense will be relevant to the attempt. In this case, Baldwin's *Another Country*, Henry Roth's *Call It Sleep*, Millhauser's *Portrait of a Romantic*, and enormous amounts of Dickens, Christina Stead, and Philip Roth. I absorbed the permissions inherent in those books. Once I'd done that, the plot grew from the characters—and out of a handful of essential situations I had in advance.

Stein: You give yourself a lot of stuff to juggle.

Lethem: At the start I meant to write a book of two halves. The first a third-person ensemble, with some degree of omniscience. Organized by the setting, á la *Girl in Landscape*. And I knew the second half would be first person. Organized by a compulsive voice. There's a strict alternation in my books. *Gun, with Occasional Music*: first person organized by the voice, by the one consciousness. Then *Amnesia Moon* is a third-person ensemble, and has much to do with landscape and setting. Then *As She Climbed Across the Table*, first-person again, another obsessive voice. Then *Girl in Landscape*. Then *Motherless Brooklyn*. You see the rhythm. So, in *The Fortress of Solitude* I extend the pattern, but the next two books are compressed into one. Following *Motherless Brooklyn*, I went back to four hundred pages of ensemble viewpoint, third-person, omniscience. And followed that with a first-person book organized by voice; those make the two halves of *Fortress*. The new book is less unprecedented if you see it that way.

Stein: If you see it that way you'd be completely insane. No one would believe that you actually sat down to write alternating books.

Lethem: But I did. In fact, the second half of *Fortress*—the section is called "Prisonaires"—has a bizarre superficial resemblance to *Motherless Brooklyn*. It's almost exactly the same length. Both begin with an adult narrator introducing himself in the midst of conflict where his "other" abandons him. Frank Minna is killed in the first chapter of *Motherless*; Abby splits in the first chapter of "Prisonaires." This loss sends each character careening through a story that, in its "present," takes only a few days. *Motherless* takes four days from the first chapter and the second half of *Fortress* takes five or six days. Both are absolutely hectic with plot and epiphanies, and both make room for an approximately hundred-page flashback to childhood, in which we learn what is truly at stake in the present. In fact, both end in cross-country car trips and climax at these rather non sequitur locations—Maine and Indiana—where the main character learns the secret-hiding-within-the-secret of the book. Both secrets have to do with the past life of an important female character at a bohemian enclave. The similarities go on and on.

Stein: Does it feel like something you've been waiting to do?

Lethem: Let me put it this way, there's a scene in this book that derives from a manuscript I began when I was seventeen.

Stein: Which scene?

Lethem: It's now smothered in a stream-of-consciousness flashback. Barely a scene, a flicker of a scene. Dylan recalls sneaking into his father's studio and painting a frame of his father's film.

Stein: At seventeen you already knew Dylan Ebdus's father was painting frames of film?

Lethem: No. The character wasn't named Dylan Ebdus, obviously. And it was then an oil painting. But I've felt this book coming all my life. More specifically, I sat down with my agent seven years ago now and told him that I'd just had an idea for a "short book" that I felt I could do quickly before I tackled "the big Brooklyn book." I told him I thought it might be a good idea because the "short book" was sort of an appealing notion and might earn me some breathing room for writing the "big one." The short one was *Motherless Brooklyn*, which I then imagined would be about two hundred and fifty manuscript pages. I thought it would be a sprint, a finger exercise, before writing *Fortress*.

There were two results. Number one is that this book is better because I waited longer. I gained tools I'd needed—so many that now it seems impossible I thought I could have written this book seven years ago. Number two, *Motherless Brooklyn* was imbued with energy from the project I was holding at bay. I thought my Tourette's detective book would be brisk and funny—akin to Thomas Berger's *Who Is Teddy Villanova?*, a linguistic tour de force. But I was delaying writing an emotional journey back to Brooklyn, and in fact I was *unable* to delay it. So those feelings saturated *Motherless Brooklyn*. And I wrote a longer and more serious book. Kind of got lucky there.

Stein: Did you remember all those details about being a kid in the city—skully and stoopball and the other street games—or did you have to research them?

Lethem: Sure, I remembered skully, I remembered all the street games. I've had full apprehension of those childhood memories all along. I wrote this book to try to *forget*. I did some research, just to confirm the external context—for instance, that Wild Cherry's "Play That Funky Music," which was emblematic in my experience, really was the number one song the week I began sixth grade in an all-black school. My instincts were usually confirmed.

Stein: Was there anything you'd forgotten? Any recovered memories?

Lethem: Just one. This book has everything to do with revisiting the uncomfortable position of growing up as part of a small white minority within a black and Hispanic neighborhood, and, frankly, that has a lot to do with enduring beatings and bullyings, as well as subtler psychic torments. I'd imagined I remembered all of this stuff, but of course I explored the memories with those friends—both black and white—I could persuade to join me in reminiscing. And what I'd repressed was poignantly simple: the shame of my own utter cowardice. Those few times when I'd abandoned another bullied kid to his fate, when I'd apparently thought, *Thank God* there's a white kid worse off than me on this playground, taking the brunt. It took friends to remind me of the lowliness of my own reactions.

Stein: Who was kind enough to remind you?

Lethem: My oldest friend, Karl Rusnak, one of the dedicatees of *Amnesia Moon*. He and I were side by side through sixth and seventh grades—ground zero, in the book's terms. I recalled a story aloud to Karl, a story of our mutual victimization, and he gently led me to the repressed punch line: I'd fled the scene and left Karl to his fate, in the hands of our tormentors.

I was helped by another associate from the neighborhood, a fellow with the elegant name of Alexander Arguelles. Alexander was always rather ascetic and intense, and mercilessly honest—I believe he's a Catholic seminarian now. We talked together in a Berkeley coffee shop ten years ago, the first and so far last time I've seen him since childhood. There, Alexander told me he'd never forget the exact tone of my keening as I cringed and abased myself on the Brooklyn pavement. I had of course been preempting attack by pretending injury in advance. I'd banished the memory, but it wasn't possible to take exception to Alexander's description.

Stein: Did you get scared by the superhero stuff once you built up the realist stuff so much? Did you know you could handle it?

Lethem: The superhero material wasn't a problem. The problem was persuading you that, say, I knew what prison was like. That's harder than persuading you that teenage boys want to fly, but that they wouldn't know what to do about it if they could. That's easy. I've spent my whole life figuring out how to talk about that. Teenage life—possibly adult life too, I'll let you know when I've lived one—is all about what you want and can't have. And then about what you receive and misuse. I don't mean to say this book was easy, but the blending of the mythic and the realist elements was hardly the deepest challenge. The teenaged human mind specializes in that blending.

Stein: What was hardest? The prison stuff?

Lethem: I'll tell you about one area of pressure or resistance. It relates to *Girl in Landscape*. In that book I noticed that despite adopting the female viewpoint, I was terrified of writing scenes that included no male witness. Scenes between two women, or three. I only managed to get Pella alone with another woman for about two pages, when Diana Eastling takes her off into the desert for a talk.

Stein: Don't we see Pella all by herself?
Lethem: That's different. You're not depicting social reality. You're just doing consciousness. It was women talking to women that intimidated me. And in *Fortress* I noticed a unique discomfort when I tackled scenes among the black characters, scenes lacking a white witness.

What else is hard? The violence is hard. The actual violence is hard. The shooting was difficult.

Stein: Because you weren't sure what register you were in?
Lethem: Because I had known about it for three years before I had written it. I rely on vagueness in my plans for creating both energy and authenticity when I attack a scene. But that plan had been so specific for so long that by the time I got there I became afraid that the characters were being shoehorned into a script. I hope it isn't so.

Stein: When did you realize that Barry was going to become an important figure in the book?
Lethem: I only had to conceive a book about two sons to know it was also a book about two fathers. Then I knew instantly that the black father would be this figure of a singer, a figure that had been pressing on my imagination.

Stein: It's hard to know where to start with the career of Abraham Ebdus—the white father, that is. He's a neglected experimental filmmaker who disconcertingly finds himself acclaimed as a paperback-jacket illustrator. Were you winking at yourself?
Lethem: Well, Abraham's film career is modeled on specific experimental filmmakers—Stan Brakhage and Ed Emshwiller—though he's less successful than either. And there is of course my own father, though my father's art—and his life, his politics—connected him to the world around him, the world of our neighborhood and its conflicts, much more than Abraham is connected. Abraham's withdrawal, his discomfort, is my own. Abraham is much nearer a writer's self-portrait than Dylan is, and so his film is more like a novel than it is like *any* painter or filmmaker's work. Like *Fortress*, Abraham's film is a record of days on a given street—Dean Street.

I suppose I *was* picking my own old scabs, those to do with the experience of receiving acclaim that is unsatisfying to the point of bewilderment. That is to say, acclaim from the science fiction community. Which, I should add, was my own fault, not the fault of that community. But the scenes set at the SF convention have a much deeper purpose than self-laceration. I'd challenged myself to tell all I knew, to tell where I'd been in the world, and what I knew about class and culture as a result. Once I saw my task in this light, the milieu of an SF convention was an unmistakable opportunity. Had I ever seen any more impacted site of human yearning, expressed through culture-making—and wasn't that the subject of my book? For an SF convention is a terribly complicated space, where people try to collectively resolve an enormous number of incompatible needs.

So, the ForbiddenCon chapters resonate with Watermelon Sugar Farm, the hippie commune at the end of the book, and with Boerum Hill itself. And with the punk community. Like them, the convention is a bohemian demimonde. As with any such, there's a desperate assertion of classlessness within it, an assertion that is crumbling around the edges, continuously. An SF convention is a gentrification that fails in the space of a weekend. The whole American premise of community fails everywhere, because it lies about class.

Stein: What's the connection that you draw in the novel between growing up a white boy in the city and getting into indie rock?
Lethem: The fearfulness with which white public-school kids in the mid-seventies, the disco seventies, clung to the possibility of punk identity. There's a scene in *Fortress of Solitude* where Gabe is confronted on the street for wearing a black leather jacket that comes out of real experience. When I tell people I used to go to CBGB's in the mid-seventies, they think I'm talking about some halcyon thing. What I mean is there was this panicked little bar where they would let the dorks come in and order a beer when you were fifteen years old. We cowered there, in a city we didn't understand.

Stein: Was the graffiti stuff part of your childhood?
Lethem: More a part of my brother Blake's. He became an important graffiti artist, one remembered in the various histories for the tag KEO. More important than any of the characters in my book. In researching the backdrop of the book, I relied on Blake for both historical and folkloric accounts of the "underground" New York of the seventies. In fact, he's a graphic designer now, still rendering a similar font on more legal surfaces.

Stein: And your sister's a photographer. You come from a family of visual artists, and you trained as one in high school. Do the visual arts influence your writing process?

Lethem: My process is dull. It's as plodding and pedantic as Abraham's film, painted one frame at a time. I'm a tortoise, waking each day to plod out my page or two. I try never to miss a morning, when I'm working on a novel. There are no other rules, no word counts or pencil sharpenings or candlelit pentagrams on the floor. Growing up with my father's art-making in the house, the creative act was demystified, usefully. As a result, I see writing as an inevitable and ordinary way to spend one's hours.

Stein: You're gregarious with other writers. Does anyone read your early drafts?

Lethem: The opposite: I'm gregarious with writers and *never* with manuscripts. I'm a very private writer, actually. I don't like to emerge from my room with anything short of a polished book. To create the illusion of seamless perfection, so I alone know the flawed and homely process along the way. I try never to show my editor, the generous and hugely patient Bill Thomas, chapters or halves. Instead I do my best to deliver a completed book, a *tour de fait accompli.*

Stein: You work on a computer. Do early drafts get printed out and archived?

Lethem: No, I never print anything out, only endlessly manipulate the words on the screen, carving fiction in ether. I enjoy keeping the book amorphous and fluid until the last possible moment. There's no paper trail, I destroy the traces of revision by overwriting the same disk every day when I back up my work. In that sense, it occurs to me now, I'm more like the painter I trained to be—my early sketching is buried beneath the finished layer of oil and varnish.

Stein: I find it ironic that you talk on the one hand about an "illusion of seamless perfection," while on the other you're so eager to discuss the patchwork of influences on the books.

Lethem: But that talk dissipates around the writing of *Girl in Landscape,* never to return. You've drawn me back into that mode because we've been casting back over those earlier books, which are, undeniably, pastiches. But there's one thing I ought to clarify. When we talk about those first three books, it's important to understand that those were all conceived—and nearly all completed—before I'd published *anything*.

That is to say that my first real book is *Girl in Landscape*. That's the first conceived after I was a published writer, the first not written by a gifted, and giddy, amateur. The first that grows organically from character and voice, embodied in dramatic situations, rather than from cognition and concept. I was a very late bloomer in some senses. It was only with *Girl* that I began to trust my emotional instincts—which now seem to me the only impulses worth honoring in my writing. *Girl* seems to me the real beginning of the writer I'm so happy to be now.

Stein: As opposed to the writer you . . .
Lethem: As opposed to the writer I wanted to be when I wanted to be so many different writers all at once.

An Interview with Jonathan Lethem

Michael Silverblatt/2003

From *Bookworm*, KCRW-FM, December 4, 2003. Copyright © 2003 by KCRW-FM. Reprinted by permission.

Silverblatt: From KCRW Santa Monica I'm Michael Silverblatt and this is *Bookworm*. Today I'm happy to have as my guest Jonathan Lethem, whose new book *The Fortress of Solitude* has recently been published by Doubleday. It's a big novel. It's his biggest book I think to date.
Lethem: Yeah. Twice as long as anything before.

Silverblatt: Wow.
Lethem: They've disguised it with nice thin sheets of paper but it's double the length.

Silverblatt: I want to find a way to go through this book, since a lot of people are talking about it but it seems to me that they're missing a lot of things. In the final pages of the book Jonathan talks about a kind of happier place. The book has been about neighborhoods, neighborhoods in Brooklyn, racialisms. The hero of the book has been one of three white children in his public school class. His parents live in that neighborhood of Brooklyn, Gowanus, by choice. They feel they're carrying on the good fight, the old fight, the integration fight. And the boy to some extent in very complicated ways is both the victim and the beneficiary of their liberalism. But by the end of the book, having taken us through many different enclaves in which race, gender, all kinds of questions get subjected to an eye that wants to see both sides of the picture, we come to the kind of art that does not have an interest in sociology or race or gender. It's typified on the one hand by the kind of experimental filmmaking that Stan Brakhage was doing and the boy, Dylan's, father is himself that kind of filmmaker, and the kind of music that Eno was trying to make during the [unintelligible] rock days. In other words, something that could appeal to popular culture conceivably but was not of or made from popular culture. Stuff that people called the ivory tower if they weren't talking about the academy but about the sacred precincts of art. And this book seems to be the book in which you investigate as far as you have away from the hermetic.

Lethem: Yeah. It's very interesting to try to pursue that thread because I think there is an argument with myself about what my writing has been for in the book. This image of the main character's father, Abraham, is a film-maker kind of in the Brakhage mould and he's painting on celluloid in this very absolute and super-essential and hermetic way. By temperament he's a hermetic guy. I was thinking about Rothko at the end of his life, painting endless black and gray canvases, purifying color out of his pictures and obsessed with this image that had reached a kind of limit for him, where he couldn't purify his art any further. Then he sort of reached an apotheosis of despair having done it. All of this of course happening in a studio on the Bowery, in the middle of New York City. A place I grew up, right around the time I was born into this city full of artists and full of sociology and full of life that I'm now finding myself drawn to depict in this book. So yeah, you're right, my earlier books are in a funny way I've been seen as someone working with—I love Stanislaw Lem's description of the junk stratum [laughter], working with pop culture junk and fooling around with it. But in fact my experiment was always pretty—

Silverblatt: You were an aesthete. [laughter]

Lethem: Yeah, a pretty hermetic one. And in this book I kind of blab all of a sudden that I'm from this place that was intensely sociological and that I'm enormously confused about it, and stimulated, to have come from Brooklyn in the 1970s. So there's Abraham all through the book trying to pretend that he's not in that place. Like Rothko painting on the Bowery. And the kid, Abraham's son Dylan, is stuck on the street and in public schools. He doesn't have the opportunity to purify or distill his experience into that kind of hermetic response. He's for better or worse stuck with the sociology of the body in motion on the street.

Silverblatt: He seems in certain ways very much in your shoes in that there is on the one hand one high tradition of disembodied art. Then there's the following after modernism position of if we are going to have a political novel, the world in which everything is going to enter and it's not going to be a sacred art piece, we are going to imagine a better world, a world of integra-

tion, a world of universal suffrage and it's part of a Utopian political ideal. This boy is the child of both of those things. His mother has been an activist and she is in a sense putting her money where her mouth is. She's sending the boy not to a private school but to the public school. And there he is, trying to make sense of things in the seventies, the eighties, the nineties, moving through those post-idealistic periods, where both politics and art get subjected to all kinds of mixing. There's not going to be purity anymore.
Lethem: Right.

Silverblatt: And that seems to be the subject of this book.
Lethem: Well, I like that description a lot. And of course you're right. I've saddled Dylan, this kid, I've saddled him with my own birthday and address, basically. By doing that I wanted to really force myself to stop manipulating experience so indirectly, but to confess a little and start naming some names as to what it was like to be in that place. Where in the early seventies this part of Brooklyn was a super-laboratory of gentrification and juxtaposition of cultures and classes, just by the chance of, there's a lot to that place that made it so. And these things were fore-grounded by my parents and the kinds of parents that Dylan has and that were typical of the families moving in. They wanted to, first they wanted a cheaper house and second they wanted to do something real and that reflected their commitment to the civil rights era. They couldn't fathom that they were in a way handmaidens to realtors. It wasn't like that then. This was before Reagan. This was before the gulf had opened up that absolutely made everyone choose up sides. There was a kind of negotiation in the middle and that middle was Bohemianism, you know? This was this Utopian space where the beautiful American pretense that things are classless and free and we're all going to get along together was being mediated in terms of art and drugs and hippiedom.

Silverblatt: It's still a period in which there are communes. It's an accusation virtually that the artists and political people living in communes are the dupes of their realtors who are using these people to clean up neighborhoods in order that eventually the people who can pay more will be able to move in. This is a story sort of like the pre-story of Soho, say—
Lethem: Right, absolutely.

Silverblatt: —or Alphabet Village.
Lethem: Or any gentrification.

Silverblatt: Right. Where what we see first is an artists' community moving in and then a kind of activist community and then suddenly the prices go up, the restaurants improve and you're dealing with another world, a politically correct world, in which the problems virtually can't be named.
Lethem: Right.

Silverblatt: I would say that the subject of *The Fortress of Solitude* is to find a language in the wake of political correctness for the conditions that preceded that in which the young people, and there are four of them who are central to this book, are in different ways shut down from speaking about their experience even to one another because the language has been foreclosed to them.
Lethem: That's a marvelous description. And I was very conscious that this book was about naming the unnamable sight, in a way. You know, it's terribly specific for me. There were these transactions that occurred that I had no name for. I would go as a New Yorker moving to California as I did, or spending time in Vermont or Canada, you get the generic question oh, ever been mugged? And for years, as light as that question seems in some ways, I was tormented by it. I didn't have an answer. Because I knew that the asker of the question was envisioning this kind of *New Yorker* cartoon of the bandit with the handkerchief over his face asking a well-dressed couple who've just come out of the theater to step into an alley and then saying your money or your life. And this had never happened to me. That wasn't, I couldn't say yes to the question because I knew that I hadn't had that. The kind of mugging that Kojak rescues you from, or Batman. And yet I'd had an enormous number of experiences that were something more than routine childhood bullying. They involved this negotiation over identity. They were like racial hazing. And they also involved surrendering my pocket money, often every day of a school year. And they always involved shame and double silencing. They were events that were—their prime characteristic was that they were meant not to have happened after they happened. You know I really like you. This isn't really happening. We're just friends. You're not afraid of me, are you? If you're afraid of me you'd be a racist. So I was dealing with this absolutely gnarled up sense of these acts that often had taken place somewhat humorously. You'd shrug them off. They'd take place between kids who knew each other. Another context might be friends or playing or the older brothers of friends. In other words, they were acts of community-making. As hostile as they were, they were a conversation. They were substitution for language. And when I was being identified as OK, you're the white boy and

I'm the black boy and this is going to happen now because this is what we do because that's who we are, I was engaging and not involuntarily in a theater, a kind of endless rehearsal of racial meanings in the wake of the civil rights era. I wanted to go back and find names for all of this material.

Silverblatt: The four boys who are at the center of the book seem to be a kind of continuum of possibility in that spectrum. There's a white boy, son of liberal radical artist political parents. His name is Dylan. There's another white boy who doesn't have a father in the home. He has a mother there. He's uncharacteristic of this group and he's in a sense a mothered boy. He's been avoiding attacks by feigning asthma attacks and eventually he's going to be the white who turns, he gets involved [overlapping voices].
Lethem: He's a super-assimilator.

Silverblatt: —with drug deals. There is another boy, Robert, who is ironically given the most Anglo Saxon of all the names in the book.
Lethem: [unintelligible] [laughter]

Silverblatt: He's the bully. And he doesn't stir from that. We're going to find him most of the time in jail. He's going to demonstrate to Dylan what it's like to have a mean face and to keep it on all the time.
Lethem: Right.

Silverblatt: Then there's the son of a once-prominent musician who is caught between worlds in the same way that Dylan is.
Lethem: Yeah.

Silverblatt: He could easily be gentrified. He belongs to a kind of art royalty.
Lethem: Right. And also just as importantly he's the only one, he's a black kid but he's the only one of them who's ever been a Boy Scout. He's actually come to this neighborhood out of the suburbs. Which is absolutely alien to the experience of the other kids.

Silverblatt: Now do these, I mean, it began to strike me as being like the couples in *Midsummer Night's Dream*. You know, blond and fair, dark and—
Lethem: Yeah.

Silverblatt: That this was a kind of quadrant for a certain focus. Am I right?

Lethem: I'm delighted by your description. I see all four of them as the key characters in the book and even though Dylan and Mingus, the most prominent pair, seem to dominate the book, I think Arthur and Robert are absolutely carrying enormous amounts of weight of meaning. I see the book in some ways, this is in retrospect, not that I was conscious as I worked, as a series of collapsing communities, attempts at communities and demonstrations of how tenuous and fragile these moments are when the black, white, and Puerto Rican kids on the block are all playing together in a game of [unintelligible] or tag or whichever it might be. And everything for a moment is perfect. It's like there's a jelling of that vision, that egalitarian, Utopian, communal reality and then it slips, turns a corner and it slips and it's gone. Again and again, the arts college, which has been poisoned with money in the book, and the science fiction convention where uncomfortable people go for forty-eight hours and build a momentary community almost like Burning Man [laughter] in a hotel somewhere and claim. You know, it's like a gentrification that lasts for the space of a weekend. Even the young men who gather in the auditorium to listen to Stan Brakhage speak and they're so nervous and freaked out because in Brakhage they've got this—

Silverblatt: Hero. [laughter]

Lethem: —vision of what art might really mean but they can't keep from going at each others' throats before the lecture is over. So that brief moment of community collapses as well.

Silverblatt: This book becomes meaningful and profound for me because I think that while in certain ways it presents itself as being something of a universal experience of growing up in a ghettoized neighborhood subjected to gentrification, I thought that the real subject was that once upon a time art brought people together.

Lethem: Right.

Silverblatt: That it somehow stopped and there was a replacement set. Comic books did instead. And that comic books had their value. The whole of pop culture entered through that crack and it became comic books, music, and movies, where once it had been the new European films that were coming in, the new traditions of a strange and avant garde novel, crazier and

crazier films and music. In other words, let's leave the racial and the class structure and explore the possibilities of art—
Lethem: Right.

Silverblatt: —and then it becomes no, it's not going to happen. Pop culture enters and you get instead the ability to enter the world, eventually Dylan's father Abraham is painting science fiction paperback covers. It's the only way he can make a living. And he enters the world in that way and he gets tributes even. You're almost feted for compromising.
Lethem: Right. Well, and that's it. Art is this deeply potent but profoundly neutral negotiation with the world that can turn on a dime to hermetic isolation, to empty compromise, to retreat from community instead of an approach. Dylan as a rock critic, when he grows up he's a writer of liner notes, he loves soul music. He loves black music so dearly and yet he's still bricking himself in like a character in Edgar Allan Poe behind a kind of wall of fetishes. He's not learning to take it back to community.

Silverblatt: Well, now we get to the absolutely complex part of the interview, and you're listening to *Bookworm*, I'm Michael Silverblatt, my guest is Jonathan Lethem, author most recently of *The Fortress of Solitude* published by Doubleday. Jonathan had been doing something really unusual, which was to create Borgesian, Calvino-esque versions of Westerns, Chandler novels, noir novels, science fiction. In other words, he was in some crazy way gentrifying genre, you know?
Lethem: Yeah.

Silverblatt: And in this book, *The Fortress of Solitude*, it's as if something has woken up. The language is no longer pared down, everything is exploding everywhere. The sentences are going for triple their normal length. The metaphors are proliferating like crazy. And this is the book that has earned you the most attention. Does this become part of the conflict, that in other words to enter the world in which yes, I'm going to divide it the way you divide it, between sociology and pop culture, and I'm going to leave art in the attic with the father. I'm going to enter the world in this way, armed with the load of language you all like and the describing of everything and the big subject, racial tension, in the period in New York in a place. It's almost as if could you have done anything more to take a big shot at it? Is this part of a conflict?

Lethem: Well, the funny thing is I see the book as more deeply related to the earlier ones than the question supposes, because it's really a culmination of a series of arguments in my work that have led to a greater and greater interest in some of the methods of literary naturalism. I mean, I've just also gotten, I've turned my interest in genres to the genre of the bildungsroman or the genre of Philip Roth. Because Roth is all over this book. But I also think that there's something very hardboiled actually in Dylan in the second half of the book. That it's another Chandler novel in its way. The second half of the book, which I call Prisonaires. Which is an ostensible quest for the best friend that turns into the bittersweet discovery of one's own inadequacies. It's basically *The Long Goodbye.* The first half of the book is another version, the childhood half of the book, is another version of the Western, the book I was trying to write and I'm very proud of *Girl in Landscape*, it's kind of a book of immigrant children in a disputed turf. So I see these deeper relationships. But of course you're right that the outward form it's taken seems so different to people.

Silverblatt: No, but it's, given that I've been following your work, it's one of those heartbreaking things. Did we always know that you write *Goodbye, Columbus* and you get an attention that you don't get if you've been writing *In Watermelon Sugar*, or a different kind of attention?
Lethem: Yeah.

Silverblatt: Sure we knew it.
Lethem: I guess that's true.

Silverblatt: Do we know nowadays that Henry Roth chose by making his book really rigorous that he wrote a classic rather than a popular novel, *Call It Sleep*, about Brooklyn, about a Brooklyn childhood? Yeah.
Lethem: Yeah.

Silverblatt: And do we know that when an author does this kind of thing, you know, that suddenly a public is going to fall all over it because suddenly they know how to talk about sociological fiction but not about art?
Lethem: Well, there's something very simple that I've learned is true. People are terribly afraid of novels. And even the people who write them and I include myself are very afraid of novels. They're afraid of what moves them the most in reading or writing. My favorite answer to the question "Why do you write?" was Bernard Malamud's. He said I'd be too moved to say. [laugh-

ter] And anyone, including myself, given an opportunity to talk about John Wayne instead of the ambiguities of the characters in *Girl in Landscape* will do so as we all did when *Girl in Landscape* was the book. Or to talk about Tourette's syndrome is much easier than to talk about language and the really insane fact that emotion inheres in the architecture of sentences. That's almost impossible to talk about.

Silverblatt: Yeah. Almost no one would say that the kind of fracturing of language because of the Tourette's syndrome in your last book, *Motherless Brooklyn*, was closer related to things that were going on in *Finnegan's Wake* than to some kind of linguistic pathology.

Lethem: Right. But Michael, I'd be failing to do justice to your question if I didn't also say that as a writer there's a real sense of giving of myself, of wanting to open my mouth and really say what I know and that there's an immense satisfaction in the personal, the degree to which I was able to comfortably fuse personal experience and testimony and personal concerns and witnessing, because there's just a tremendous amount of witnessing in this book, into the work, and that people are, they know me better as a result. That's not small. That's a deeply satisfying experience.

Interview with Jonathan Lethem

Sarah Anne Johnson/2005

From *The Very Telling: Conversations with American Writers* by Sarah Anne Johnson. Copyright © 2005 by University Press of New England, Lebanon, NH. Reprinted with permission, pages 121–42.

Q: How did you get started writing and what did you do to develop your craft?

A: Like every single person you've ever interviewed, I was a voracious reader. I grew up in an artist's household. My father was a painter. It was in the air. It was my family's milieu. My first memories are in his studio watching him paint. My mother was a great reader, a bohemian, and a brilliant talker. Language, literature, painting, the idea that you would make artifacts and that you would love books or music, was innate. This was an enormous advantage. So many writers I know had to fight their way through to a life choice that was considered esoteric or exotic.

For me it was a given. Most particularly, that I would paint seemed very natural, and I did for a long time. As a kid, I was developing the temperament of a maker of artifacts. Everyone thought I was going to be a painter. I thought I was going to be a painter. I went to a special school for it. I drew and I painted all the time. I modeled myself on my father. He is a very natural, well-adjusted artist in that he loves to be in the studio, loves to make stuff. He has a very healthy devotion. He works every day.

So, here I was, developing the lifestyle, while devouring books and discovering an appetite for language. At some point there was a transference that was almost subliminal. I realized when I was eighteen that I was meant to write fiction, not to paint or sculpture or draw. I'd been fooling around, almost covertly, with some short stories as a teenager. And I wrote a novel, or what I called a novel, when I was fifteen years old. I was given a manual typewriter by my mother for my fourteenth birthday, and I spent the next summer typing out this 120 page manuscript on ripped-out notebook paper. Of course, it wasn't any good, but I didn't even want it to be good. I just wanted to get to the end. It was exhilarating. It was bewildering. In some way I was already understanding that I was beginning to do what I was always going to want to do. From then on, I knew I was a writer, though I didn't slough off the external idea of myself as a painter until I was eighteen and I got to Bennington College.

In the middle of my freshman year, I began another novel, which still wasn't going to be any good, but I was trying now. I lost interest in everything else and stopped being a good student. I dropped out of college to finish this book, and by that time there was no turning back. I've never done anything since then but try to write fiction and gradually succeed at putting together something that anyone would want to read.

Q: Since you left the support of the writing program at Bennington, how did you continue to develop your writing?

A: I was twenty-two when I finished that novel, and I was pretty clear that it wasn't viable. Almost as a ritual I did send it out a couple of times. I began some short stories that were better, and some of those were published, and others became material that I would incorporate into my second published novel, *Amnesia Moon*.

My apprenticeship was always a matter of reading and writing according to my own agenda and appetite. I threw over almost every chance I had for institutional support early on. In fact, Bennington College was one where the writing teaching was explosively interesting. There were friends of mine who were writing there and having almost ridiculously prodigal success: Bret Easton Ellis, Donna Tartt, Jill Eisenstadt.

Q: What made you leave Bennington?

A: I loved Bennington, but I was also freaked out by it. I'd never been to private school. I was a public school kid. I had this bohemian ethos that I'd absorbed from my parents world, which was misleadingly classless. I was kidding myself about the fact of privilege. It was a very jarring confrontation for me with that fact. I'd existed in a bohemian demimonde where the circumstance that my parents were lower-middle class would never have registered on me. The cultural advantages, the richness of their lives and their friends' lives, and the richness of our existence in New York City, disguised for me the fact that we were poor.

So, I didn't completely identify with Bennington, but I was excited by it in other ways. It was a school that had attracted a lot of self-defined future bohemians like myself. In that sense it was a perfect setting for me, but I couldn't resolve my discomfort. There was also the practical matter that I was amassing a lot of student loan debt to be there. Once I began writing and liking that better than classes, I just looked at the situation and decided that rather than beginning writing four years in the future with $30,000 in debt, I could leave school and focus on writing immediately, with a smaller debt load.

Q: What did you do to keep yourself going? Were you able to create a support system once you moved to California?

A: There were moments in my twenties when I did feel lonely for precisely those things I'd been so cavalier in tossing aside. I scratched around for some people in the Bay area who I could swap manuscripts with, in order to alleviate that typical writer's loneliness. I had some colleagues and a writer's group and that was very important at the time. When you aren't good enough to have editors focusing hard on your work, you need amateur editors who can give you feedback, so I sought that out informally.

Even after I published my first novel, and my second, I was quite isolated and naïve about what writers did when they met other writers. I was deliberately marginal. I believed I was meant to be a writer who worked outside traditional structures of prestige. It wasn't a moral issue for me, but an aesthetic issue. Writers like Patricia Highsmith, or Phillip K. Dick, carried this sense that they were exiles within their own literary generations. I cast myself as one of those, which is a somewhat perverse thing to do. It's a fetish to choose exile, but I did, and I achieved it for a little bit. I published several novels that found their way to readers who treated me as a cult artifact, while not being reviewed, for instance, in the *New York Times*. I've already experienced the inside and the outside, which for a writer as young as I am—I'm forty-one—is probably unusual. There's certainly no shred of dark horse-ness in how I'm published now. I'm given every chance by my publisher to be taken seriously, and I enjoy that, now that I have it. But I'm grateful to have known both sides of legitimacy, to have functioned as an outsider for a bit.

Q: What precipitated your transition from outsider to insider?

A: It mostly changed for a variety of reasons, which all happened concurrently. I moved back to New York. I switched from Harcourt Brace, where I was being published in a noble and upstanding but quiet way, to Doubleday, where I was published ambitiously by an ambitious young editor.

Q: How did you connect with the new editor?

A: My earlier novels had a cult following and my agent received calls from time to time asking whether or not I was tied down anywhere or if I was available. The editor who became my editor as of my third novel is still my editor. That's a long relationship in the contemporary publishing landscape. People lose their editors all the time. I'm seven books into my very fortuitous relationship with my editor at Doubleday. He's one of the editors who mentioned early on that he'd like to look at a manuscript if I was ever free. I adored my editor at Harcourt Brace, but for whatever reason, I wasn't thriving there, and so I was restless.

Michael Kandel, my editor there, was incredibly important to me because in lieu of graduate school, he taught me to become a scrupulous line editor of my own work. He was an atypical acquiring editor in that he also did copyedits, so he worked with me all the way down the line from working on the big things, down to the commas and corrections.

Q: When he gave you feedback on the bigger issues in a manuscript, was that helpful, and did it change how you looked at your work moving forward?

A: I'm always open to another angle of view on the larger choices I've made in a book, although I tend to do a lot of things that are unconventional and deliberate and about which I feel a great deal of confidence. I often welcome critique and then say, thank you, but I'm nevertheless just going to do it this way. What was crucial about that relationship with my first editor at Harcourt was that he made me think about bearing down and applying a kind of pressure to the sentences, making them crystal and making them sing.

When I moved back to New York and switched to Doubleday, I was becoming much more interested in discovering things like what it was like to go to Yaddo, or applying for a grant. I'd never applied for a grant or a fellowship. I'd never reached for anything like that. I didn't think it belonged to me, then I began to reframe that and I thought, why not me? This led me into more friendships with writers who were published in ways that were more or less analogous to the ways in which I was being published. I became less shy, less perverse about wanting to know how it all worked and how I could make it work for me so that I'd make a good living from what I was doing and enjoy the glamour of being taken fairly seriously.

Q: You made it your own.

A: Yes, and I had a lot of nice help doing that in the way I was being published and from the first people I got to know at Yaddo, or when I was invited to give readings at places like KGB. The energy from that was thrilling. I was suddenly having the response I failed to have when I was at college with Bret and Donna. Being around other people who are provoking you and inspiring you by their ambition is a charge. I want that.

Q: *Fortress of Solitude* is full of wonderful details about the prison system, graffiti art, the music industry, and street politics. *Motherless Brooklyn* narrates the escapades of a detective with Tourette's syndrome. How do you go about researching material for your books?

A: With Tourette's syndrome in *Motherless Brooklyn* I had to acquire a lot of knowledge about something that was extremely specific, specialized, and that I started by knowing nothing about. I had to master Tourette's syndrome. I had to read everything, from the brilliant and evocative and poetic Oliver Sacks essays on the subject, to self-help books along the lines of: "So You Have Tourette's," or "So Your Family Member Has Tourette's." I had to understand it scientifically, to an extent. I'm not very good with scientific material, but I tried to grasp the neurological ideas and the latest thinking on what was occurring in the brain. I had to surround the topic with real research. It was one of the only pieces of study I've ever accomplished in my life, because I was never a good student. Even when I was in classes, I was the kind of student who slipped through by bluffing.

To that point all my fiction had come almost one hundred percent out my own rhapsodic fantasizing about the world, combined with the influence of other fiction, but I'd never read nonfiction to figure out what I was going to do with my work. It didn't seem to have any bearing on my work, which to that point took as its subject my own sensibility, my imaginative and observational insights combined with the example and influence of other kinds of literature. I was like a painter. Painters don't read nonfiction books to figure out what they're going to paint. I first came out of that attitude about the arts, one which exalted the imaginative act. The idea that there would be information in my books that would resemble an essay or an article on some topic seemed absolutely irrelevant to what I was going to do. Those were the parts of books I was always bored by. I hated explanations for things, whether they were actual explanations or laboriously worked out fictional explanations. As a reader, I was always rushing past them to get to the next piece of emotion or language or dialogue or imagery. So I thought, I'll write books that consist only of imagery, language, and conversations. This bias shaped my early work.

Q: So *Motherless Brooklyn* was a departure from this bias.

A: With *Motherless Brooklyn* I changed frameworks in a couple of ways. I latched on to the external idea of Tourette's syndrome. I also decided that I wanted to describe the streets of Brooklyn. That meant having to give over more of my energy as a writer, not to explanations, but to extensive visual descriptions, which I'd also been bored by: *he was wearing such and such,* or, *the trees cast a shadow on the building.* Now suddenly I did want to write about the trees casting a shadow on the building. I began to be a writer who slowed scenes down more and offered more visual information of various kinds. Needless to say, the corner I turned in *Motherless Brooklyn* became a whole new world in *Fortress of Solitude.* All the methods that I'd ignored—making reference to the real world, explaining things, researching things, doing meticulous visual panoramas—I wanted to do all of that all at once. I shocked myself by my appetite to use all of these methods that I'd excluded from my fiction to that point.

Q: The use of brand names or pop iconography has long been a matter of debate. Did you have any ambivalence about using this language in your fiction?

A: I'd always thought it was embarrassing or awkward to put real brand names of things in fiction, and then I backed into it in a couple of places in *Motherless Brooklyn* because Lionel Essrog was a guy who liked to name stuff. He didn't want to say, *I ate a hamburger.* He liked White Castle hamburgers. That difference is so small but it's so enormous at the same time. There I am writing about White Castle, which is a real company. There's the imagery that it provokes about American cultural history, the history of franchising, the role of franchise restaurants in the urban environment. You're evoking all of this meaning that's sociological. It's not necessarily all going to be made explicit, but it is ingrained in the use of the real name. Lionel Essrog didn't want to just do this with White Castle hamburgers. He wanted to do it on every other page. He wanted to talk about *Mad* magazine and the songs of Prince. I was suddenly finding my fiction enclosing the real world, grabbing onto it and using its energy and aura.

Fortress of Solitude represents my embrace of this method, to the power of a hundred. If one chapter in *Motherless Brooklyn* could take a lot of energy from describing a song by Prince, what would happen if every page of a six-hundred-page novel were bursting with references from music to film to street names? What if I just enclosed the world I grew up in inside the book, unapologetically? That's what I did. It required enormous amounts of research, but none of it was as deliberate or scholarly as when I researched Tourette's. When I researched Tourette's I was taking one subject that lay completely outside myself and mastering it. For *Fortress of Solitude* I was doing internal excavation. I was researching my own life. I was remembering things and then stirring the memories at deeper levels by recapturing some of the details. I spent time dreaming my way back to Brooklyn in the seventies. I'd remember famous headlines from the newspapers and then I'd have the newspaper in front of me and I'd read it and it would take me even deeper into this relationship to my own memories. I was also doing this in conversations with old friends and family members. This was crucial. That book could never have been written without intimate interpersonal research. I was spending a lot of time with guys I went to school with talking about our school days. In some ways it's a collective oral history. I could never have recaptured all of those tales, all of those images, all of those feelings without hearing from these other guys. That was the most important research I did for that book.

Q: How does a novel idea come to you: in a voice, an image, or a character? For example, why did Lionel Essrog have Tourette's?
A: I hit on the idea of Tourette's because I'd read the Oliver Sacks essay, "An Anthropologist on Mars." Then, I happened, by very good luck, to see at the Roxy movie theater in San Francisco a documentary called *Twitch and Shout,* by a filmmaker Laurel Chiten. It was a forthright and humane look at the lives of people with Tourette's. By the time I left the theater, I knew I was going to write about this subject. I couldn't have told you why it was so important to me, but I knew that it was something that I was going to have to incorporate.

Q: Even on the level of language it seems to have struck a nerve.
A: It was very, very opportune. My response to it was personal, in that it reminded me of some of my own cognitive operations, the way I respond to language, the way I like to invert and destroy words.

Q: There's a riff element.
A: Yes, there's a kind of play that I was already doing, and doing somewhat compulsively. I liked it, I didn't have any need to get rid of it, and I didn't think of it as a symptom, but it *was* involuntary. The fact that there was this category of experience called Tourette's syndrome that consisted of uncomfortable and involuntary verbal riffing and inversions and repetitions and

punning created a sense of terror and identification in me. I could see the activity I called "writing" in a light where it might be unwilling, or helpless.

The other thing that was going on was that I was rediscovering my connection with Brooklyn, and I realized I wanted to move back. I experienced a sentimental urgency to proclaim that Brooklyn was where I was from. The way people talk there, the way they're louder and more sarcastic, the way they're more impetuous in their talk: that's what I'm like. That's why I'd been uncomfortable in California, I decided, because everyone was so careful and damped and gentle in the way they spoke. I was constantly being responded to as if I was out of control when I just thought I was being emphatic. People would take a step back and act like I was always a bit too much.

So, I began to make this provocative and exciting analogy between being a Brooklynite in California and being someone with Tourette's syndrome. What is it to dwell in a world where you're always saying too much? Those two things began to map onto each other, and that was when I began to have something exciting to offer.

He became a detective because I love detective stories. I was looking for a traditional form because the linguistic contents were going to be so radical. I wanted a familiar receptacle to pour them into. It seemed incredibly funny to me. He'd be the opposite of the hardboiled detective, who is defined by his verbal control, his mastery.

Q: What is your process like for working on a novel? How many revisions do you generally do?

A: I wrote four novels on a typewriter, where a draft is an actual physical thing. I'm glad I learned to write in that manner, where a draft is a separate pile of paper, rather than on a computer where drafts merge together in this amorphous, oceanic flood. They drift in and out of each other. It was good for me to learn to rewrite by handling every sentence over again, by retyping it. But now that I have a computer I could never imagine going back. I don't obey the physical reality of drafts at any level. I'm always changing things, doubling back. My process is oceanic now. On the other hand, some things have been true from the beginning and are still true now: I always go from the beginning to the end, and I never jump ahead or write scenes out of sequence. I want to experience the book the way the reader experiences the book. I don't want to indulge any sleight-of-hand in that. I want to be discovering the story word by word, sentence by sentence, turning the page and meeting the story the way the reader meets it.

I probably still write three drafts, but the first two are combined. I write the book from beginning to end very, very slowly. By the time I reach the last page, I'm actually almost done. I'm one brief revision away from turning it in to my editor. The image I came across recently that seemed perfect is that I feel like a snail leaving its trail. I work extremely slowly but leaving behind a very thick and complete slime as I go. My pace can't be hurried. What I leave behind in my wake is very complete, and like a snail, I can't jump at all.

Q: Do you feel impatient?

A: Not anymore. I've experienced this process—beginning a novel and finishing it—eight times now, and when you reinforce that experience enough times, you begin to build into your body the expectation that you'll get there. All that leaves is the morbid superstition, when a book is going well, that I might die in a plane crash and no one would have any idea what happened after where I left off. The snail would've left a slime trail that just ended and there would be no indication of what comes after. That seems very sad to me, when I like what I'm writing. But my confidence doesn't falter anymore. Unless the snail is dropped from an airplane, he'll get to the end of his trail.

Q: How is the process different when you're working on short stories?

A: The stories I've produced I see in two different lights. There's a kind that I began writing and that I've written a few times recently but I've mostly stopped, that are more novelistic. They're more like compressed novels, or like first chapters for novels that will never be written.

I love the immersion and the fullness of the experience of reading a novel. Early on as a reader I wasn't drawn to short stories, with a few exceptions. So, as a writer, I wrote what I'd been reading. I wrote things that felt like fiction to me, and fiction felt like the novel. Even when I tried to be a short story writer early on, I'd come up with these things that were like thwarted or impacted or super-compressed novels.

Then I developed a love of the short story. It was a subsequent part of my reading life. So, of course, it was a subsequent part of my writing life. I began to learn to write things that were fifteen to thirty manuscript pages and introduced fewer elements and complications. They're sprints. The working method is different. They're written more in a burst, where as the others are written more in that snail crawling way where I'm getting into a world and exploring it in like I do with a novel.

Q: You've called *Motherless Brooklyn* your farewell to plot. Can you say more about this?

A: *Girl in Landscape*, the book before *Motherless Brooklyn*, is, I think, my most honest and substantial engagement with the novel form, in that it's fully an exploration of character and emotion, and the interactions of an array of characters, irrespective of any kind of exoskeletal plot driving the story from the outside. Not that those characters aren't dealing with external circumstances, but the way the story develops is as an expression of the characters' existence, their dwelling inside the world I've put them in. Whereas in earlier books, I had a big idea and I put my characters on stage like puppets in a show in service of my big idea. Now, in fact I think many of those earlier characters are delightful and have a lot of warmth and life to them, but ultimately they're mastered by the exoskeleton of concept.

In *Girl in Landscape*, I realized that the character-driven writing was better for me. It was more like the writing I loved most. I was learning to do it and to trust myself without the superstructure of concept. I knew this was what I'd primarily want to do for the rest of my life. Having reached that point, I realized I'd stop having puppet shows. It's like the difference between putting on the fullest and most human puppet show you can possibly put on and being a method actor on stage. With *Girl in Landscape*, I was a method actor on stage during a play *being* the character, and that's how I wanted to feel when I was writing, always.

Having come to this conclusion, I immediately doubled back, in part because the language of *Motherless Brooklyn* required a familiar container. That book obviously has a very strong exoskeleton of plot: that whole elaborate, ridiculous mystery that has to be solved. There's no version of plot more prominent and distracting than a mystery that needs solving. Clues must be distributed through the book and an explanation must be revealed at the end. For me it was like playing the old song one last time. Maybe playing the best I ever had, because I'd learned a lot about how to plot a book and how to make a concept really appealing, but I also knew that I wasn't going to do that after this farewell. And sure enough, *Fortress of Solitude* is written a thousand percent in what I've called the method-acting technique, where character and emotion are what drive the book.

Q: Lionel's linguistic rants offer readers a scatter-shot glimpse of some internal logic, and they let readers know more about Lionel and how he sees himself in the world. Did you know that these rants would provide that opportunity or did you discover it in the writing?

A: I discovered it very early in the writing. The first page of the book is the first thing I wrote. I stared at that page for a while, regarding it as a conundrum. Could I really write a book that began with those sentences? It was a very different kind of writing for me. There's a lot of energy required. I realized that he was going to have to reach that kind of crescendo again and again in the book, but also if it stayed in that voice all the way through, it would intolerable to write, and if I managed to do it, intolerable to read. Instead, I had to look at that first page as a battery. I figured there would be fifteen to twenty of these "Tourette's rhapsodies," where the voice rises up and pours out. The book would be punctuated by these rhapsodies, on a series of subjects. It was a writer's discovery, but it was an initial and formative discovery.

Q: It must've taken a while to perfect his voice, and his idiosyncrasies.
A: Once I met Lionel and heard his voice in those first few pages, it was very appealing and very real to me. It was a variation of my own natural voice. I didn't have a lot of hesitations. I applied editorial pressure to the book as I was writing it, and immediately after. I cropped parts where the puns or the free-associations seemed too easy, a little pat, or a little schematic, but that's just editorial work. I was never in any crisis of doubt about the voice because it was self-maintaining. It had a motor.

Q: You make references to the genres that influenced *Motherless Brooklyn* through out the text. Lionel asks, "Have you ever felt, in the course of reading a detective novel, a guilty thrill of relief at having a character murdered before he can step on to the page and burden you with his actual existence?" What does the narrative gain from these self-reflective references?
A: It's a dubious choice, isn't it, having material that analyzed the nature of detective stories in a detective story? On the other hand, I was discovering the pleasure and the value of self-consciousness in narrative voice. This goes back to the fact that he wanted to talk about *Mad* magazine, Prince, and White Castle hamburgers. It didn't follow that someone like Lionel could be so explicit and generous with his cultural references and so extensive in this cultural vocabulary and yet be oblivious to the references that would be most germane to him and his own aspirations.

Why would someone like him want to be like him *unless* he'd read Raymond Chandler? If he was going to think articulately and vividly about everything that came across his path, it was only fair that he should get to say that he reads books. It was an inevitable by-product of the contract I'd struck, that I was going to allow this character to be totally interested in his environment and talk about everything that amused him, from the magazines in the store, to the sandwiches being made at the counter. Leaving fiction reading out of that would've seemed like an imposture.

Q: Do you ever feel disappointed or surprised by the requirements of what you call the contract you've struck in taking on a book?
A: There are times in the latter stages of a book where you realize you can't do everything you wanted to do at the outset. You can only do so much on a given page, with a given voice. In the expanding size of my last couple of books you can see me reaching to enclose more and more of the world, and of what I can say as a writer. *Fortress of Solitude* is an attempt to devise a book that can say anything I wanted to say, but even a book that large develops its own kinds of exclusions. As enormous as *Fortress* is, it's starved for other things. There are no women in the book. People sometimes complain to me about that, and indeed, I felt very lonely for women as I wrote that book. Without women on the page, it was like a starvation diet. Yet if my subject was isolation and fathers and sons and broken families, I had to keep that bargain.

Q: The word "motherless" describes the Minna Men, including Lionel, and Dylan Ebdus in *The Fortress of Solitude* and his friend Mingus Rude are both motherless. What draws you to writing about characters whose mothers are absent?
A: My mother died when I was fourteen. She began to be ill when I was eleven, in and out of hospitals and having brain surgery. It was a loss that occurred in slow motion, so that I got to think about as it was going on. I don't know if that's easier or harder for a kid to go through, but whichever it was, it was definitely not a sudden, sharp loss that could be isolated and denied to then be contemplated later. It was something to dwell on as it was unfolding. I had to participate in losing my mother over a period of years. That's a big experience. In my early work there are metaphorical versions of incomplete families, incomplete tribes, and incomplete worlds, even before I start writing directly about motherless-ness.

It's easy to say: I lost my mother, therefore I became obsessed with loss. But I don't think losing my mother was actually the beginning of that sense of loss, or the only source of its resonance as a metaphor or motif in my writing. The reason loss proliferates in so many ways is that I was already quite focused on the notions of broken families, broken tribes, broken cities, before my mother was sick. Her dying only confirmed and deepened and made personal a suspicion I already had about the world. That suspicion comes from several places. It comes from my grandmother and my mother's Jewishness. I was raised in a family that commemorated and mourned the Holocaust. It came from coming of age in the Watergate era, when our society was explicitly broken. My parents were political radicals. The Vietnam War and Watergate obsessed them. I felt that I lived in a broken land. New York City was itself a broken place, where loss was manifest. Everything about this world I grew up in evoked the idea that there had been a great and complete and glorified past and now there was a ruined present and we were living in the shambles of something formerly great. When my died, my family echoed this sense of destruction and loss. However horrible, it was also strangely natural to me: structures are complete and then they fall apart. It felt to me that the deep story of existence had played in miniature within my family. That's one reason that in my work I first projected this strong feeling not on descriptions of families or individual lives, but on descriptions of culture, city, and history.

Q: Your most recent books are all set, at least in part, in Brooklyn. Your characters are involved in tagging, are the recipients of racial discrimination, struggle with nervous disorders, compulsively read comics, and struggle to survive in a potentially violent combination of race, class, and culture. How do your own experiences inform your fiction?

A: In *Fortress of Solitude*, I was energized by the idea that I would write an autobiographical novel. I would admit it was one, and I would make it one. I gave Mingus and Dylan my street address. I put them right in the crosshairs of my memory so that I wouldn't be fooling myself or anyone else. That's the block I grew up on. I wanted, for a change, to be caught in the center of the autobiographical impulse as a writer. Nevertheless, I'm a fiction writer by temperament, by instinct, by training. The book is loaded with red herrings. I'm constantly credited with experiences I haven't had, some of them quite comically specific. People are sure they've read all my music criticism, that I must have some extensive history as a record reviewer. They'll remember, falsely, that they'd seen my byline in *Rolling Stone*, over a record review.

That's one, relatively superficial example. But the book can be very misleading. A more profound version is the Dylan and Abraham relationship, which does describe some aspects of my own father/son relationship, yet almost none of the external circumstances resemble my childhood. Dylan and Abraham live together in a mute isolation alone in a giant house. I was surrounded by talkative siblings. We lived in a semi-commune. My father is a painter whose studio was always filled with live, nude models and fellow artists. As you know from the essay collection, it was almost an over-whelming hive of human possibilities. The loneliness in the Abraham/Dylan experience has nothing to do with a depiction of my childhood. It's tricky. What I performed, I think, was the Philip Roth trick of pouring so much autobiographical feeling into the fiction, and raising the specter of direct confession, so that the reader feels at every point that they must be being told something terribly intimate.

The other thing to emphasize is that I really did absorb and regurgitate my siblings' and my friends' experiences. Dylan, Mingus, and Arthur are re-ceptacles for collective lore. No one of them maps to any one other person; rather there are dozens of people who rightly feel a claim on those charac-ters, because they see parts of themselves and their experiences reflected in those characters. The list of acknowledgements at the end of that book is not a trifling thing. It's an important list. Lastly, there another thing that's overlooked when a book seems autobiographical: how strongly it may be influenced by other fictions. *Great Expectations* is in *Fortress. Portrait of a Romantic* by Steven Millhauser, too. The character of Arthur comes right out of Millhauser. Henry Roth's *Call It Sleep* was crucial too—Roth's depic-tion of the child's experience of life inside his house and life in the street as two opposite worlds. My earlier books are very transparent in terms of liter-ary influence. But in *Fortress*, because of the passion of the autobiographical feeling, this fact tends to be disguised.

Q: What are the challenges of writing about these conflicts in the place where you grew up and where you live?
A: If I'd thought about it, I'd have been paralyzed. I knew that the only chance for me to find the voice that would be allowed to write the book was to put aside any question of speaking of these matters objectively. Instead, I had to give total authority to intimate experience, the life of the body, the life of one child moving along a sidewalk trying to get to school on a given day. I'd let any wider implications enter on their own steam from the readers' projections, from my own helpless reactions. But as a conscious strategy I'd stick to testimony, through fiction, of intimate experience. When I thought about race, I didn't think about race. I thought about Dylan and Mingus. I didn't think about black and white. I didn't think about any contextual or conceptual structures. I thought about what does Abraham think when he meets Mingus? What is Mingus feeling when he tries to introduce Dylan to Robert?

Q: Some writers need to write about the place they grew up in from a distance. Lynn Freed said, "Estrangement is a necessary ingredient to your work because it gives you the perspective of another world from which to examine your own." But the opposite seems true for you—you moved to the west coast and didn't start writing about Brooklyn until you moved back to Boerum Hill in 1997. Comment?

A: I agree with the quote completely. The fact that I returned to New York and then wrote about it is a little misleading. Estrangement is the deeper truth. It's the long estrangement of being away from New York City and rejecting it for a decade, that enabled me to get to this material. If I'd been there continuously, I'd never have been able to write about it. It was the objectifying estrangement that allowed me to write about it. Even then, the majority of *Fortress of Solitude* was written outside of the city in German hotel lobbies, in cafes in Toronto, and Yaddo. It seemed to depend on that exile, that sense of yearning back toward the place.

Q: Even though the main character of *The Fortress of Solitude*, Dylan Ebdus, is a minority among the black students in his middle school, he's still white and he will eventually enjoy privileges beyond those of his black classmates. First, was it difficult to write about characters from different ethnicities and income levels?

A: It's uncomfortable. It's the most uncomfortable possible material, but I was writing about discomfort, so I had to make a radical embrace of my own discomfort, not so that the book would be easy, but so that I could convey my discomfort and encode it in the book. I think it can be very unsettling for people to read. The result is an incompleteness. If you frame those questions, they're terrible to live with—that's why we push them out of view. In order to do this book at all, I had to decide to be incorrect, rude, and blatant. I had to name things that weren't ordinarily named. That's one reason that the superhero element was so important, because it's so embarrassing and ridiculous—I realized that the whole book had to be ridiculous. They'd have to be named Dylan and Mingus. I had to be unafraid of being broad and exaggerated and ridiculous in every way because this was a book about looking at what's flinched from. It's not about subtle postures. It's about confrontation.

Q: Dylan experiences a kind of reverse-racism, where he clings to his older, black friend Mingus for a perceived status that Dylan can't have because he's white. We learn near the end, when Mingus is in jail, that his "status" was an illusion created in the microcosm of their young lives. What challenges did you face in depicting the racial inequalities of this time and place? Were you ever concerned about getting it right?

A: As I say, I stuck to intimate testimony, my own and others. This isn't to say that it's all factual and that my authority is derived from facts, but that my authority is derived from my total investment in these characters and their absolute reactions. People asked me after *Girl in Landscape* how I could write from the point of view of a thirteen-year-old girl menstruating for the first time. If I'd conceived it as that question proposes, I couldn't have written a word. But I never thought that way. She wasn't some representative thirteen-year-old girl. She was Pella. I met her. I found her. I made her my own. I lent her enormous parts of my own personality and sensitivity. It wasn't a task of solving the problem of how a thirty-five-year-old male could write about a thirteen year old girl, it was a question of telling Pella's story, since I was the only one who knew it.

Q: Abraham's relationship to his art, his philosophies and eccentricities feel so real, as if he dropped onto the page whole. Your father was an art professor and a painter and you grew up around his work, yet you've said that Abraham is as much you as he is your father. How did Abraham materialize on the page?

A: I'd been thinking about a certain kind of experimental filmmakers, the purists from the fifties and sixties like Stan Brakhage and Jonas Mekas and their ilk. There was one, somewhat less famous but who I was compelled by, named Ed Emshwiller. In certain external circumstances, Emshwiller had Abraham's career. He was an experimental filmmaker who painted images on film, and he made his living doing science fiction art. And this split, the fact that neither of the two realms in which he dwelled cared about the other, so that he had this doubleness, seemed to say something about the lives of artists. For, nearly every artist is at some level located between these poles: an absolute, fixated, obsessed relationship to their artistic impulse, and trying to be viable, trying to communicate, trying to make a living, trying to do something that other people will respond to.

I was very interested in this idea that art was both a very selfish activity and a desperate attempt to connect. For the happiest, luckiest artists (like myself) those things align very closely. I carry on writing the most perverse and obsessive things I care to, and yet they also seem to matter to my audience, and I make a living. Whereas many people feel that the thing they do that matters most to them is not the thing that people want to give them money for, or even to talk about. Abraham suffers this disparity to a ludicrous degree. The two poles of his creative life are so distant they're not even in the same medium. As an image of the dislocation of an artist in a commercial culture, this was quite moving to me. I was also interested in the kind of temperament of the kind of artist who creates a hopeless, modernist object. I was thinking about Beckett, Mark Rothko who painted increasingly dark and simple—gray on white forever. I was thinking about Conlon Nancarrow, who retreated to Mexico to punch holes in player piano rolls because the music he heard in his head was unplayable by human hands.

I was also thinking about the beauty of my father's devotion to his work, and some of his disappointments as his commercial viability dwindled. All of those lives are conflated in that character. And then, more accidentally, Abraham became a figure I identified with enormously myself, because the work I invented for him, painting these little frames day after day, became a confession of my own method of writing this long novel, incrementally filling in one little item at a time on this seemingly endless canvas. I was describing myself writing the novel while I was writing it. Even Abraham's relationship to the street, his distance from it, his fascination with it, the way he feels that he is capturing the life of that block in his film even though no one would know it from the outward result. That seemed to me a confession of how close my work had always felt to a depiction of Brooklyn, even before I wrote about that place explicitly.

Q: I want to go back to what you were saying earlier about pop iconography. There has long been a debate among writers, especially in writing programs, whether or not to use references from pop culture. You've managed to use references to music and comic books to deepen character and create resonant details. Are there times when you've written details that you've had to omit because it didn't add to the work? Is there some standard that cultural references, or any detail for that matter, must live up to in order to be included?

A: I'd really not done it, until I suddenly did it. It was Lionel Essrog who tricked me into it, because he loved to name things. I used to have, without thinking it through very well, that same prejudice: that there was some cheap authority when you mentioned a brand name, but costly in the long run because it would date and nobody would know what you were talking about—although there were writers, like Ann Beattie, who I adored, who made use of the method. I thought I was excluding it from my work for a high reason. Then I realized that *Fortress of Solitude* would need to have that method at its center, for I wanted to create a time capsule of the world I grew up in.

Some readers had pointed to the pages of *Motherless Brooklyn* that featured Prince and *Mad* magazine as their favorites. There's something talismanic and beautiful in naming, and I thought that if it had been charged for Lionel, maybe it could be charged in this book too. Again, I had to embrace and authorize myself to do something to the point of absurdity. There are so many cultural names in this book. To console myself, I thought about Dickens. His novels of London feature an inordinate amount of references, street names and bits of jingles and names that advertise products that I can't know of, but because they're conveyed with total authority, and because it all means something to the characters, I can accept it. It builds up my sense impression of this world. With *Fortress* I thought: if I'm lucky, maybe I can get away with this and it will have the same kind of authority—not because we know what the names mean, but because the names themselves become an edifice of language, a reconstruction of a world.

Q: The first half of the novel is written in an omniscient point-of-view where readers are privy to the thoughts of many characters, while the second half of the novel is told from Dylan's point-of-view. Why did you decide to use these two different viewpoints for the different parts of the novel?
A: I knew from the outset that this book had to have a before-and-after quality, and that there had to be a strong rupture between the two. The paradox of the subject matter was that I wanted to simultaneously write about how close at hand and deeply influential on adult life childhood experience can be—and about how remote and irretrievable childhood experience can feel, at the exact same time. I had to encode that closeness and distance in the technology of the book. When the characters are thrust out of childhood at the end of high school, when Mingus kills his grandfather, I had to make it feel as though they'd never get back to that place, and yet that they'd never left it. I had to make the reader feel as estranged and upset as that yearning to return to an irretrievable place feels in life. The result is a sort of breach of the contract with the reader. Many are angry that I shift when I do and the way I do. They want to go back. That's a feeling I meant to arouse, however uncomfortable.

In the first half of the book, though the characters are suffering, there's a golden glow that makes everything okay. Whereas the feeling in adulthood, in the second section, is that nothing is okay. In the last part of the book, everyone seems so estranged and inconsolable that you want to make them go back to the way they were. But rescue is impossible.

Q: You break out of the first person near the end when we hear from Mingus what his life has been like and how he landed in prison. How did you arrive at this decision to briefly step out of the established point-of-view?

A: Yes—but that comes from a radical disproportion in the first part of the book. You experience everyone's point-of-view except for Mingus's. The whole first half of the book surrounds the question of Mingus's subjectivity but never penetrates it, because that's the mystery of the book. What is Mingus feeling through all this? When you finally have access to Mingus's subjectivity, it corresponds to Dylan being able to take Mingus off the pedestal, of Dylan's allowing the possibility of him being a damaged, feeling human being, rather than a kind of superhero. It's a missing piece of the first half of the book, one which arrives just barely in time.

Q: You've said that form is present in a short story in a different way than in a novel because of the compressed structure. Can you say more about this? What appeals to you about the form of a short story?

A: I'm more naturally a novelist. I like the commodious form of the novel best of all, the one that takes in all kinds of forms and unifies them and permits digressions. But I can engage, with great excitement, with the more rigorous, more visible, more skeletal form of a short story, which relates to other short-form items, like the song, or the folk tale, or the joke. They're like little mechanisms or toys. I get excited about how to pull that off.

Q: You edited *The Vintage Book of Amnesia*, an anthology of writings about memory loss. What inspired your interest in amnesia?

A: I'd already been writing about it for a while before I noticed that it was an obsession. It was one of my most pregnant metaphors for the kind of loss I feel present in the world. In my first two novels, I used amnesia to describe the fundamental state of brokenness in the world. In fact, I was confused about memory when I was younger, simply because I have a better memory than average. So, I was certain that anyone who told me they couldn't remember something that happened—if I remembered it—must be lying. My first assumption was: of course you remember, quit fooling. If it's in my memory, it's got to be in yours. I formed an impression that forgetting was a vague but universal conspiracy against me. It took me a long time to understand that people could honestly forget.

I then became fascinated with the extent to which our worlds are comprised as much of forgetting as remembering. For, after all, it's necessary to suppress and eliminate and edit for emphasis, if only to make sense of the world. All of our experiences of ourselves are fundamentally vast fictions, in that they consist of exclusions and emphasized memories, strung together to make a coherent version of self, version of family, version of life. I started to realize that these images had a lot to do with what I liked about story and how storytelling related to experience. Novels are exciting to me partly because they are a version of how we narrate our lives.

So, I'd been an accidental connoisseur of the amnesia story. I'd written a couple, and I had all of these favorite novels that were amnesiac plots. This was a motif in fiction that I liked. Editing the book was as simple as looking around my room and identifying all of the amnesia books and stringing them together. I enjoyed declaring a genre, one that hadn't existed before my declaration.

Q: Is there anything that holds them together beyond the theme of amnesia?
A: With a couple of exceptions, everything in the book takes the idea of amnesia and either turns it into a metaphor for life or for fiction making. There's a lot of very gently meta-fictional writing in that anthology. Amnesia, as a motif, leads you into problems areas. For fiction itself is amnesiac. When you open a novel or story, you are in the exact condition of the corniest amnesia story ever told. You wake up in a room, it's blank and white, you don't know who you are, or why you're there. If you identify with the character, you're slowly filling in the details like an amnesiac slowly figuring out who they are.

Q: In *The Disappointment Artist*, you've gathered several of your cultural essays and revealed some of the wealth of obsessions that inform your work. Does writing nonfiction about your obsessions feed you in a different way than using these obsessions in your fiction? How?
A: This was an important book in terms of discharging the energy residing in of a group of obsessions that had characterized my fiction up to a recent point. Central enigmas that I was wrestling with in my fiction. By the time I finished *Fortress of Solitude* and certainly by the time I finished those es-

says, I was tucking them into bed to go to sleep for a while. To name them so specifically, and with such scrupulously honesty, was a finishing touch, a culmination of the work that *Fortress of Solitude* represents.

Q: You've written many introductions to reissued novels, including *Poor George* by Paula Fox, *The Man Who Was Thursday: A Nightmare* by G. K. Chesterton, *On the Yard* by Malcolm Braly, *A New Life* by Bernard Malamud, *It Happened in Boston?* by Russell H. Greenan, *The Man Who Lost the Sea: Volume X: The Complete Stories of Theodore Sturgeon* by Theodore Sturgeon, *Dombey and Son* by Charles Dickens, to name a few. How do you get asked to write these introductions?

A: After I'd done a few introductions, and it was clear that I was willing to do them, I was asked to do many more. It's part of the ecology of publishing that editors at Penguin Classics or Modern Library are always looking to put a newer spin on something that they're reissuing by getting someone younger than the previous introducer—for these things hang around a while. When I wrote the introduction to the G. K. Chesterton, I replaced an introduction written by Kingsley Amis in the sixties. Not that Amis is irrelevant, but it might be right if you're going to reissue a classic every fifty years or so, it may be appropriate to invite someone contemporary to explain why we remain excited about the book.

I see this work as a curatorial impulse, the same one that used to be expressed for me by my work in an antiquarian bookstore, where I'd cultivate and groom the literature section. I was excited by modern first editions and by finding obscure authors and out-of-print books, so writing introductions to books I love feels very much like another version of being a bookseller.

Q: What do you do to prepare for writing the introduction?

A: It's hard work to justify for the money you're paid—not that they aren't as generous as they can be! To do a good job you have to read and reread an awful lot. For that reason, of course, it's tougher to do a Dickens than a Nathanael West. The amount of reading and secondary sources is enormous. For *Dombey and Son* I spent six months doing the reading and about two weeks on the actual writing. Suddenly I'm doing all of the scholarship that I never bothered with as a student.

Q: And you pick books that you'll get something out of in terms of your own work?

A: It's usually something I've read at least once and am looking forward to rereading, or something that bears on what I'm working on now, something that's inspiring. For example, when I wrote the introduction for Malcolm Braly's *On the Yard,* a brilliant novel about prison, it was right when I was writing the last sections of *Fortress of Solitude,* and the Braly told me things I needed to know. It was as though some guardian angel had steered me to that book.

Q: What are you working on now?
A: As I've suggested, I feel that I've discharged a set of motifs and images that have consumed me for four books in a row. The book I'm writing now is a celebration of my freedom from those concerns. It's set in Los Angeles. It involves no parents and children whatsoever. It's not full of cultural specifics about the seventies or any other era. It's exists in a blurry fictional space, one that's vaguely contemporary, but it doesn't really matter. My characters aren't record collectors or DJs. They don't have that naming impulse that runs through Ebdus and Essrog. They're a hapless group of musicians trying to be in a rock band in Los Angeles. It's basically a romantic comedy. A piece of deliberate frivolity. There's nothing resembling an autobiographical stance, although I love the characters and they feel very intimate to me. The main character is a woman, so it's a compensation for the masculine deprivation chamber of *Fortress of Solitude.* She's not only the main character but she's the viewpoint character, so there's a woman in every sentence of the book. It's a way for me to spend some time in a more female universe.

Q: What would you say to new writers working on their first stories or novel?
A: The most germane bit of advice I have is to not bog down in writing one thing over and over again early on, but to finish something and move to the next, and then to do that again and again and again. I suspect that even by taking three years on one novel at the outset, I was grinding in one gear for too long. It's better to finish a great number of things. Learn what it is to write a beginning, middle, and end, whether that means a series of stories or writing a first draft of a novel and then writing another first draft and another. Err on the side of writing things and letting them go and working on next things, and you'll learn much more quickly.

A Conversation with Jonathan Lethem

James Schiff/2005

From *The Missouri Review* 29, no.1 (Spring/Summer 2006): 116–34. Reprinted by permission of James Schiff.

Jonathan Lethem is the author of six novels, including *The Fortress of Solitude* and *Motherless Brooklyn*, the latter of which won the National Book Critics Circle Award and was named novel of the year by *Esquire*. He is also the author of two short story collections and one volume of essays, and his writings have appeared in the *New Yorker, Rolling Stone, Esquire*, and the *Paris Review*.

Lethem's fiction has been described as inventive, incandescent, visionary, and wickedly funny. He is, perhaps, best known for bending and conflating genres—whether stitching together science fiction and hard-boiled detective conventions, mixing *Alice in Wonderland* absurdism with campus satire, or integrating elements of fantasy into otherwise realistic fiction. In ignoring conventions and genre boundaries, Lethem has expanded the range of possibilities for fiction. In addition, perhaps as much as any serious writer in America today, he has been influenced by and has integrated into his work elements of popular culture and genre fiction. He knows his comic books and sci-fi paperbacks as well as his Kafka and DeLillo; he knows his *Star Wars* as well as his Godard. He also has an amazing recall of what he has read and seen. Talented and inventive, Jonathan Lethem is a highly charged novelist who has absorbed a good deal of popular culture and literature, and in so doing, he has generated an art unlike that of any of his literary contemporaries.

During a recent visit to Cincinnati, Lethem was interviewed by James Schiff, assistant professor of English at the University of Cincinnati and author of several books on contemporary American fiction. What follows is based on an interview that took place before an audience on the campus of the University of Cincinnati on March 3, 2005.

Schiff: In your new collection of essays, *The Disappointment Artist*, you write about your artistic influences, and also about your parents and their larger circle of friends. In contrast to most of your literary contemporaries, your childhood was spent among painters, musicians, and writers. I'm curious if you can remember a moment or an experience in which it became clear to you that you wanted to write fiction.

Lethem: Yeah, I had an unusual head start as an artist, generally, which is that I grew up in a painter's household. My father was and still is a painter and a lot of my parents' friends were his students or colleagues, and so this activity—specifically, going into the studio every day and trying to make paintings—seemed normal to me. It was just everyday, and something that I could aspire to, but it wasn't esoteric; it wasn't a remote possibility, it was something very everyday and available. I can't remember a time when I didn't think I was going to be an artist of some kind. Specifically, at the beginning, I thought I would paint too, and this was different, I learned, from the way most writers or artists grow up. They're usually in families where even if making art is regarded as an interesting possibility, it's somewhat esoteric, seen as impractical or unlikely. For me, it was inevitable. In fact, it would have been very strange, I think, for my parents if I hadn't been creative in some way. My brother grew up to be a graphic designer and my sister's a photographer, so I fell the furthest from the tree by switching to writing. But even that was in the ballpark, because my parents were very literate. My father's painting itself is very narratively based, full of symbols and at times even language—some of his styles include words on the canvas.

My mother was a big reader and a great talker, very dynamic. You've mentioned my talent for recall—well, she was famous for her memory, and memory is a real novelist's gift. I think it's the most important natural gift I inherited, her capacity for recall—not in a photographic sense, not a pure, scientifically accurate recall, but a recall that centers on an interest in emotional situations, conversations, language, affect, people's styles. She was socially brilliant; a great talker, raconteur, and joke-teller. I grew up in a house full of anecdotes and descriptions of friends—everyone had a nickname. We'd savor how different friends of the family, or relatives, were great characters. We shared an instinctive narrative curiosity. I think if my mother had lived, she might have turned out a writer. Certainly a lot of her friends thought of her as a kind of proto-writer, even though she didn't write anything. But she was so verbal, and so interested in stories, that people expected she would do that. Too, her books were available to me, and her love of reading was imparted to me very early on. I grew up in a house where writing was a very accessible ambition to latch onto.

The mysterious thing, harder to locate, is when I sensed that I was not going to paint. Because that was the first thing I was doing and it was the obvious role to play: the art prodigy. I'd inherited some of my father's raw gifts. I had a good eye, I could draw in a way that impressed grownups. And when you're a kid, anything you do that gets attention, you do more of. So I was eager to draw and paint, and I enjoyed it. But it never meant as much to me as the relationship I felt to the books I was reading. The inkling that I might tell stories, or write, felt more personal and important to me. In fact I tried to write some short stories when I was eleven, twelve, thirteen, but it came on really strong a couple of years after that. In the last essay in *The Disappointment Artist*, I describe the moment when, for my fourteenth birthday, the last birthday while she was alive, my mother gave me a manual typewriter. She sensed my desire to write and gave me this gift. Within a year she was dead, and I had begun, at fifteen, during summer vacation, a novel, a 125-page manuscript that I typed on torn-out notebook pages with blue lines and hanging chads along the edge. I wasn't concerned with quality—I was just impressed with myself for typing 125 pages of anything at fifteen. By then, writing was the only thing I seriously wanted to do. Yet I was still playing the role of the art student, because it was such an appealing role, and because that same year, the year I'd turned fourteen and my mother died, I'd gotten in to the High School of Music and Art in New York, which is the official school for little art prodigies to attend. I was still painting by the time I got to college four years later. It was only then, at eighteen or nineteen, at school in Vermont, that I threw over the painting completely, and said, "Okay, I'm a writer." I came out of hiding. Up to then I'd been furtive about that identity, though I had a typewriter and my room was lined with books.

Schiff: More so than other authors, your writing appears to come specifically from your reading, yet the way you have described it, particularly with your mother and the conversations and atmosphere within your house, these experiences also played an important role. So often, one's early stories and novels deal with adolescence and seem to work in an autobiographical, coming-of-age, even mimetic fashion, yet yours don't. So I'm curious. Did you write any coming-of-age fiction early on and decide not to publish it, or did you begin by doing really different kinds of things?

Lethem: When I first decided I wanted to write, I had an image of the kind of writer I wanted to be. Of course, it was a misunderstanding in some ways, of both what my own tendencies or gifts were going to turn out to be, and of the nature of some of the writers I meant to emulate. I thought, quite foolishly, that the world of writing was divided between, let's say, the Philip Roths on one side, who work from thinly concealed personal experience and are personally present in everything they write, whether by autobiographical narrative or an unmistakably personal voice, or both, and then there are those writers who use their imagination, who are storytellers and inventors, who offer a generosity of invention. They present concepts and images—in that sense they might be seen as being more like visual artists or cartoonists. They say, "Here, look at this!" They're not interested in presenting themselves.

Needless to say, this duality is quite artificial and exaggerated. Yet I invested in it, and I thought that the writers I liked went on the side of the inventors, who refrained from writing about themselves. They were instead putting on a great show. I thought, "That's what I'll be." I simply didn't value the autobiographical impulse in my own work, even when I saw little traces of it—it always emerges, of course. Everything is personal, finally. But in the early going I always validated the imaginative act. I wanted to produce fascinating characters who were not myself, situations that were not familiar but exotic, diverting, and strange. Readers, I hoped, would marvel at them, the way I marveled at Italo Calvino's stories, or Stanislaw Lem's novels, or Borges, or Kafka, or at some of the American science fiction writers I was in love with, or the gripping plots that I encountered in Graham Greene and Patricia Highsmith. Now, I know what you're thinking: Well, wait a minute—some of those are very-personal writers. This was precisely the fault line in my theory. Obviously, when you read Kafka, you encounter a voice that's intensely personal and autobiographical. He may have translated that impulse into exotic metaphors or unusual situations, but he's still presenting—as much as Philip Roth or any writer who ever lived—his own experience of the world, very directly. Granted, if you look at someone like Borges, the writer may be somewhat better concealed, but he's still present. If you look at any writer, Highsmith or Greene, whomever, the work is intensely autobiographical or confessional—but not directly. They don't wear confession on the sleeve of the work the way someone like Philip Roth or Thomas Wolfe says, "I'm here. This is me. Love me."

Well, needless to say, I would turn out to be a writer who was wholly incapable of disappearing or hiding. So this proposition—"Oh, it's not going to be about me, I'll instead offer you great stuff to look at, great stories to follow"—began to break down the instant I wrote. But that misunderstanding explains what you've observed: that my work starts by seeming to dam the autobiographical impulse, and then allows it to leak in, increasingly, until it floods the place.

Schiff: If we could go back to the early stories that you began publishing in the late 1980s, when you were in your early twenties, I'm curious as to what we would find and what you would say now. What would embarrass you about these stories, and what would you still be proud of?

Lethem: I was excessively showy, and not always interested in offering reasons someone should want to read my work apart from the fact that I was juggling a lot—many of those stories are verbally dexterous stunts. There remains more than a trace of this impulse in the earliest work that got into hardcovers, a couple of the stories in the first collection, and in aspects of the first three novels. They may be more the work of a conceptual artist or a verbal stunt man than they are very emotionally satisfying to read. On the other hand, I was always a little bit warmer or more personal a writer than I could admit. In some ways, the best thing about those early stories is the way the emotion gets in anyway. And that tension that's produced by my thinking that I was going to turn out to be like Mark Leyner, someone who is simply riffing all the time trying to blow your mind with sheer concepts. You can see me very briefly trying to turn out to be Mark Leyner, but I just wasn't ever capable of it. First of all, I don't have that degree of conceptual invention. I have some. But I also have lots of other stuff I'm interested in, and I always, from the outset, wandered in other directions.

Schiff: Unlike so many of the writers of your generation, you were not, as far as I know, ever involved in a workshop environment. I think you described yourself recently as being a "sophomore on leave from Bennington." Did that give you some freedom and allow you to take more risks than other writers?

Lethem: I'm always hesitant to boast about bravery or risk, as though I was out there in a dangerous situation. I didn't conceive of it that way at the time. In fact, I think leaving school involved a certain amount of cowardice. I didn't want to be in a writing workshop situation because I felt that I had to protect my work from critique. I felt I was doing something different, and perhaps also suspected I wasn't as far along as some of the writers I'd be in workshop with. I had the odd luck of being a freshman and sophomore at college with a couple of the most exaggerated writing prodigies of that moment, Bret Ellis and Donna Tartt. This was a very small school, so we all knew each other and I certainly knew what they were up to. Through high school I'd been allowed to think of myself—partly because of my parents' milieu—as talented and prodigal, but I was not, when we were all eighteen or nineteen, near the level of these writers. I felt intimidated. Part of dropping out of Bennington to go off to California to write consisted of arrogance or bravery: "I can do this on my own." The rest was ego failure, from encountering the level of accomplishment of the writers at Bennington. I couldn't fully confront it. I'd already been working at used bookstores when I was a teenager, and I had something in my temperament of the autodidact. I enjoyed training myself as an outsider. I'd never been a very good student. Yet I always read more than the people who were doing well in school. I read eccentrically, the things I wanted to read. So, for better and worse, I decided to train myself.

Schiff: Your career seems so established now, yet—and I say this for the benefit of the younger writers here in the audience—I'm curious as to what you were feeling, say, fifteen years ago, during that period in which you were working as a clerk in a bookstore. Did you ever give thought to doing anything else, or what your life would be like if writing didn't work out for you?

Lethem: I couldn't let myself think about failure because I had no real advocates. Only an instinct that it was possible to devote your life to an art form. My father's example was crucial because he never made a living from his painting throughout his entire adult life. I felt that was legitimate. It was far less easy than striking it lucky, but he was no less a serious painter for that. Truthfully, I maintained a kind of double-think. On the one hand I was prepared to go on being a book clerk and write for as long as that took. If I published marginally, and still had a day-job when I'm fifty, that was fine. I'll still be a writer. On the other hand, I was working as hard as I could to make it turn out otherwise. And the instant I had a few thousand dollars saved from the advance on my second novel, I quit my day-job. I got a little ahead, and made the leap. But I had to be very willful. I believe that's your question. It maintained a certainty that I was meant to do this as much or more than anyone else. I was also quite selfish about my time and energy, and no Mother Theresa. I didn't start a family. I was single-minded. I was a grind. I suppose I sacrificed some of the fun of being young in California in the 1980s; I could have gone out more, could've had a little more fun. But I was dogged, instead.

Schiff: Were you getting feedback from anyone at that point?

Lethem: I found some writers who were sympathetic to what I was doing, and we swapped manuscripts. Having cut myself off from graduate school and from other kinds of institutional support, I was left a bit lonely and hungry for validation and contact—even just people to share rejection stories with. So I found a few. Berkeley and San Francisco were not lacking in aspiring writers, and I made a little writer's group for myself.

Schiff: Your first volume of stories, *The Wall of the Sky, the Wall of the Eye*, is a rich and at times bizarre collection, full of futuristic, surreal tales. For those unfamiliar with these stories, one features a dead man returning from hell to support his family, while another depicts a futuristic NBA in which a young white player, by donning an exosuit, can acquire the playing skills of Michael Jordan. But there are two stories in particular, "Five Fucks" and "The Happy Man," which are especially multilayered and unusual. Is it true that "Five Fucks," a story which recounts how a woman, after spending the night with a stranger, discovers that two weeks have passed, was a response to Bruce Sterling's observation that any time anyone has sex in your fiction they're punished?

Lethem: I knew he was right, but I decided to deal with that criticism by a sort of judo method, by moving in the direction of the line of force of his criticism. I decided to write the ultimate "sex is punished" story. Perhaps then I'd be done with the motif. So I offered up a series of nightmares–one-night stands that cause reality itself to crumble apart. Every time these two characters meet up, the world is further degraded by their meeting. That was a very important story. It was the last one I wrote for that book, to complete it. The story has the same relationship to that collection as "The Beards" has to the current book of essays—it's the moment when I can see the book that I've just about written, and I'm searching to write a piece that will culminate it, to make a complete book. I wrote it as a deliberate sampler of possible styles, but that story also emerged at a moment when my control of style had suddenly increased significantly. I'd written a couple of novels. They're not incompetent stylistically, but I was still working in the dark in some ways. At that moment, when I wrote "Five Fucks"—and I was also in the course of writing *As She Climbed Across the Table*, which is a book I still associate with learning to master my craft—my sentence-writing was suddenly more firmly under my command. So "Five Fucks" was partly a stylistic showcase. I said, "One chapter of this story will be in the style of Thomas Berger, one will be Italo Calvino, and one will be George Gissing." But I was also looking at the use of the fantastic in those early stories. Up until that point I was still thinking that the imagination could generate metaphors or concepts that were not personal. "Five Fucks" represents an admission that if a story is any good, it's because it is a container for my anxieties, my emotions, my own personality. That's all that's ever worked. So I allowed myself to write a story in which I collapsed those imaginative images into a completely personal subject matter.

Schiff: You've talked before about how your stories and novels derive from other writers. I know that *Girl in Landscape* arose from Shirley Jackson, Carson McCullers, and others. This notion of riffing on others seems pervasive in your work. I'm curious about *Motherless Brooklyn.* Where does that come from?

Lethem: *Motherless Brooklyn* is less easy to describe in terms of influence. In a structural sense, I think that book has a strong resemblance to *The Catcher in the Rye, Confederacy of Dunces,* and *Flowers for Algernon.* Which is to say that all these books function as examples of the "geek genre," in which an incredibly sensitive, beautiful main character is misunderstood by everyone around them. But the reader knows how great they are, and hence the energy in the book derives from our awareness that they're smarter and more sensitive than the people around them, who are treating them so badly. I think *Motherless Brooklyn* is fundamentally a geek book in that way. Stylistically, though, it's not like any of those books. Stylistically, I was thinking of the masters of New York slang, like Ring Lardner, and, more recently, Richard Price, people who deal energetically with New York's street language. That also means DeLillo, whom I've mentioned a number of times as being very important to me. He doesn't do it terribly often, but when he does it, it's masterful—the very beginning of *Libra,* the chapter set in the Bronx where the bullies harass Lee Harvey Oswald at the zoo, shows you that if DeLillo cared to be, he could be a great novelist of New York street language, like Jimmy Breslin cubed. In a way, Lionel Essrog is also Bugs Bunny, the character who's verbally going off in every scene, who's running crazy rings around the Elmer Fudds of the world. That also relates to the detective in Chandler's novels. Marlowe doesn't have defenses or weapons in the world against the criminals and cops who are always bullying him, apart from his humor. The reader gets all his jokes even if the characters he's talking with don't. In a way, you could look at Philip Marlowe as another geek, another Holden Caulfield, to whom the reader wishes to say, "Why can't they see that you're so much smarter and more alert than they are?" Yet the other characters go on ignoring Marlowe's superiority, so the reader has to love him all the more, precisely because they alone understand him.

Schiff: You mentioned DeLillo. Did his novel *Amazons*, written as a collaboration and published under a pen name, influence *Motherless Brooklyn*?
Lethem: Yes! *Amazons* is a book Don DeLillo wrote under the pseudonym Cleo Birdwell, ostensibly a memoir by the first woman to play in the NHL. And DeLillo has never allowed it to be republished under his real name, because, in fact—I asked him about it once—he claimed quite obscurely that it was written with someone else, and "she" doesn't want him to say who she is. I suppose he's diffident about the book. A very funny book if you can find it. Often misshelved in the sports sections of bookstores because, by all appearances, as I said, it's a memoir of the first woman to play in the NHL. I was a bookseller, and I still have a fondness for outré items. I love the way *Amazons* doesn't exist in any real way. It's a conundrum. People who love DeLillo don't know about it—you show it to them and they're bewildered.

It was influential on *Motherless Brooklyn* because there's a character with something called "Jumping Frenchmen." That's the syndrome. It's basically Tourette's. Cleo Birdwell, the hockey player, is one of these Betty Boop–like characters who sleeps with every player on the team. She's ingenuous and easily led. When challenged to a game of strip Monopoly, she says, "Okay! Sure!" and plays strip Monopoly. So at one point she falls in with this guy who has "Jumping Frenchmen." He leads her to a conference center where they're having a giant support group, the national convention for sufferers of "Jumping Frenchmen." She sits watching this panel where, at first, everyone's orderly and talking about the syndrome, then one person begins to jump, and then everyone starts to react to the person who's jumping, and soon the whole room is full of "Jumping Frenchmen." I stole that quite directly for the scene in *Motherless Brooklyn* where Lionel goes to a Zen monastery, and everything's calm, and he's thinking, "I can stay calm, it's gonna be all right," then he begins to tic, which sets off all sorts of reactions in the people who are trying to meditate in the room. *Amazons* is one of the funniest books ever written, it's *painfully* funny. It shows how DeLillo is such a talent that if he'd chosen to he could have been uproarious in book after book. He's obviously tempering that impulse in favor of doing other things most of the time.

Schiff: *Motherless Brooklyn* must have been a fun novel to write. There's a good deal of pleasure in it. Did it feel as if things were clicking when you were writing it?

Lethem: It was a great pleasure to write, and I knew I was doing something that was special for me. The big change was that I was writing about Brooklyn and New York City for the first time. I took a much greater interest in the texture of my real surroundings than I had before. The earlier books are all set either in California or a sort of cartoon desert, a Nowheresville, like the flat scenes that pass behind Fred Flintstone's car when he's driving. Suddenly I got interested in talking about real stuff—sandwiches, sidewalks, the subway—because the project dictated it, and because I'd moved back to New York and was falling in love with Brooklyn again. But Lionel Essrog's voice was also very giddy, obviously; and it was freeing. If you look at each of the four novels that precede that book, I've got minor characters exiled to the edges of the book who are in charge of "speaking crazy." In *Gun, with Occasional Music*, it's the babyheads; in *As She Climbed Across the Table*, it's the two blind guys; and in *Girl in Landscape*, it's the aliens themselves, the Archbuilders. It was a minority impulse in my writing, this instinct for sub-Joycean wordplay; I'd always assign it to minor characters. It was as though I was afraid that if I let that impulse take over a book, it would wreak havoc—because I also wanted to tell an orderly story. So I relegated this instinct to walk-on parts, Shakespearean fools with a couple of scenes. In *Motherless Brooklyn*, by coming up with Lionel Essrog, this character with Tourette's, I suddenly had my excuse to let a wordplay character run amok. Give him the book. What would happen if he wasn't only a minor character, but the major character, and also the narrator? What if I just handed the reins to this instinct in myself? It was a liberating, lucky choice to come up with: a very rational excuse for irrationality. The book remained orderly in that I was crediting it to Tourette's syndrome, and that I had the traditional structure of the detective story. If you have to provide clues and a solution, then the plot is going to be very visible to your readers.

Schiff: The creation of a sense of place that you mentioned with Brooklyn is even more intense in *The Fortress of Solitude*, and I'm curious as to why you think it took you so long to write about Brooklyn?

Lethem: For ten years before I tried to begin, I had ideas of writing a big book about growing up in Brooklyn, and conflating that with a story about a real but pathetic superhero. The book I was visualizing, of course, I couldn't write. I had this big foggy book hanging there, yet I didn't have the tools to execute it. I needed to collect more techniques. I had to become a better writer to stand a chance of doing justice to this image. So in a funny way, *Motherless Brooklyn* was written partly as a conscious effort to set the ground for writing a bigger and more serious book about Brooklyn. At first

I meant to do it in a relatively fast and silly way, a kind of giddy valentine to where I grew up. Then I'd have opened the door and begun to talk about this place and all its complexity, in order to write the longer, more ambiguous, more complex book.

This question of the order of the acquisition of my own tools has a lot to do, of course, with my tastes, my appetites as a reader. When I was a teenager, I read stuff that was very inventive and conceptually strong. So, at the outset I was good at writing stuff that was conceptually clever. Yet even in those years when I was writing those first books, so prominently imaginative and inventive, I was beginning to devour Richard Yates and Philip Roth and Christina Stead, writers who used mimetic textures, who reproduced versions of the everyday world. So I began to acquire some of these tools by reading more writers who used those methods. That part of my own inclination as a writer was scurrying to catch up with the other one. It was like I was a fiddler crab with one overdeveloped claw, while the other one was still rather small.

Schiff: One of the wonderful things about your sequence of fictions is that you don't repeat yourself. You keep on changing, reinventing yourself. It's also interesting to note that as your writing has become more powerful, it's become more popular. There's a wider acceptance. Given that you were raised in a political and artistic atmosphere of some resistance, how do you feel about the relative acceptance of your work? And do you see your recent work as less experimental, less radical?

Lethem: There are certainly angles from which you could view it as less radical, but I don't think that corresponds, exactly, to popularity or critical acceptance. I also believe that in other ways it's much more radical. *The Fortress of Solitude* is more radical than *Motherless Brooklyn* because I'm smashing together in a far more intense way my commitment to the fantastic and the commitment to realism. The two poles are each developed to a greater extent, so the attempt at their reconciliation is more violent. That juxtaposition, which is so uncomfortable for many readers, has been made unavoidable, unmistakable. In *Motherless Brooklyn*, my conflations are more gently integrated and beguiling. The language is the fantastic element, which means that people, if they prefer, can regard the book as realistic—though it's quite absurd to believe that these guys are lurking around Brooklyn in trench coats acting like detectives, or that there are Zen Buddhist Mafiosi. It's a total fantasia, yet it doesn't challenge the reader's sense of reality in the same way that *The Fortress of Solitude* does.

But anyway, I don't really measure whether I'm happy with what I'm doing with how radical it seems to me. I've always believed I was a more traditional writer than people often make me out to be. Critics are excited to declare that someone's breaking ground or conducting a radical experiment, but I've always believed that my work was firmly sourced in traditional novelistic technique. I'm hardly interested in throwing over most of the things associated with the traditional novel. I like plots and characters, and I like the reader to identify with my protagonist—even if I often wish to make that identification a challenging or confusing choice. Consider someone like Donald Barthleme, a true radical: he's really throwing away a lot of what fiction does well, traditionally, and giving you something quite amazing in return for your commitment to his experiment. By that measure I've rarely been so radical. I've simply got this one, perhaps irritating, notion that I push again and again, which is that metaphor and symbol and linguistic experiment are not so very different from a "fantastic element," or a magical intrusion on the lives of the characters in the story. All of these—metaphor, symbol, and magical intrusion—are different ways in which reality and dream come together. In fact, this is basic to literature. All stories are collisions of reality and dream. Language itself is a fantastic element. So you can't keep from being metaphorical or surrealistic. The moment you commit to storytelling in language, you've done it. I just keep pushing that line, and placing the line in different areas within different works. That, I suppose, is what passes for my radicalism, but it's not that radical. It's an argument that's been conducted by writers for centuries, from *Tristram Shandy* through Cervantes and then to Pynchon and DeLillo and Barthleme, and so on. And Philip K. Dick. I happen to exemplify that issue, to make it really prominent in my work. But I love traditional means of storytelling, and I don't need to be thought of as an innovator because I doubt that I really am.

Schiff: Because you're interested in other genres, particularly visual art, and because of your background in comics, I'm wondering how curious you are, as you're working, of how the plots or language that you're handling might be treated differently in those other art forms, and does that come into play at all in the way you think about craft?

Lethem: I'm very influenced by film. I think narrative film is a close cousin to the novel in really interesting ways. It's also divided from the novel in very specific ways. But it has a very fertile relationship to the novel, more so than painting, and certainly more than music, both of which are so much further from narrative. Sometimes I look at the history of the novel in the twentieth century and it seems to me to be defined by its resistance to film. At the century's outset there appears this incredibly facile way of depicting characters and situations and scenes—and almost immediately upon its arrival the greatest novelists all migrate towards the things that novels can do that films can't: voice and subjectivity and tricky point-of-view. The defining innovation in the novel in the twentieth century may be unreliable narration. With that particular innovation the novel has located a very specific form of interiority, one which film periodically attempts to reproduce, and fails utterly.

Painting and music, which are very influential on me, are much harder to talk about. It's harder for me to isolate the resonances, the ways in which they're influential. If I look at my early stories now, a lot of them look to me as though I was on some level trying to write versions of surrealist paintings, by painters like Magritte and Ernst—painters who employ pictorial paradox, who use realist methods to depict impossible images. I was attempting to write stories that have that same hard-edged weirdness to them. *Girl in Landscape* and *Amnesia Moon*, the desert books, are very strongly connected for me to Mark Rothko's paintings, to the way certain abstract painters depict the horizon line (but then deny that they're painting landscapes). Just thinking about space, human space, the act of walking across a room or a desert floor, towards a horizon line that defines the human space. This is also something that relates, for me, to Beckett—characters on an empty stage. But these are very elusive resonances. With music, you can think about the poetry of your lines, the music of your lines. Certainly in *The Fortress of Solitude*, by trying to write in so many different voices in the same book, I was hoping to be like a great radio station where you hear remarkable transitions from one kind of intoxicating music to another. Some of that comes again from reading DeLillo, reading a book like *Underworld*, where there's a tremendous musicality to the language, especially in sequences like that Lenny Bruce chapter. Or some of Philip Roth, where he just lets the voice fly. In *The Human Stain*, for about five pages, the female character identifies with crows, and thinks to herself "I am a crow." The voice just goes on this riff, like an incredible song. Opening my fiction to these musical possibilities was late in coming for me. I had to think about structure and plot and character for a long time before I could let myself just fly. But that's where the music comes in.

Schiff: Clearly science fiction is a big influence on you. I wonder if you could talk about the critical disdain in academia for science fiction, and also about how science fiction has infiltrated mainstream fiction. I'm thinking of cross-over books by writers like Margaret Atwood, books that resemble science fiction yet are also considered literary or mainstream fiction.

Lethem: It's a difficult conversation because, for the most part, when people start talking about science fiction, they are talking about status, about the reception of things. To even use the word evokes the critical quarantines that are kept on stuff that might be sub-literary or para-literary, and therefore threatening. Why, even the jackets of the books look bad! There's a tremendous reluctance to think beyond the discomfort that has produced the quarantine.

What becomes exasperating is the routine assertion that when, for instance, George Orwell produces *1984* or Don DeLillo produces *Ratner's Star*—or any one of hundreds of other examples—they were doing something categorically different from the activities of the writers under quarantine. Oh, no, the cry arises: That's real writing! Please don't sully it with this déclassé association. Well, if every admirable result from setting a story in the future, or from using images of the fantastic, or extrapolative concepts, isn't science fiction—because it's too good—then all that's left to represent the label are the failed attempts to use those motifs. So, of course, the genre is contemptible. In my opinion there's no meaningful critical borderline at all, and I don't think there has been for a terribly long time.

So all you're discussing, then, is status and reception. And that's a loaded subject, because . . . well, you wouldn't want to claim that it's in any way as important as racism, but when we begin to analyze it, we discover it functions by the same illogic as racism: a seeming need for people to feel better about themselves by having something that's beneath them. To complicate it further, we also discover the self-willed exile of the minority population: the way in which outsider identity becomes defiant—the brand of the outcast worn as a badge of subcultural credibility. Which therefore propagates the problem from within the outcast community as well. In fact, I think there's a tremendously defiant victim-identity within parts of the community of readers and writers of what's called science fiction, one that forms just as difficult a threshold as the resistance from the other side. Anytime people define themselves by the outlines of their own rejection, it's made easy to go on rejecting them. To go any deeper into this would be pure sociology.

Because I grew up in a bohemian demimonde, hippiedom in the 1970s, that wasn't so terribly different in its function from the science fiction community (both believed that their difference arose from the superiority of their beliefs), I migrated into that community very easily at a certain point.

But I was baffled by its lack of interest in confronting this issue from within. Even the most interesting science fiction readers didn't seem completely eager to see the continuity of their interests with literature at large. When I'd say "I'm not only influenced by J. G. Ballard and Philip K. Dick and Thomas Disch, I'm also thinking a lot about Calvino and Borges and Kafka," they'd become as irritated or confused as, say, an academic critic might be by the same statement. This was totally unsatisfying to me. Briefly I took up the imaginary, nonsensical role of spokesperson in the cause of eradicating this boundary. But that's really not my job, and anyway it's well beyond anyone's capacity. Now I merely smile or frown, depending on my mood, when I see, for instance, a review in the *New York Times* of Margaret Atwood's book, one which ties itself in laborious knots to say: "Well, this may be very good in certain ways, but of course it's not literature." Well, what the fuck is literature? It's everything good that anyone's ever written. There's no other definition. But the fact that the *New York Times* has to keep reinscribing this boundary, so that everyone can be confident that we're superior to the folks on the other side of it—this problem may not be solvable in our lifetimes, portentous as that may sound. This difficulty is as embedded, in its weird way, as racism. It has to do with status anxiety, and with the insecurities of the people who reinforce that boundary—unfortunately, from both sides.

Schiff: As a writer, what haven't you done yet that you'd like to do, and what might be next for you?

Lethem: The easy part of that is to tell you what I'm doing next. In my new work I'm trying to throw over a lot of what I've previously been doing. *The Fortress of Solitude* was a long, four-year project immersed in memories of a place. It's about being from somewhere, about being a child, and it's about families; though the families in it are largely destroyed ones, families are very much its subject. It also has a lot of danger in it. I recently noticed how, different as my books may be, they all have mortal stakes. The risk of death. There's usually a gun pulled at some point. Even in the mildest, sweetest of my books, *As She Climbed Across the Table*, life and death is at stake, because the universe might collapse into one point, or characters might enter a black hole and never return. So I wanted to write a book with no mortal stakes, because that's not really where I live my life. I don't actually face death very often. So the new book restricts itself to social and psychological stakes. The issues for my characters are: will this person fall in love with me, will I be liked by my peers, will I have enough money to go to the rock show on Saturday night? I wanted to write a romantic comedy, basically, and I wanted to forget Brooklyn for a while, so it's set in Los Angeles. I also wanted to forget family for a while. There are no parents or children—so far nobody in this book shows evidence of even having a sibling. They dwell in that kind of twenty-something space where your family is the last thing you think about—you're into your friends and romances and aspirations, but never call your parents. I also got tired of really specific cultural references. *The Fortress of Solitude* involved tremendous research into pop culture. I had to establish what movies were on the marquees as my characters were walking down the street, and what songs were coming out of the radio, and what headlines were in the tabloids. And the essays I've been writing are also entrenched in the same cultural specificity. I've abandoned that. These characters in Los Angeles are dumb about these things. They're trying to form a rock band but they don't even listen to records very much. They're spaced out. I've tried to ignore chronology. The book is openly anachronistic. They float in a vague, mid-nineties Los Angeles that doesn't make any real sense. Another reverse I'm attempting—*Motherless Brooklyn* is a very male book. There are a couple of women in it, but they're on the edges, very embattled in this male world. *The Fortress of Solitude* is even worse. For eight hundred manuscript pages, women are barely in evidence, and this was actually quite lonely for me. I missed the women. So, I'm trying to write a chick-lit book. The new book is told from the point of view of a female protagonist, in third person. In that sense, there's a woman in every sentence of this book—to make up for how my readers may have been longing for a female presence. I certainly was.

Birnbaum v. Jonathan Lethem

Robert Birnbaum/2005

From *The Morning News*, October 19, 2005. Reprinted by permission of Robert Birnbaum.

Since I last spoke with Jonathan Lethem, author of six novels, the most recent of which is *The Fortress of Solitude*, he has published a collection of stories, *Men and Cartoons*, and *The Disappointment Artist*, a book of what can loosely be called essays. He has also recently won a MacArthur Fellowship and has begun splitting his residence between Maine and Brooklyn. He is currently working on another novel and considering adding a dog to his family.

On any given weekend in the summer, the literary population of metro New York is significantly diminished and, consequently, Maine's is swollen by an inexorable seasonal exodus. As I live in Exeter, N.H., just off Interstate 95, which is a major artery twixt God's own cement and what many claim is paradise, I have occasionally benefited from the summer shifts. This past summer I managed to catch up with Lethem, whom I missed when he was touting his recent essay book. Comfortably ensconced on the shores of the Squamscott River, in the company of my moody and protective Labrador, Rosie, and away from the diabolic pressures of the book tour, we chatted about literary this and literary that.

This conversation represents the third in what may be correctly regarded as an open-ended dialogue. Unfortunately, we never got around to talking about one of Lethem's great passions, the New York Mets, though off camera we both expressed a high regard for hurler Pedro Martinez and dismay at the way Red Sox fans have viewed him since his departure for New York City. I expect we will pick up this thread in the future—most assuredly when Manny Ramirez joins Pedro in the National League.

Robert Birnbaum: So, we talked last—almost two years ago?

Jonathan Lethem: I think it was more than that. Maybe not. I guess it was in the thick of the hardcover tour for *The Fortress of Solitude*. So that dates it to October 2003.

RB: We were going to reconvene for your essay collection, and things didn't work out. And we connected after that, and you gave me the impression that you had things on your mind—
JL: [chuckles]

RB: —maybe not of great urgency, that were pressing on you.
JL: I vaguely recall. There had been a wave of reactionary vibrations in the reviewing environment that disturbed me. I know you were upset by some reactions to some books. I'm remembering from the emails, it might have been along those lines. It's probably just as well that I didn't race into conversation with a head full of—

RB: [laughs] —vituperation.
JL: Yeah. I'm sure some of it will reemerge.

RB: Since the novel, you have published some stories and published an essay collection, which is something of a hybrid. Certainly they are essays—but not exactly.
JL: Call them sleight-of-hand pieces. I began by pointing outward at some cultural object and then kind of looped around into confession. And, through the book, increasingly so. Once I established the pattern, I realized what I was up to, and began letting the pieces become increasingly confessional pieces. By the end of the sequence—which is how I think of it, a sequence of essays—it seemed to me I had written a backdoor memoir. Not a comprehensive one, more a series of glances, a series of entrees into memoir.

RB: These were written for the purpose of being in one collection?
JL: The pattern emerged and then became more and more deliberate. I'd never written essays. I never thought that I'd want to. I had an exaggerated sense of the novelist's role as a tale-teller, an imagineer. I'd written four novels and any number of short stories before I even attempted any rudimentary essay forms—like a book review or a record review. I'd done practically nothing in a nonfiction voice. Never used a first-person "I" that was sincerely—or ostensibly—direct. I backed into it. After I'd finished *Girl*

in Landscape, I found myself not completely satisfied. I was proud of the book, I thought it expressed everything I could in fiction about my feeling for John Wayne and the John Ford films, and yet there was something left unexpressed. That was, to actually say: "I love these movies, and it's confusing to love these movies." So I began writing the essay that opens the book, "Defending *The Searchers*." Really, just a self-portrait of myself entering four different moviegoing experiences. A description of what it had been like to watch *The Searchers* and end up upset four different times. By the time I finished it—well, I liked the piece very much. Yet it was anomalous. I hadn't written it for anyone. It wasn't commissioned. No editors expected essays from me. Because everything I wrote was fiction.

RB: I was focusing on your having said that you wrote it and there had been no commission?

JL: Yeah. I just sort of stared at the piece. I offered it to a couple of places, but because it was this hybrid, and I hadn't established any precedent for it, not one bit. Certainly from a journalistic view, there was no peg. No one thought that John Wayne was hot news that year.

RB: *The Searchers* is a perennial in top 10 movie lists.

JL: Sure, to the people who care, it's always news. That's how I felt. Yet as it happened, the piece was a kind of a floater. It was on my desk for a couple of years before I published it. I stared at it, and it was a provocation to me. I thought, "Well, maybe I could do that with something other than *The Searchers*. What if I did the same thing, confess my obsession, but with another cultural object?" Because really that's what these essays are about— being a fan, being an obsessive. And so I took the next occasion. Someone asked me to write about *Star Wars* for a book of essays, and I thought, "Well, let's see if I can repeat the trick." So I wrote another confessional piece, built around the moviegoing experience. Why did I care about that movie when I cared about that movie? Why did I go to see it so many times? Again, I liked the result. So I repeated the trick a third time on the subject of Jack Kirby and Marvel Comics. And by the time I had three of these things, I felt it was an inviting mode for me as a writer. So suddenly I was an essayist, in this funny hybrid-confessional form. And I thought, "OK, I'll find four, five, six more chances and I'll have a book." At that same moment, I began to imagine a piece to conclude the book—"The Beards" was its eventual title—one which wouldn't dwell on any single cultural object but on the nature of my obsessions generally, as they play out over a whole range of material.

RB: Is there writing you didn't include or you discarded?

JL: No. There were subjects that I at one point imagined would have to be included. I thought, "Of course there has to be a Bob Dylan chapter." But my relationship to Dylan's work became too big—it wasn't proportionate to the book. So someday I'll write a whole book about Dylan. Or else I'll leave it to the few glancing pieces I've already done, here and there.

RB: Have you read Greil Marcus's *Like a Rolling Stone: Bob Dylan at the Crossroads*?

JL: I think it's terrific.

RB: You must have read Dylan's *Chronicles*.

JL: Yeah.

RB: I found it to be an odd, awkward read, though I enjoyed it. I liked the audio version read by Sean Penn, which gave me a better feeling for it.

JL: You felt more invited?

RB: Yeah, I didn't access it well on the page.

JL: I liked the prose a lot. It seems to me that the key to that book is not to demand of it that Dylan's being precise about the past, but instead see it as an enormously generous snapshot of Bob Dylan at this instant. This is how he feels, today. In that way it's akin to a song like "Highlands" at the end of *Time Out of Mind*. It's like Dylan opening his journal to you. And saying, "Here's a day in the life." So, *Chronicles* is how he feels about all these different moments in his life now. It seems to me very warm, very generous.

RB: What do you make of the review that Brent Staples published in the *New York Times* last week on *The Disappointment Artist*?

JL: I was in Europe and couldn't get a hold of it when it was published, so I happened to receive people's reaction to it, over email, long before I read it myself. Which was an interesting thought experiment because—

RB: My first question was, "Why publish that now?" Not that there should be a time limit and in fact I liked that—

JL: Oh, I didn't care about the schedule. The *Times Book Review* has freed itself to be late more recently, a good thing. I myself actually turned in a very late piece—I reviewed the Kafka study *K* by [Roberto] Calasso three or four months after it was published. It's not a bad thing. It breaks the spell of everyone necessarily hanging on that review, at the instant of publication, to set the tone for everything else. It might free us and also free up the *Times* from any sense that it's somehow in charge.

RB: Maybe it's a break with the industry's conventional wisdom that a book has a six-week window—so this was not tied to the publication date.

JL: Well, technically, I'm sure it makes publishers miserable. But the Staples piece was a funny one in that I got nothing but—the piece was totally positive in every surface sense, and yet I got nothing but commiseration on email. People saying, "Too bad about the piece."

RB: It's as much if not more about him than about you.

JL: I suppose. I don't hang on any single review the way I might once have. I never have pretended not to read them. You do lose interest in them. There are a just few basic stances that most reviews fall into, though the exceptions are fascinating. You're so struck when a review is compelling to you. But reviews that I might read with fascination if they were of someone else's book, trying to parse them—when they're of my own book, about which I've already thought so hard, in a process which ended a year or more earlier, I'm rarely engaged. I put them in the drawer.

RB: American newspaper book reviewing seems to be insubstantial, and for me the only reason to read them is for a particular writer, not for news or judgment about a book. The magazines are just a hair better.

JL: They're "notices." The word that the theater trade uses is the right one— notices. People were last Sunday put on notice that my new book was to be found, if they hadn't spotted it already. That's all that matters.

RB: Why are newspapers so stingy with how many books they notice? Do these things actually sell books?

JL: Sure.

RB: I mean the good versus the bad.

JL: I don't know. I can't tell you. But they go together, in my experience— piles of them clippings accumulating goes together with people telling you your book is selling [laughs].

RB: Some critical mass has to be achieved.

JL: To be serious about it, my guess is that, for a reader or browser, you get curious about books you've heard or seen mentioned a third or a fourth time. You suddenly think, "I better find out," "OK, this is out there." Something you hear mentioned once you can forget about; four times you begin to wonder if you're on the outside looking in. Whether you've lost a step. So, notices are good.

RB: The short-story collection, the essays, so here you are and here it is summertime—are you sitting by idly doing nothing?
JL: No, I'm writing a novel.

RB: A novel!
JL: I figured out what to do—after *Fortress*. It took a while.

RB: Were the stories diversions while you figured it out?
JL: Both the story collection and the essay collection gather approximately seven or eight years worth of work. So, both books were written before, during, and after the composition of *Fortress*—if that's not too confusing. The essays began immediately upon completing *Girl in Landscape*, so that's dated very specifically. I began in '97. The stories reach back a little further. The oldest may go back as far as '95. But the preponderance of the work in both collections was done during the years of writing or the year of [chuckles] promoting *Fortress of Solitude*. And both are closely related to the big novel. Both could be seen as elaborate afterbirths.

RB: Appendices?
JL: I don't mind looking at them that way. The thematic freight of *Fortress of Solitude*, all that Brooklyn 1970s, fathers and sons, pop-cultural ephemera, the nature of fannishness or cultural obsession, is reflected in both the story collection and the essay collection. They're under the same umbrella. And in terms of my own workshop, they represent an attempt to push the last of that material out the door. What comes next is quite different.

RB: At the moment do you look at—where is the seam or break in your career trajectory?
JL: There's a big one right now. A lot of people are led, understandably, to thinking of *Fortress* as a break with what preceded it. In my view, though, it's the opposite. *Fortress* is the culmination of what I'd been doing to that point. It recapitulates almost every interest and every concern of the early books, and utilizes all the tools I'd accumulated, all the methods and motifs I had been exploring and gathering.

RB: They think that because it's more personal and—

JL: —yes, and because it's twice as long as the other books, and because it has a more extensive commitment to mimetic tricks. Since it's so personal, it can seem that I must have shaken off what I was doing in order to get to that place, but actually what I'd been doing led inevitably to that effort. It's the work that comes next that's a real break. Precisely because I've now discharged a lot of my original material by exploring it in this immense fiction—and then going even further with the essays, explaining some of the personal material that fueled that fiction. So, I'm not bloody likely to need to transpose childhood trauma into Marvel comics again—for perhaps the rest of my life [laughs again].

RB: Can you recall the content of your first novels?

JL: I think I can. I might be surprised if I flip them open. You fool yourself into thinking that you really know exactly what's inside. And if you do a reading tour, there are a couple of sections that you end up memorizing and those stand in, in your memory, for the whole. Occasionally someone quotes a paragraph from *As She Climbed Across the Table* or *Girl in Landscape* and I don't recognize it immediately. But what I guess I'd call the *gestalt* of each of the books resides very clearly with me.

RB: Are you propelled by or moved by some desire to be original, to never repeat or recapitulate or cover old ground? Do you even think in those terms?

JL: The way you framed the question, I'd say no. First of all, I think my so-called originality—which is just as often called my "surrealism" or my "postmodernism" or what-have-you—tends to be overstated, at the expense of how deeply traditional my work is. Any innovation is a sort of howling red flag. Though I doubt red flags howl—a three-word mixed metaphor. It's in the nature of the innovations to demand disproportionate attention and description, when often they comprise 10 or 15 percent of what I've tried to do. In fact, I think I've demonstrated an unwavering, and quite extensive commitment to character, narrative, and emotion, beginnings, middles, ends, the sturdiest of traditional methods—I'm hardly on some avant-garde frontier. There's simply one thing I do, and it's not out of—as you proposed in your question—any restless urge to be original or provocative. Instead, it's a helpless instinct, one I've been expressing from the very beginning in my work, and I suppose I'll never quit: That is, to push together realistic character and emotion, and naturalistic or mimetic textures, with the stuff of dream, fantasy, symbol—and to make the fit between these different areas very prominent. Aggressively prominent. This conflation of the realist and the anti-realist, which—if you believe me as a critic of my own work, which you have no obligation to do—isn't something I, as a writer, can propose to either do or not do. It's a helpless act. It's how writing feels to me, and I've produced versions again and again, in different combinations and different proportions each time. When you look at *Motherless Brooklyn*, the language, the Tourette's, is the fantastic element. In that book the linguistic distortion, the metaphor, runs amok as if a dream of language has broken out in a typical hardboiled detective novel. Obviously, in *Fortress of Solitude*, the superhero is the metaphor that breaks out of the metaphorical and runs amok, distorting the reality. The better I succeed at making this rupture prominent, making it apparent what I want to do, the more satisfying it is for me, and the more provocative or even irritating it can be for readers who don't like it, who can't accept it. But I'm not trying to do anything that seems to me to be radical. I'm trying to do something that seems necessary—to express the way experience itself—memory, desire, perception—is, like language, like fiction, comprised of what we'll agree to call, quite clumsily, a realist and an anti-realist tendency. Life itself is made up of things that we experience as prosaic and things we experience as dreamlike, or disruptive, or metaphoric, or hallucinogenic. And so I've always wished to push some version of those distortions I sense pushing at the surface of everyday life into prominence in the work. Whether it's a fantastic element, one that created a resonance with science fiction, or fantasy, or magic realism, or a linguistic or metaphorical distortion, or a neurological distortion, or whether the distortion is archetypal, symbolic—say, the superhero plopping into the everyday realm—for me it's the same chase. I'm on the same trail.

RB: Maybe another way of asking that big, sloppy, puppy dog question that I tried is: As you create a larger body of work, how self-conscious are you about—

JL: About not repeating myself?

RB: No, but thinking about, "Have I learned something?" Maybe it's not as concise a thought as "Am I a better writer?" or something like that. Perhaps, "Can I do this?"

JL: In retrospect, I do look at things in those terms: tools acquired, capacities acquired and made use of. I'm very pleased with myself when I see I seem to have been studying a method both in my reading and writing, and then I suddenly put it in play. One reason I didn't do very much with the evocation of place for so long was that I hadn't read a lot that I loved that was as deeply engaged with setting. Because it always begins with reading, of course. When I started out, I read so much on the Borges, Calvino, Kafka side of things. I hadn't, for instance, read ten books by Philip Roth where he brings Newark to life. I couldn't have done Brooklyn the way I did in *Fortress*, because the synapses didn't fire along those pathways yet. I hadn't acquired those instincts as a reader.

RB: You had to read Roth as opposed to—I don't get the sense that you've had that kind of personal experience or reflected on that kind of personal experience. That you really thought about where you lived and traveled. You had to read it to get it?

JL: No, I don't mean that I—I'd been waiting for ways to talk about that street, Dean Street in Brooklyn, forever. I'd been making attempts. I'd been metaphorizing it, expressing those feelings in ways which seemed direct only to me. No one would have thought I was writing about Brooklyn or race, yet I was often writing about a dystopian urban environment. I was often writing about versions of otherness and identity. In fact, I almost did nothing else. But to speak of it by naming it [chuckles] as I did in *Fortress of Solitude*, I had to absorb the example of writers less like Kafka, and rather more like Philip Roth—to stick with the same vivid example, although there are dozens of others—who employ the power of giving the world its real name. It was an epiphany for me when I realized the power of giving things their actual names. I thought there was a kind of fictional law that you had to make up everything. If a character in my early books listened to a song or went to a movie, I'd make up the song or the movie. I thought nothing should be nonfictional in a fictional space. It's a false morality I was imposing. But I believed in it. I felt it passionately: That I should invent everything inside the space of my novels.

RB: The naming of some specific real world thing gives it an additional potency?

JL: The writer transports himself into a different linguistic space, and the reader is carried along. When, for instance, Dickens gives London streets their real names and when Roth gives Newark streets their real names, there's a conjuration of memory and time and space that the reader experiences, whether they know these are the real names or not.

RB: Or even whether there is an accurate description—

JL: Of course. And if it's fiction, it's almost always less transparently auto-biographical than it's taken to be. This is something I learned from Roth as well: You can derive tremendous energy for yourself as a writer and for read-ers in their experience of a book, not only by gathering material from your real life, [but also] from raising the question of whether or not something is autobiographical. In Roth this tension often stands in place of traditional plot mechanics for generating readerly fervor. You're always having to think, "This might be real. But it might not be. He could be fooling me." In *Fortress*, I switched not only to honest autobiographical methods but as well to manipulative autobiographical chimeras, where I seem to be saying, "This is me." And then I pull away. I become deceitful, and the reader responds to that as well, with irritation perhaps, but curiosity. They're being teased with the possibility of confession.

RB: Is that what you want from your reader? If I'm watching a movie, do I want to be conscious that I am watching the movie?

JL: Once I'd allowed myself to be unflinchingly autobiographical in the emo-tions, I also came to an understanding between myself and my editor, and myself and eventual readers, that I wouldn't choose to be coy about this, and claim the book was somehow unrelated to personal experience. I grew up in that place. I was deriving a lot of energy from writing about schools I attend-ed. Putting my characters, planting my characters' feet on the sidewalks that I walked growing up. Unless I was going to vanish and never speak of this work, and temperamentally, I've never been inclined to vanish. I knew my publisher would be bewildered if I proposed to vanish—never tour, give no interviews, do a Pynchon. That wasn't likely, and so I was certain to be read from the very beginning in the context of an array of information. People were going to know that this was a semi-autobiographical novel. To pretend otherwise, to think they weren't going to encounter this book in company of reviews, profiles of me, even dust jacket copy that implicitly speculated on the novel's relationship to my life, would be ludicrous. So, I proposed to capitalize, just as Roth capitalizes on this energy that is created by the reader's curiosity, even if it's subliminal or awkward or embarrassing. Read-ers may not wish to feel that they're reading a novel but also learning about an author's life, but they'll nevertheless be captivated. Of course there are readers who never want to think about that. This wasn't going to be a book for them.

RB: There is that recurring issue of all that's relevant is what's on the page.

JL: It wasn't that I was thinking that I could control those externals. All I care about is what's on the page. I care about the book and I also feel a compulsion—it's not a responsibility toward anyone except toward myself— a compulsion to ensure that any given text is an absolute self-enclosing, self-describing system, that needs absolutely no apparatus or information brought to it for it to function. It should be a machine like a perfect space probe, one capable of being self-sustaining in a vacuum, forever. But, having committed to making the text function that way—and I always do—it would be a kind of bogus naiveté to pretend that innumerable readers would not be encountering this work alongside at least some hint, some whisper that I grew up in Brooklyn, that I went to public schools, etcetera.

RB: A porous, permeable self-contained entity.

JL: Well, no, not porous. Rather, think of this space probe as an object available to projection. It's not porous. It's absolute. But, like a gleaming surface, you can have all sorts of things broadcast onto it, projected onto it. And it was a certainty that any book promoted as heavily was going to enjoy, or suffer, projections. If I were to extend this insane metaphor even further, I'd claim that cleverly inscribed on its outermost surface were runes designed to engage brilliantly with the projections—

RB: Um—yeah.

JL: I think we pushed that one to the very brink.

RB: [laughs] You still live in Brooklyn—an area that has a very high writer population per capita.

JL: It's almost grotesque.

RB: You said something about living—there's the writing, which is a big part of your life. When you live in Brooklyn, what's your life experience outside of writing? What do you do?

JL: I don't know how to answer that.

RB: Is your living always tied to being a writer? How conscious or self-conscious are you about what you do? Do you skydive?

JL: I don't skydive but I, of course, do any number of things that would stand in the place of that. So, let's say skydiving. I'm reluctant—it seems like the high school yearbook to list my relevant hobbies, my non-writing hobbies.

Here's the thing—I've just published a sort of confession about my obsessive cultural appetite, the book of essays. And in a funny way, I think I've gotten dodgy about certain personal question because that's the new book. It says exactly as much as I want or need to say. I go to movies all the time. Big surprise!

RB: That's seems to be an expected writerly thing to do.

JL: You're tough. Okay, let me try to surprise you, minimally. Few people expect that I am as fervent a baseball fan as I am. That every morning I read the sports section before any other section in the paper. At night in hotel rooms on book tour, I have to go to the sports channel to find out how the Mets did. Well, now I sound idiotic. But, hey, man, I've got a life. And of course, Brooklyn has to do with every part of my life. It's where I live. Not a symbol, but a place. I grew up right there and that's just happened to become a part of what I write about. It's not actually my fault if Brooklyn functions as a cultural token. I'm a regional writer, testifying about a place I'm helpless not to think of, to dream of.

RB: When you talk about a life that is including things that are [more] specific, that are real, then one becomes curious about what those things are that you are seeing and experiencing and most of all utilizing to make stories and tell stories. Not that I really want specifics—just to know that you are doing something other than sitting in a room all day and writing, or trying to.

JL: Sure, of course. But I'll wrestle with your question a little more. Because the fact that *Fortress of Solitude* encompasses prosaic reality in a way—it opens up this aperture and swallows up all sorts of . . . to the point that many people who liked my briefer books think it's kind of tiresome. That it describes far too much everyday detail.

RB: So much for short attention spans. Ian McEwan wondered how short attention spans allowed for the consumption of big books like *The Da Vinci Code*—he speculated that attention spans might not be a matter of biology but of culture.

JL: That's good. The fact that it [*Fortress of Solitude*] happens to encompass everyday life doesn't mean that I only just recently began to live everyday life. You can't dodge experience. I was as fervent a Mets fan when I was writing *Girl in Landscape*, a book set in completely propositional space, where the Mets never could have been mentioned. I was just as devoted to my team as I was while writing *Fortress of Solitude*, where I'd created a different sort of propositional space, one made up of all these deceptively prosaic details, and where the Mets were welcome. But here's the crucial point: both *Fortress* and *Girl in Landscape* are artificial realities. Fiction is a gigantic construction, a bauble. A novel is not life. That's why it's so pointless that this relentless baiting goes on, where "realist" fiction is pitted against "anti-realist" fiction as though one of the two has made some kind of commitment of integrity to be real, a responsibility the other has abdicated. Listen: every novel is a piece of wrought plastic. Readers may not wish to dwell on this fact, and I feel no necessity that they do, but writers, in order to be intelligent about the innate properties of their medium, must come to grips with it. Fiction, like language, is innately artificial and innately fabulous. It's made of metaphor. Language itself is a fantastic element. It's not possible to plant words in the ground and have seeds grow up and feed on the results. It's not part of the biological or mechanical world.

RB: Our training inclines us to look at realism as the truth because we can readily identify these things—
JL: As opposed, say, to the feeling of emotional identification that occurs when you read Kafka's *The Castle*?

RB: There is some laziness possible when one reads certain texts.
JL: Look, let me be brutal. When you encounter the argument that there is a hierarchy where certain kinds of literary operations—which we'll call "realism," for want of a handier term, though I'll insist on the scare quotes—represent the only authentic and esteemed tradition, well, it's a load of horseshit. When you see or hear that kind of hierarchy being proposed, it's not a literary-critical operation. It's a class operation. In that system of allusions, of unspoken castes and quarantines, mimetic fiction is associated with propriety, with the status quo defending itself, anxiously, against incursions from the great and wooly Beyond. When "realism" is esteemed over other kinds of literary methods, you're no longer in a literary-critical conversation; you've entered a displaced conversation about class. About the need for the Brahmin to keep an Untouchable well-marked and in close proximity, in order to confirm his role as Brahmin. Once something has been relegated or outcast or quarantined from propriety, you're seeing a kind of burnishing of class credentials, a hastening to the redoubt, a drawing-up of the drawbridge of the castle, because the moat is too full of terrifying fish and fowl. A critic who expends much energy on delineating quarantines—"This sort

of material is legitimate" is testifying as to their own anxieties as to whether or not they themselves are on the legitimate side of some imagined moat or gulf. "We're going to draw a line here, and feel very relieved and superior about the people on one side of the line and very disappointed and sorry for the people on the other side." It's not a literary critical distinction of any usefulness whatsoever.

RB: I notice some writers will insert "fictional" facts—
JL: Hmm.

RB: They'll create places and flowers and all sorts of things and that's taken notice of as if the rest of it is of a different metaphysical status.
JL: Now we're arriving at the bug [that was] in my ear when I said we should talk again. It's all coming back. Certainly, yes, there's a kind of relentless bad faith expressed when reviewers or critics remark on one element in a novel as though it's a remarkable piece of metaphor or surrealism, as though they've never encountered such a thing before. They're shocked, just shocked that something is being proposed—they act as though it is utterly unfamiliar to them, what they really mean is that they object to it on principle, on class or political grounds like those I just described. So, by reacting as though the incursion were new, instead of familiar, it permits a kind of disingenuous head-scratching: "Hmm, perhaps this new method is of interest, or could be, in the hands of the most serious of writers. We'll have to watch closely and see." You saw this happening when Roth's new book was reviewed. Roth's use of the "alternate history" was treated, in certain quarters, as though, first of all, Roth himself had never written a book that challenged mimetic propriety— suddenly *The Breast* didn't exist, suddenly *The Great American Novel* didn't exist. Suddenly *Counterlife* didn't exist. To write about this thing with a ten-foot pole, and say, "What's this strange method? What have we got here? One of the great pillars of strictly realist fiction has inserted something very odd into his book. We'll puzzle over this as though it's unprecedented." It was as though there had been no Thomas Pynchon. As though Donald Barthelme, Kurt Vonnegut, Angela Carter, Robert Coover had been thrown into the memory hole. Was there never a book called *The Public Burning*? Do we really have to retrace our steps so utterly in order to reinscribe our class anxieties? Not to mention, of course, the absolute ignorance of international writing implicit in the stance: where's Cortazar, Abe, Murakami, Calvino, and so very many others? Well, the status quo might argue, patronizingly, those cute magical-realist methods—how I despise that term—are fine for

translated books, but we here writing in English hew to another standard of "seriousness." Not to mention, of course, the quarantine that's been implicitly and silently installed around genre writing that uses the same method as Roth's with utmost familiarity. Well, the status quo might argue, sounding now like an uncle in a P. G. Wodehouse novel: Ah, yes, well, we all know that stuff is, how do you say it, old boy? Rather grubby. No, I say, no. This isn't good enough, not for the *New York Times Book Review* and the *New York Review of Books*, in 2004. Let me say it simply: there is nothing that was proposed in Roth's book that could be genuinely unfamiliar to a serious reader of literary fiction of the last twenty-five years, thirty years, fifty years. To treat it as unfamiliar is a bogus naiveté—one that disguises an attack on modernism itself, in the guise of suspiciousness about what are being called post-modern techniques. It actually reflects a discomfort with the entire century.

RB: Seemingly smart and savvy people fall prey to this impulse.

JL: I agree. Which is why I was so exercised. It's not remarkable when some well-meaning but misguided, not particularly well-read reviewer from a not-trendsetting newspaper says, "Oh wow, what have we here? Roth's history isn't real history." But when responsible critics with access to the wealth of methods and motifs and strategies that have been employed in contemporary fiction, American fiction, play at being unsettled by the deployment of such an overtly familiar technique, what they're doing is retrenching. They're pulling up the drawbridge. I think there's a lot of that going on right now.

RB: To what do you ascribe their motives?

JL: OK, let me go hang myself here. I'll speculate on their motives, too. Remember we're talking about a collective gestalt abreaction. If I'm right—let's just for the sake of argument, let's say there *is* a kind of reactionary shudder making its way through the literary community, from newspaper reviewing to magazine reviewing to perhaps even some of the blogosphere—there's what feminism would call a backlash phenomenon going on. What would the motive be, for such a thing? Well, if you permit analogies to things like identity politics, you'd say some bulwark or status quo is feeling itself threatened. Which in turn means that the very success of writers like Pynchon and DeLillo and Angela Carter, and the pervasiveness of their influence is what's threatening this status quo. For, much like feminism, if the argument had no influence, if these methods all represented failed experiments, if they led nowhere, led only to unreadable novels, then there would be no reason to draw up the gates. In fact, that's what's being proposed by the false naiveté: that these activities were circumscribed, that they consisted only of a brief period of avant-garde provocation, one with no influence, that had no resonance or relevance. If those writers didn't have hundreds upon hundreds of delighted successors who have made free and ready use of their methods, the status quo wouldn't be unsettled. Unsettled by what they attack under the name post-modernism and what—if you accept my argument—is in fact modernism itself! It is the success, not the failure, of the revolution, which has caused the nostalgic hand-wringing for the "good old days"—as always, the non-existent good old days—when literature was the safe preserve of the "realists." What are we hankering for? Examine the logic and see where this impulse ends up. Let's see, if we chide the writer who makes reference to low-brow material, who appropriates cultural material—because appropriations are a bit like sampling in rap, really borderline plagiarism, everyone knows this—we'll have to roll back to T. S. Eliot. Oops, we have to throw Eliot on the scrap heap, too—apparently he risked some high-low mixing, and some appropriations. Forget Joyce, of course. We'd better go even further back. Once you begin looking at the underlying premise—a blanket attack on the methods that modernism uncovered—the kind of bogus nostalgia for a pure, as opposed to an impure, literature, what you really discover is a discomfort with literature itself. A discomfort with writing. A discomfort with the kinds of exuberance, with relevance. What's really being called for is a deeply irrelevant—literature as a high-brow quilting bee for people who are terrified, in fact, by its potential vitality, influence, and viability. American writing, its roots in Poe, Twain, Melville, and extended through Faulkner and, for gawd's sake, everyone else—is encompassing, courageous, omnivorous. It gobbles contradiction, keeps its eyes open, engages with the culture at every possible level. But boundaries being crossed make the inhabitants of the increasingly isolated castle of the status quo all the more anxious. If we're free to use these methods, allowed to talk about everything we know, if we are allowed to describe the world of advertising, the world of capitalism, the world of pop culture, the actual world where the elements described as of high- and low-brow are in a constant inextricable mingling—if we let down our guard, where will our status emblems be? What credentials will we burnish? How will we know we are different from the rabble outside the gates? Again, it's sheerly class anxiety that is expressed in these attacks. And, as well, a fundamental discomfort with the creative act, with the innately polymorphous, the innately acquisitive, curious, exuberant, and engaged tendencies in the creative act itself.

RB: Does that suggest a steady downward spiral of the critical conversation?

JL: Well, I don't know. We're in a bad patch, that's all. A reactionary shudder is moving through the collective mind. It's not about reading. That's the problem. It really is about—I'm repeating myself—class anxiety. Once you have an eye for this you spot it in odd places. I read a review in *Book Forum* where a critic, quite incidentally, in attacking Michel Houellebecq, said in an aside, "But then again, the French regard Hitchcock as art." Well, now, wait a minute! These battles were fought and won. These victories were decisive ones, fifty years ago. There's no rolling that back. Hitchcock is art. So if you pin Hitchcock's scalp to your belt: "Not only have I seen through Michel Houellebecq, the charlatan, but in fact I'm going to tell you that the auteurists were wrong and Hitchcock is low-brow and unsavory," you've discredited yourself so absolutely that you deserve to read nothing but Trollope for the rest of your life. What's left, then, in the residue of a reactionary environment, is cult hysteria. Houellebecq is typical of the provocative, absurd figures that flourish in conservative times. In place of intelligent conversation everything is pushed to extremes. On one side we have the castle with its drawbridge raised—the vast environment of what's actually going on in the world of writing and reading stranded outside the preserve—and on the other end we feature ludicrous figures of cartoon provocation. I personally don't find Houellebecq that thrilling, just as I don't find Lars von Trier the most nourishing filmmaker. A von Trier or Houellebecq dedicates far, far too much of their energies, their creative energies, to sheer provocation. You see a kind of mirror image of the reactionary impulse, a moral scold from the other end of the spectrum. The only message a Houellebecq or von Trier can convey is "Western society, and all that your propriety comprises, is totally bankrupt." Well, fair enough. The problem is, I'm not terribly nourished in being scolded for being a citizen of contemporary Western culture. I can't help it. I'd like to know a bit more than the fact that I am to be ashamed. You get only a very brief charge out of going into a von Trier movie and being told how bankrupt everything is.

RB: The danger of becoming what you are fighting.

JL: Man, I'm really full of lectures today.

Seattlest Interview: Jonathan Lethem

Courtney W. Nash/2007

From Seattlest.com, April 17, 2007. Reprinted by permission of Courtney W. Nash.

Jonathan Lethem understands what being an unabashed fan feels like, and we are an unabashed, dorky fan of his many books and recent essays. When we heard that he is non-exclusively sharing some of his short stories for $1 to be reused in other works of art (films, songs, etc.) and he is giving away the option to his new novel *You Don't Love Me Yet*, and releasing the ancillary rights after five years, we realized he was moving even further into territory very dear to our heart. We chatted with him in advance of his appearance at the Seattle Arts and Lecture series Wednesday night.

Q: Taken collectively, your recent forays into alternative copyright feel somewhat revelatory for you—how far back was the seed for these ideas planted, do you think?

A: The truth is, my real origins as a . . . whatever I am now, a copy "left" provocateur, is rooted in all of what I do. Almost everything I do is because of my appetite as a consumer. For what I like. All the things I write about tend to come from something I adore or that I respond to from the ancient past.

Q: In *The Disappointment Artist* essays, there seemed to be some cringing on your part about your adorations.

A: Sure, well, it isn't simple to just get crushes on all sorts of cultural stuff. Because you have to sort it out later and figure out what you can get behind or not. In the case of this stuff, it is rooted in my responsiveness to collage art and sampled music . . . to openly sourced material. I always liked when I was watching movies or reading material when somebody would be appropriating something or paying homage to something and be really obvious about it and do so unapologetically.

So it originates with my pleasure in these things, and my sense that there

133

was no contradiction in celebrating sources or influence, and being original. The kind of Bob Dylan paradigm was the one I believed in, that you could be the master thief and the originator and that those things were two sides of the same coin.

Q: So does it matter that there's not any original ideas left?
A: Well, only if you look at it in the kind of either/or approach, which I believe is a mistake. Originality itself is sourced. It comes from the idea that culture is a conversation. To wish for anything else is a kind of death impulse. To say that things shouldn't come from other things is to want there to be no things.

Q: As an artist, how do you reconcile that with a culture that's so dogged about ownership?
A: It's irritating. It's a problem. But another mistake is to be a purist, to try to offer some other legal philosophy that would be more ideal, that would exactly describe the reality of the life of artists and their audiences, and their relationship to cultural production. And it's probably not the case; laws are a really evil and imperfect attempt to describe and account for what goes on, and how we would prefer it to go on. Art is impossibly rich and contradictory, and you can only understand it on a case-by-case basis.

Q: Regarding that and your *Promiscuous Materials* project, you opted not to use a Creative Commons approach because of certain "contours" of your projects, is that what you're talking about in terms of a case-by-case basis?
A: Yeah, I think what's important there is for people to invent their own ways of doing things and to recognize that there is no single plan or system that is going to answer every need. One of the important things that I was trying to understand and express is that art-making is this impure act—it's a muddle of egotistical and selfless impulses, a muddle of commercial and gift-oriented transactions with the world at large. And artists are already always giving stuff away. They may not think of it that way, and they may be encouraged by their life in a commercial culture to feel that they are clutching very dearly to the things they produce and to try to squeeze every justified penny out of them, but the fact is that . . . If I have a per-word value on my work, if I accept the top-dollar I've ever gotten out of, let's say *Rolling Stone*, is the ultimate value of my words, then the fact that I'm speaking them to you now is a horrific act of giving them away.

Q: That you could write them then, and then go speak them for much cheaper in Seattle a few weeks later?

A: Exactly, what a discount I'm giving, right? And there's all sorts of other ways in which this paradox is played out. If I write a short story and I manage to place it in the *New Yorker* then I'll be very pleasantly remunerated, but instead if I manage to get it in say, someplace I'm also equally pleased with like some literary quarterly, then what is my story worth? Do I think that its value just changed so radically, or do I think that I wrote it because it is a transmission of meaning and energy that's important to me per se? And this other thing that might happen to it where some dollars move around is only one very small feature of the phenomenon of my wish to write it or the world's potential reception of it.

Q: Have you chosen a filmmaker for optioning *You Don't Love Me Yet*?

A: No, not at all. I'm here in LA where rumor is everything, and I'm hearing that I must have picked someone already. There's a sort of cynicism going around of "Oh yeah, that game is rigged, it's all over." It's the opposite—I'm helpless to look at the proposals right now because I'm traveling so much at this point. I'm really going to keep to my promise to not even really look at everything coming in until probably the end of April and then I'll give it away on May 15. Anyone thinking about it should definitely be encouraged.

Q: We've been fascinated by the people who are asking if you're worried that someone will do something bad with your book.

A: It's kind of a funny idea because selling your film rights doesn't ensure that bad things won't happen. And anyway, I've always felt there was a weird misunderstanding where people want you to be defiantly protective of a book. But you know what? First of all, even if you tried, you're not a filmmaker and your energies wouldn't really be rewarded if you tried to breathe down the necks of people adapting something of yours, and if you adapt it yourself or try to direct it yourself, well then suddenly you've become a filmmaker instead of a writer. So unless that's your wish, this is a great area to practice letting go.

Q: When you wrote *You Don't Love Me Yet*, did you have this idea for optioning the book at the onset?

A: Well no, the idea came over me at some point. While I was writing this novel I'd been accumulating the material that became that essay in *Harper's*, and thinking more and more about this stuff which is why you saw the leaking of that subject matter into the book. But I didn't figure out that I was going to do the *Promiscuous Materials* site, let alone the free option. It does seem to me that it came along at the right time, but this novel has a certain receptiveness to a film: it wouldn't be that expensive to make, it's in an urban setting.

Q: In fact, it felt almost written for a film interpretation; some have even called it parenthetical to your other novels.

A: Yeah, well this is a thing that comes up when you write a big book and then . . . I mean, people have called *Motherless Brooklyn* a big book, but the book isn't that long. And it's a pretty giddy book, too. If I'd written *Motherless Brooklyn* and then this one, all that people would say is "Oh, this is a writer who is always trying to make us laugh." It's totally about *Fortress of Solitude* that people are having this impression. It's just so rare, and people are disconcerted by someone going from the massiveness and apparent weighty subject matter to something that is a romantic comedy. But this book, first of all, is very closely connected to other books I've written, like *As She Climbed Across the Table*. And second, it's really *Fortress of Solitude* that sets this expectation, because *Motherless Brooklyn* is not so big and in fact it's a comic novel too.

Q: On that note, we have to ask: what's up with the kangaroos?

A: I'm just kind of making a . . . I stumbled into using the Los Angeles zoo when I was researching this book and I hadn't intended to put animals in it but suddenly they became important to me and I ended up with the kangaroo. It just made me laugh, to repeat myself in such an odd way. Knowing that it would seem like a shout-out to *Gun, with Occasional Music*, but it doesn't really have any kind of deeper pattern.

Q: It just struck a note, and we do tend to read into these things, perhaps too much . . .

A: Yeah, the connections between the books, the little jokes that knit them together, are in a way embracing the people who have followed me from one bizarre project to the next. It's my way of saying, "Look, you know that I've done a kangaroo before."

Q: As a bad animal metaphor, the kangaroo seems like a white elephant, in the context of you viewing art as a gift that is exchanged, it's that funny thing that comes back around again and again.

A: That's good, I like that.

Q: You can appropriate that if you want.

A: I think that repurposing within something is . . . I'm now a middle-aged novelist and I've done a certain number of things and I can fool around with my own cache of images and jokes a little bit. It's like that way you begin to see your own material up for grabs, too.

Q: Is your perspective on sharing your work something that's come with age and time for you? Or is it just something more easily grasped by people of our generation who grew up listening to sampled music and other shared sources?

A: It's an interesting paradox. Something that people have said to me when they wanted to be a little bit critical or skeptical is "Oh well, this is very easy for you, you've got a solid career and you're doing well so you can afford to give some things away. You're flattering yourself, but what about a young hungry artist who desperately needs to attain recognition or solvency?" And the funny thing is, I understand the thought. But the fact is that most of the people who do provocations of this kind, most of the people who are active in giving things away, are exactly young unknown artists working on the fringe. You see this in the web culture a lot, and that's why I thought there might be a place in this for me, but that's kind of rare. If you look at this as a sort of movement, I'm really quite late at arriving as a participant and I don't really have anything that revolutionary to say. Public advocates like [Lawrence] Lessig and people publishing in a blog context, most of your readers are very familiar with this stuff. People like Siva Vaidhyanathan made this point, and artists like Negativland and all sorts of web-based appropriators get it. But the reason I thought there was a place for me was that it is not common for more established artists working in these more traditional forms—and the novel is a very ivory-tower, privileged form, it's not like novelists are under attack, we're not getting cease and desist letters.

Q: But you did mention with the *Promiscuous Materials* project that most of that is for the short stories and song lyrics, and you still reserve the novel as something separate to a certain degree.

A: There are a couple of reasons for that. One of the critical things that I wanted to enunciate, once I figured it out, is that it's not an all-or-nothing thing. To let it become one was to play into the . . . because if copyright abolition is what's at stake, then for that purpose the Author's Guild and the RIAA should be up in arms. Because if there's to be no copyright and no protection, then what we'd have would be a sort of train wreck. But what's important to recognize is this: between the two extremes that have been staked out is this enormous middle ground where you can embrace a greater freedom of connection between artists, more movement of cultural materials, a larger and healthier public domain and still have adequate protection and adequate incentive for artists to make stuff. So yeah, I've benefited in lovely ways from the notion of intellectual property; the options I sold on earlier novels kept me writing at times when I would have been forced to go back to a day job, forced to go back to a, I don't know, masturbation boutique. It's precisely understanding that I get to sell some things that makes me want to give other things away.

Q: That evokes the metaphor you used in the *Harper's* article of art being like public land: belonging to everyone and no-one simultaneously. That gave me a new perspective on the phenomenon of the "cultural collective" that really made sense.

A: Yeah, this image of the collective commons is a very vibrant one once you realize how it kind of applies to everything. The airwaves, which have been completely privatized and auctioned off by the government—how on earth could those belong to anyone? And the Internet, which when you talk about things like the inquisitive attempts of the cable companies to privatize the Internet by wrecking neutrality, these are all commons issues. And they can all be analogized to a public park, or a public road.

Q: And naming it was important. In the *Harper's* essay and *You Don't Love Me Yet*, you touch on that quite a bit. What is it about the power of naming something?

A: It's something very vital to me about that. And names connect with negotiating identities. In *Fortress of Solitude*, at one point I realized that one of the subjects of the book is multiple names. Every character has multiple names: a name, a nickname, a tag. Barrett Rude Jr. is a member of The Distinctions but he wants to be Barrett Rude Jr., and Mingus wants to be "Dose" but he also lets Dylan be "Dose" and everyone is transacting their place in the culture, their place in the world, by making up a name. And Arrowman, every superhero has two names. And *You Don't Love Me Yet*, is a book about daft characters, or extremely unrealized characters—it's almost a book about lacking names, the provisionality of names and what it feels like to not even be sure you've got one. I'm very interested in the constructed nature of identity, and the way selves are made up via a series of negotiations, with roles and masks as disguises. One of the other subjects of *You Don't Love Me Yet*, to the extent that it has serious subjects in it, is this making yourself real by pretending. The way how becoming something in life, especially this bohemian ideal of self-creating, is all about pretending to be something, faking it before you can become real. It's the tender, pretentious, ludicrous quality of people pretending to be something by wearing disguises, by playing dress-up.

Q: That reminds me of the conversation you had over at *Seed* with Janna Levin [a cosmologist and author], where you talk about not being able to get to truth per se, but instead surrounding it.
A: I'm very fascinated with that topic. People who are philosophically minded will get perturbed, because they will say that somehow I'm alluding to now relatively discredited French ideas, that there is no there, there is no anything. But I don't really mean that, I'm just so aroused by . . . my awareness is so activated by this feeling that there's a slipperiness to mind and memory and language. That there's this way that we make identity out of these tools that are so unstable. They are full of projection and magic and metaphor. It's why when talking about contemporary writing, the idea of realism is so mixed up, because language isn't photography.

Q: It's symbolism.
A: Yes. It's infected with magic, and crazy, digressive, metaphoric, projective, wishful energy, and just to use it is like a tool that you're trying to operate that's not made of iron, but is instead made of mercury. And it infects everything, and makes you crazy. And memory itself is a kind of language, it's . . .

Q: Mutable and changeable.
A: Exactly. And it's negotiated. It's infected with wishfulness.

Q: How did you find yourself researching neuroscience and memory?
A: Well you don't even really have to research to be interested in this stuff, because they're just coming out with it—something is announced every five minutes that they've just discovered that we're even more preposterous than we thought. Memory scientists are persuaded now that when we remember something, we don't go back to some original stored file.

Q: There is no file!
A: There's no file, what we do is remember the last time we remembered it.

Q: And then it changes by remembering it.

A: So memory is just a series of rehearsals, for a show that never goes on. This isn't to say that I'm with Derrida, who I basically have never been able to understand, you know "Nothing is everything so it's all OK." We just need to constantly understand how much we're awash in our own subjective, fantastical consciousness. This is why people are so interested in stories, even if they distrust them. It's why fiction and film . . . it's how we understand ourselves. By the same token, we're all storytelling at some time.

Q: That's a theme that is in so much of your writing, that powerful phenomenon of identifying so personally with something in art.

A: Absolutely. It's everything.

Q: It's that feeling of, "Hey wow, that's me." In the book, everyone is thinking that at the same time.

A: Yeah, when the song plays.

Q: It's kind of the same thing with sports—you're something of a sports fan, right?

A: Oh, a huge sports fan. That's a powerful collective.

Q: So our co-editor Seth, who is something of a sports genius, wants to know: Where and with whom were you for Game 7 of the World Series last year?

A: [laughing] Well, I was with Christopher Sorrentino, my fellow long-suffering Mets fan, and I don't know why he knows to ask this, but we were on the third base line. So: a beautiful, perfect, unforgettable view of Endy Chavez's catch, and everything after that should just go undiscussed.

Q: And lastly, Michael van Baker wants to know: If push comes to shove, could you take Amis?

A: On what playing field are we talking about, just purely a brawl? Or do I get to choose weapons? Because we could go at it at snooker, and I would probably get my ass kicked. But if I got to pick, I would go with schoolyard basketball, one-on-one, in which case I could kick Martin Amis's ass up and down the block.

An Interview with Jonathan Lethem

Michael Silverblatt/2007

From *Bookworm*, KCRW-FM, July 19, 2007. Copyright © 2007 by KCRW-FM. Reprinted by permission.

Silverblatt: From KCRW Santa Monica, I'm Michael Silverblatt and this is *Bookworm.* Today I'm happy to have as my guest Jonathan Lethem, whose new novel *You Don't Love Me Yet* has just been published by Doubleday. He's the author as well, to talk about the books in the latter half of his career so far, of *Motherless Brooklyn, The Fortress of Solitude, Men in Cartoons,* which is a collection of stories, *The Disappointment Artist,* a collection of essays, and now, *You Don't Love Me Yet.* We haven't seen him around here since *The Fortress of Solitude* so we'll be talking about a number of things he's been up to in addition to this novel.

Now this novel is about a band and it's set in Los Angeles and it has as an epigraph lyrics from two songs, both of which are called "You Don't Love Me Yet" by the Vulgar Boatmen and by Roky Erickson. Erickson is as you know a famous doozy, a kind of thrilling basket case and I found immediately that the novel is about the opposite kind of characters. These are not kids who are out of their minds with drugs and genius and possibility. They're kind of drifting into the business of alternative band, but why? [laughter]

Lethem: Right. Well, they're very much Bohemian wannabes. And they're in a milieu where everyone suspects everyone else of being a fake but would never make the accusation because they've got their own bad conscience to consider. But on the other hand, they're also in a milieu where they have to generously be aware of the possibility of genius arising at any moment. They sort of know, and I believe they're right to think, that by faking they may fake their way to something worthwhile. It's a group of characters who are full of impostures and pretensions and yet I feel very tenderly toward them because I think they're making a kind of authentic if faint exploration and they have at least their yearning to guide them.

Silverblatt: One of them, the songwriter Edwin, has Alex Chiltern as his hero and he wears a big star tee shirt and yet his kind of claim to genius is a writing block.

Lethem: Yeah. [laughter] His reluctance is his credential.

Silverblatt: That's right. And it seems like in addition the lead singer, while sexy, is more concerned with the sick kangaroo he's stolen from the zoo and is keeping in his bathtub. It's almost as if this is setting out to be a kind of rock novel that's an anti-rock novel.

Lethem: I think it is an anti-rock novel in the sense that these characters never penetrate the music industry and they also never clearly penetrate the realm of art making, or if they do it's despite themselves and for one instant. This is very much a book of almosts. I think of it as being as much a day job novel as it is a rock and roll novel. But for me there's a poignancy to this distance between the way they want to view themselves, the way they hope they'll appear in others' eyes and the banality of their striving and the way they spend their days squabbling over the band's name and enacting their day jobs, working putting together cappuccinos or swabbing out the cages in the zoo.

Silverblatt: Now they seem though to be surrounded by reminders of a different kind of obsessional minority world. When they go to the radio station on the day of their almost discovery it's to KPKD, which I assume is Philip K. Dick.

Lethem: It's a joke about Philip K. Dick for sure, yeah.

Silverblatt: Yeah. And that sense of the landscape being littered by people who used to be, in an obsessional neurotic way, compulsive creators who didn't have control over it—

Lethem: Right.

Silverblatt: —and now we're looking at a world in Los Angeles full of people who are trying to control one another, in particular a guy named Falmouth.

Lethem: Falmouth Strand.

Silverblatt: Yeah.

Lethem: The conceptual artist. There is sort of an array of figures, most of them older men, around this band and some are just symbolic names, as you say. Philip K. Dick is floating there in the distance and Alex Chiltern.

But others are these music industry types who have both a worldliness and a cynicism but also a sense of daring or possibility, danger, attached to them that again it intoxicates, bewilders, threatens this young group. I think I'm fooling around with the image of myself in a way as an increasingly decrepit [laughter] figure. You know, the complainer is a kind of stand-in for any forty-something who still identifies in some way when they glance at people in their twenties. But I think the truth is that my post-collegiate life is an exotic time, a very distant time. Whereas in *Fortress of Solitude* when I contemplate childhood itself, I am really trying to bridge an almost interstellar gulf. There's this strange almost religious feeling of mystery about those selves. I still feel that my twenties were yesterday and yet I was that callow person. That's one reason for the self outing of the author photograph on the jacket of this book is to confess that I was that thin and pretentious and my poses were just as comic and transparent, and yet somehow in that shameless, helpless striving I did deepen myself. I found the way. Yet if I'd met my forty-something self at that time I would have been just as suspicious as these characters rightly are of the strange men that hang around the band.

Silverblatt: I think that you've begun to explore a subject that's quite interesting to me. In *The Disappointment Artist*, which is your collection of essays, you're writing frequently about things that, when you say about Vonnegut and Brautigan et al. that you're almost afraid to reread them because of what one might find there. That phenomenon of being the voice of a generation and the detritus of that generation is starting to have greater sentimental value than artistic value. Then there are things that belong to other generations. You have an essay, not about *The Searchers*, but about the pain one feels when showing that movie to contemporaries in college and they're not getting it, they feel it's just a Hollywood movie, it's a racist movie, look at these corny sequences and you're trying to figure out how do you induce them into the order of its meaning? In other words, as things become meaningless culturally how do you retrieve meaning?
Lethem: Right.

Silverblatt: As this band, you know, there's no poster in this book that will tell the reader these four young people are a little vapid, a little bland. They're surrounded by a world that's more interesting than they are and maybe if they're lucky they'll become interesting—
Lethem: Right.

Silverblatt: —but we have to pick that up from the effluvia of the book, yeah?

Lethem: Yeah, it creates a lot of anxiety I think in the reader when they realize that full identification with these characters might be [laughter] an experience too shallow to be tolerated. So I think you're onto something, absolutely. In fact, these four characters might be more or less the people who I could never convince to watch *The Searchers*. But then again, I think I'm also contemplating the dilemma of my rapidly receding tokens of culture. This book is set more or less in the early nineties and I already can drop the names of the bands I was listening to in that period and have a younger listener believe that I'm making all the names up. They're so utterly forgotten. And this is for a receptive listener, someone who believes themselves to be interested in indie rock [laughter]. What if one day I have as great a difficulty persuading someone that Big Star matters, as I did with *The Searchers*? Now that may seem like a strange or very low-stakes anxiety, but in a way I'm toying in this book with the reduction of the stakes.

Silverblatt: [laughter]

Lethem: The question is, what matters to you? Dare you risk embarrassment? Embarrassment is almost like the feat of death might be in another context, in this book.

Silverblatt: I'm Michael Silverblatt, this is *Bookworm* and I'm talking with Jonathan Lethem about his new novel, *You Don't Love Me Yet*. Part of the subject is the subject for a writer, which is that we've lived in a series of rapidly collapsing writer generations. The blank generation, the Brat Pack, a whole series literally supplanting one another, almost with an alarm going off every seven to ten years—

Lethem: Right.

Silverblatt: —and you may be the first generation to notice this sufficiently to be able to be writing about the voice of a generation as that generation loses its cultural voice.

Lethem: That's wonderful. I hope you're right. [laughter] I hope you're right.

Silverblatt: Why do you hope I'm right?

Lethem: Well, that we might be alert enough to ride the crest of the wave rather than be subsumed in it. Of course, it's terrifying to realize how disposable every form of culture is. I think one of the things that gives shape to my effort as a writer is my old life as a bookseller, and not a bookseller in a Borders or even in a good new bookstore like Cody's or whatever the equivalent would be here, Book Soup, but rather I worked in used bookstores. I was an antiquarian. I dwelled in these shelves full of the great forgotten books and lived among them as though they were all living presences and believed in them. I was never reading in my time. I was always reading twenty to thirty years behind my time, at least. So that when I came up for air in the very few writing classes I took in the mid-eighties and realized that for not only the students but even the teachers Lawrence Durrell and Henry Miller were not hot news [laughter] but were in fact vaguely mawkish, forgotten names, influential to no one, I was utterly bewildered because I had surrounded myself with a previous literary context and I believed in it, I animated it with my affection utterly. Well, so what is it to be a collector of forgotten, not that those names are unrecognizable, but many others are. What is it to care about things that are being supplanted awkwardly, hurriedly?

Silverblatt: And the way in which things that seem breakthroughs and of great importance are turned if not into literary ephemera into cultural ephemera, that we lose the thing that we thought was going to be the inheritance for the next generation, except you have a generation perhaps that has stopped accepting inheritances.

Lethem: That's an interesting way to put it. I've been thinking a lot about inheritance and the meaning of inheritance itself, the operation of legacies as a legal entity, because I've been thinking about intellectual property and the way literary heirs control the meaning and the transmission of authors' lives. Which, it's a very strange thing when there's no notion of a public domain, when no one can put value on essentially the un-copyrighted material, the only thing that's understood is the commodity. Well, then the only writers who live are the ones who are, paradoxically, guarded most covetously by their heirs. Which is precisely the opposite of say the way Shakespeare or Lewis Carroll was transmitted, where there were hundreds of editions and hundreds of permutations and the work was up for grabs, it belonged to everyone. We were all Lewis Carroll's children.

Silverblatt: Think of the days, too, when a song, I guess most prevalently a song like "Stardust" now you could gather twenty or thirty different versions of that song and some of them came out the same year.

Lethem: Right.

Silverblatt: It was a song that every band wanted to play—
Lethem: Yeah.

Silverblatt: —because everyone wanted to dance to it.
Lethem: I suspect if you accumulated versions you'd actually have it in the hundreds.

Silverblatt: Yeah. One of my favorites. But the question that you've been addressing with copyright is, is copyright still a meaningful activity in the age of the web, which supersedes copyright on the one hand and kind of joyously opens the possibility of influence rather than ideas like plagiarism?
Lethem: Well, I'm very interested in kind of provoking a re-examination of some of these terms. I mean, what bothers me about plagiarism is not that I don't believe there can be such a thing. Anyone can identify the fringe activity where something is appropriated joylessly [laughter] and unimaginatively and deceptively and we can all condemn that very easily. But what fascinates me is that people work so hard to ignore the resemblance between that activity and what artists do routinely, necessarily, all the time in their procedure, which is grab onto stuff, move it around, transform it. And when the same thing is done and value is added and influence is acknowledged, this is culture-making. It's not some minority activity. This is culture-making at its most central. This is what people do. It's not that an act of art making is either a commodity transaction or a gift transaction, to use Lewis Hyde's vocabulary, the author of *The Gift*. But that it's innately both. If I do what I do, do what I mean to do when I offer a book into the world, sure, I'd like to get paid. But if it's any good at all I hope to transmit something far more valuable than the $23.95 you've shelled out at the bookstore. I want it to sink into you and become a part of you and trouble you. It's something ideally I could never be repaid for and I wouldn't want to try. So it's a gift and a commodity at the same moment. And this is what artists do.

Silverblatt: Let's go back into the novel *You Don't Love Me Yet*. That book is signaled by an epigraph of lyrics from two different bands with the same title, "You Don't Love Me Yet." And in the book there's a man, at first anonymous, who calls on a complaint phone line and the woman who is taking his complaints in this conceptual art project recognizes the things he's saying as unique, interesting. His word is "itchy" [laughter]. She starts to write them down and pretty soon they're song lyrics. When he hears them it makes them his songs.
Lethem: He stakes his claim on them, yeah.

Silverblatt: Yeah. As if there hasn't been any process of transformation between the statement of the idea and its existence as a song. And interestingly, this band more or less seems to agree with him. At least they let this fifty-year-old guy into their band.

Lethem: Well, they're very, typically vulnerable, as we are in this present atmosphere of accusation and constant undertone of panic. Plagiarism anxiety floats everywhere. They are completely susceptible to the accusation that they've appropriated these lyrics. Of course, I think it's impossible not to read that character as uninterested in the lyrics as such. He's found a wedge into the band. It's a way for him to exploit their guilt and insert himself into their lives. And he's a very parasitic kind of creature. But there's this joke being entertained at some level of the narrative, not that these characters themselves could articulate it, about the value of a phrase. Since his job, his day job, is writing bumper stickers or slogans that could be on a coffee mug, technically a five- or six-word sequence could be a million-dollar idea for this guy. On the other hand, here I am in your studio, Michael, spilling out hundreds upon hundreds of words free of charge [laughter] and I'm supposed to be in the business of selling my words. So what are they worth? I'm giving you an awful discount today, don't you think?

Silverblatt: Well, talk is cheap [laughter]. It's a novel in which then the idea that context determines value . . . in a sense. And that the man who has become a conceptual artist by the end of the book is back to sketching because he realizes very quickly in this book that he can't control contexts.

Lethem: I think that's a lovely way to describe it. It's very much about the shiftiness of cultural capital, but also I think about the awkward doubleness in the identity of the artist, in the role of the artist. They're always—and this of course connects the book very strongly to *The Fortress of Solitude*, where all the artists in that book are kind of superheroes. They're both famous and sublime and extraordinary somewhere, whether they're a soul singer or a graffiti artist or, in the case of the father, painting paperback book jackets, they're celebrated and recognized. But they're also always squalid and secretive and unfinished and incomplete. They have their secret identities. They have their stigmata. And the artists in *You Don't Love Me Yet*, who are in some ways much less realized or less satisfying artists, what this book I hope captures is the strange disparity between the selves that they almost bring into being, the glory of being on stage and being lusted after and adored, with the stumblebum imposter nature of creating that identity, the prosaic, awkward daily lives that they are stuck with most of the time.

Silverblatt: Now given what we've said, art theft, context is value, plagiarism, one would expect a novel like a DeLillo novel, full of sharp surfaces and bristling cultural cynicism. Instead, the whole is cast as a kind of puppy love novel [laughter]. It's a kind of romantic comedy. It's almost as if its originality consists in the degree to which its ideas don't touch its characters.

Lethem: I think that's a lovely, lovely way to describe this book. Very generous. Yeah, I think at the same time that I was letting these ideas in I was treating them, I dare say, in a dangerously cursory fashion myself. I only let them in the door. The rest of the time I expended my energies on proving the animal existence of these characters, letting them eat and make love and sleep and laugh. I was very, very interested in portraying Los Angeles as a menagerie of sleepy twenty-somethings. In that sense it's maybe a bit of a chick lit operation or another word for it might be it's an emo-novel. [overlapping voices] Emo is the new, come on, oh you're so out of it, Michael.

Silverblatt: Totally out of it.

Lethem: It's the new music movement. Emo. It's something that is used to describe this kind of infinitely damaged, tender, self-pitying singer/songwriter stuff that is very popular right now, with the young folks, and of course, as with any nascent movement in popular music, some of it's genius and some of it's worthless. But the label amuses me because it speaks of a generation that is kind of overtly, self-consciously post-irony. You know, we're emo, we feel everything. So I wanted to see if I could write an emo novel. I mean, these characters, you speak of hard surfaces and Don DeLillo, I wouldn't dare to bring a satirical instrument to bear on these characters because they're too—

Silverblatt: Hurt.

Lethem: —they're too hurt already. Yeah. To bring the operation of satire to bear on these characters would be like stubbing out a lit cigarette on an ant. You would just hear this brief sizzle and that would be the end. There'd be no more character. So while they're in a kind of farcical world I also try to treat them as lovingly as possible.

Jonathan Lethem and Lydia Millet

Lydia Millet/2008

This interview was commissioned by and first published in *Bomb* Magazine, Issue #103, Spring 2008, pp. 30–35. Copyright © *Bomb* Magazine, New Art Publications, and its Contributors. All rights reserved. The *Bomb* Archive can be viewed at www.bombsite.com.

Lethem, who won the National Book Critics Circle Award for his fifth novel *Motherless Brooklyn*, grew up in Brooklyn and Kansas City and trained as a painter before turning to writing in his early twenties. Recently he's offered some of his short stories for free to filmmakers and others who wish to adapt them, through his own version of the open-source movement, which he calls the *Promiscuous Materials* project. He also recently married for the third time and in May 2007 had a baby son, Everett. His most recent novel is *You Don't Love Me Yet*, out in paperback from Doubleday.

Like Lethem, Lydia Millet has a young child—two in fact; a four-year-old girl and a boy born a few months ago. She is the author of six novels, the latest of which, *How the Dead Dream*, was published by Counterpoint in January and is planned as the first in a trilogy. Millet, who won the PEN USA Award for Fiction for her early book *My Happy Life*, grew up in Toronto and now lives in the Arizona desert where she writes and works for her husband's endangered species group, the Center for Biological Diversity.

Jonathan Lethem: I was thinking I'd like to begin by asking you what you're reading at the moment. I'm reading *Darkmans*, by Nicola Barker. I would give you a brilliant, extensive impression of it if I weren't completely exhausted from putting the baby to bed. We've lit a fire and *The Princess Bride* is on television, so my brilliant extensiveness will have to wait for my next email. Still—what are you reading?

Lydia Millet: I'm an ADD kind of reader. I usually have a few books going at once. But like you, I have a baby, and mine is only three weeks old. So reading time is at a minimum and all there is for me right now is Alan Weisman's *The World Without Us*, a Christmas present, which is both nonfiction and a bestseller. Both abnormal for me. But I'm caught up in it. It's fun. Who wouldn't like to know what the world would look like after a highly selective apocalypse limited to homo sapiens? The premise, if you don't already know it, is: how would the earth fare if you snapped your fingers and all the people were instantly gone? Raptured off skyward, or spontaneously combusted? Of course our fall is more likely to be a long plummet, but it's still a great conceit.

Plus, did you know that a tire is one giant single molecule? That's what Mr. Goodyear and his vulcanization gave us. I mean a whole tire, one molecule. You could have knocked me over with a feather.

JL: I've been eager to get my hands on that Weisman book. Am I right that it projects its human absence onto the island of Manhattan, or was that just a delightful dream I had—or an old *Twilight Zone* episode I am generously crediting in recollection to my dreamlife? As it happens, I'm working on a novel about a version of Manhattan invaded by weird harbingers of animal life—specifically, an out-of-control tiger (I warned you I was predating on your extinction-of-species beat, didn't I?). The recent news from the San Francisco zoo weirdly trumped—or, if you prefer, as I do, to think of it in terms of Robert's Rules of Order, "seconded"—my motif. I'll be trying to get my mind around that one-giant-molecule notion as I drive into town on the recently and irregularly plowed Maine roads on my four molecules today, in order to send this email from the signal at the library.

And yes, like you, I usually have too many books going at once, and I'm always vowing to simplify, to unify. As I am with projects. It always appears that I am on the verge of knocking out the last few extracurricular assignments—reviews, essays, stories for anthologies (or written interviews . . .)—and becoming what I idealize, the "pure novelist." I never am pure. Another commitment, made in some sleepwalking or Ambien-trance-state, always emerges on the horizon. I suppose this is just life. The novel is a very impure form, so why should the making of novels be concentrated like the tasks of Zen monks? Probably Zen monks are always knocking out little side assignments too.

Anyway, mine right now are: 1) Write an encyclopedia entry on Thomas Alva Edison, Eadweard Muybridge, and the introduction of the motion picture, and 2) Write a poem "about the death of something." I've suggested, perhaps perilously, that I'll be writing about the death of my cynicism. The problem being that it is a somewhat zomboid creature, capable of rising from the grave at the suggestion I write a poem. At the moment this seems to be happening on a daily basis.

Perhaps inevitably I'm falling into a sort of diaristic style here. I guess there isn't going to be any margin in pretending that we're doing anything other than what we're doing—acting as if we're doing an interview when we're really writing emails. What's an interview, anyway? The only times I'm sure I'm in one I'm sure I hate them.

Conversations are better—almost anything is better. It also seems to me that, by the nature of this sort of pretending, we already know each other. Though we've met, briefly, this, in fact, feels like our real introduction.

But—disclosure here, or what Hollywood would call "the backstory"—I did get in touch about two months ago to say that I'd just read *How the Dead Dream* and was completely transported. Two months later it still occupies the spot of the best book I've read since the last time I read a book so good. (Which was possibly *Remainder*, by Tom McCarthy, which shares some peculiar virtues with yours.) I read your novel in one long sitting, in loose photocopied galley pages, on a train between Cologne and Berlin, stealing them from my German editor as he was reading them beside me. He was on chapter three when I started. Then I caught up with him and passed him (no knock on his reading speed—English is his second language). Does this make my life sound exotic? Sleight of hand, if so. Our first baby arrived this year and those three days of my German book tour were about the only exotic ones of the past year. The rest was beautiful boring domesticity.

I do have one extremely specific question for you about *How the Dead Dream*: Were the early chapters influenced, by any chance, by Steven Millhauser's novels about childhood—*Edwin Mullhouse* and *Portrait of a Romantic*?

LM: To answer your question about influence, first, it's been so long since I read *Edwin Mullhouse* that I can't remember it anymore, so my best guess is, if my book looks like that book, I stole from it unconsciously. The way I always steal is the way most writers steal—we can't help it. Language and consciousness are so permeable. Sometimes, though, I want to steal and fail to steal, such as with Thomas Bernhard, whose style I always consciously want to imitate but can't bring myself to because it's too singular, too theft-proof.

Edison you say? I wrote a story about Edison, which was in *Tin House* just now, about his role in the electrocution and filming of Topsy the elephant—

which has been converted to a heartbreaking short video anyone can see on the Internet. Brief, grainy, heartbreaking—the great beast falls in slow motion to its knees. . . . That part of my story was true, but then there was a made-up part about Edison lusting after a drug-addict Hungarian manservant.

Lately I'm captivated by animals. I find that any literature that isn't populated by them seems dry to me. Animals are like rock stars, they have that charisma. So I'm delighted there are tigers in your Manhattan. In my misbegotten screenwriting career (in a nutshell, the usual story: I wrote several scripts and no one ever bought them), I once wrote a kind of blockbuster feature about an apocalyptic scenario where plants and wild animals take over Manhattan—nature runs wild and the city is gone in no time. It was a mess, but I liked it. According to Weisman, the subways would be some of the first things to go, in the sense that they'd be flooded right away. The subways are vulnerable, the bridges are vulnerable. Central Park would revert to swamphood, if I recall correctly. Right now I'm at the point in the book where he talks about the Panama Canal and how it would cease to exist. The canal was Teddy Roosevelt's baby, and arguably the largest feat of earth-moving engineering in history. But apparently it would be gone long before Mount Rushmore, which bears Roosevelt's pince-nez. Weisman calculates Rushmore could last seven million years. If aliens landed once we were all gone, Rushmore might be one of the last traces of us remaining. Perfect in a way. After all we're a tacky civilization.

And about your upcoming poem—if you were a cynic, I'm glad that died. Cynicism is boring, finally. Like words without animals or music without rock stars.

JL: Your approach to influence is very traditional and probably appropriate: to forget it. (Not that I'm claiming to be sure the Millhauser is reflected in *How the Dead Dream* . . . but it was for me!) I have a strange tic which sometimes serves me well but may in fact damn me in the eyes of readers and critics who don't want to be irritated by self-consciousness: I remember influence. And then, usually, mention it, either inside the text, or in some outside remarks, or both. In a way it's probably a form of excessive literalness, that I feel the need to keep pushing attention—my own, and others'—to the fact of literary intertextuality. It should be a thing I can take for granted by now.

I like your description of Thomas Bernhard's innate resistance to being anyone's influence. I think of course he would prefer not to be, or claim to prefer it (I read an interview with him in *Harper's* Readings section that was hilariously over the top in its nihilism toward writing and writers generally). I've often thought that Thomas Berger and Don DeLillo were the two writers who held the greatest sway over me yet whose prose most resisted my appropriation—perhaps Christina Stead qualifies too. Yet I go on trying to morph my prose into theirs all the time. That sustained tension of the resistance becomes itself a kind of energy or fuel I like.

I remember seeing that death of Topsy film, in all its shocking horrible glory, as part of a documentary about the history of Coney Island in the great days. I had no idea then it was an Edison film, but then I hadn't arrived at any personal interest in Edison at that point. (Anyway, Edison himself didn't really "direct" most of the Edison films). Did you know that the science of keeping premature babies alive in little heated tents was developed not in a scientific or medical surrounding, but as a Coney Island sideshow? "Come pay to see the marvel of tiny squirming embryos, fighting for their lives!"

LM: No idea. That trumps tires being one giant molecule.

JL: As for animals, your words are music to my ears. Novels need animals. I was recently reading an essay by Mary McCarthy, a quite brilliant, free-ranging one that she first gave as a lecture in Europe, called "The Fact in Fiction." At the outset she defines the novel in quite exclusive terms, terms that of course made me very nervous: ". . . if you find birds and beasts talking in a book you are reading you can be sure it is not a novel." Well, as the author of at least one and arguably two or three novels with talking animals in them, I felt disgruntled. McCarthy is one of those critics whose brilliance dedicates itself often to saying what artists shouldn't do—like the equally celebrated and brilliant James Wood, with whom I disagree constantly. For me, the novel is by its nature impure, omnivorous, inconsistent, and paradoxical—it is most itself when it is doing impossible things, straddling modes, gobbling contradiction. But anyway, when I lived with McCarthy's declaration for a while, I found myself replying, "But in the very best novels the animals want to talk, or the humans wish the animals could talk, or both." And that's certainly the kind of book I'm trying now. The tiger and the other animals in my Manhattan are desperately hoping to say something to the humans, and the humans, some of them, are listening hard. The failure of the conversation is, as in your own book, most tragic.

LM: It sounds great. The animals that want to talk, the people that want them to . . . exactly. But to the critics—it's so easy, and so exhilarating, to denounce things. Isn't it? But prohibitions like that—"It's not a novel if it has talking animals in it," "It's not a novel if it has philosophy in it"—besides being snobbish and condescending, serve more to elevate the critic than to advance or innovate the form. In fact, I think it's a sign of an art form losing power in culture when its arbiters try to define it by its limitations, what it can't or isn't allowed to do. Shoring up the borders of the form, in other words, to isolate it and make it puny. Novels should do anything and everything they can pull off. The pulling off is the hard part, of course, but my feeling is if you don't walk a line where you're struggling to make things work, struggling with ideas and shape and tone, you're not doing art. Art is the struggle to get beyond yourself. And if you want to use talking animals to do that, and you can make them beautiful, nothing is verboten. Look at found art, I don't know . . . visual artists like George Herms or the Kienholzes or people like that, Warhol before—the avant-garde, the innovative, has to include, not exclude. Once you exclude you're calcifying. You're well into middle age and headed for death.

JL: Well, I adore this rant. You said it, so I don't have to.

LM: I want to know more about the book you're working on. Can you give me a teaser? Is it a wild tiger? A zoo tiger? An imaginary tiger? A tiger like the one in that *Life of Pi* book about the guy on the raft? Is it a so-called genre-bender, like so much of your work? Is it apocalyptic?

JL: Well, in the omnivorous tradition, I'm tempted to say yes, all of those: wild imaginary zoo tiger, and the book an apocalyptic genre-bender, yes, all of it, yes. And, in the other tradition, of nervous novelists who only have a couple hundred pages of draft and are afraid of talking too big about unfinished work, here's what I can tell you: this one is a sprawling, aggravated, unreliable black comedy set on the Upper East Side, with a tiger on the loose and other animals lurking. The tone is contemporary, possibly "realist," but the events shade increasingly toward the kind of ontological horror-story I associate with H. P. Lovecraft and Philip K. Dick. The main characters are a retired actor (really a former child star), a dyspeptic and paranoid cultural critic, a hack mayor's aide, and a ghostwriter of books—her specialty is in as-told-to books by injured athletes, frostbitten Everest climbers, and so on. I'm very happy with it so far.

LM: I can't wait to read it. Especially the parts with the paranoid critic.

JL: Did I mention he has a wandering eye? I don't mean as in "an eye for the ladies." I mean one of those eyes that migrates wildly in his head while you are trying to talk to him.

LM: Speaking of which, can I ask you about your latest book, *You Don't Love Me Yet*? Which is the story of some would-be rock stars? I want to ask the obvious autobiographical question, since we don't know each other yet. And maybe I should be scurrying around the Web trying to figure this out for myself, but I'm just gonna ask. Did you ever want to be a rock star? Are you a rock star manqué?

JL: Oh, yeah, *You Don't Love Me Yet*. May I admit that nothing is further from my thoughts at the moment than that book? Well, I can at least be polite and answer the simple question: I was the lead singer (or lead mutterer) in a rock band in San Francisco for about four months. I think we played three or four "gigs," which were of course all parties thrown by forgiving friends. Our name was the pronunciation-suspect "Emma The Crayon." It never should have been allowed to happen, in the sense that my muttering never reached even the Lou Reed level of speech-singing, which I suspect should be policed as a basic threshold for credibility at the microphone. I have since retreated to the cowardly vicarious role of lyricist for some of my friends' bands. I'm collaborating with Walter Salas-Humara of the Silos on an album's worth of songs right at the moment.

LM: You're so lucky. I wish someone would ask me to write rock songs for them.

JL: Well, it seems to me from where I stand that there are a lot of musicians out there who thrive on collaboration with writers. If you're really looking for it, I bet I could scare up some kind of arrangement for you. Maybe we could even create a kind of clearinghouse for these needs, like a dating service. Call it VICARIOUS ARTS, LTD.

LM: The Mekons did a collaboration with Kathy Acker. Though it wasn't my favorite project of theirs, I desperately wish that had been me. If you can hook me up with the Mekons, I will be your slave forever.

JL: Ah, why don't you just shoot for the sky? Can you think of a rock band that has less need of writing help than the Mekons? Let me see what I can do.

My question for you now is: how does it feel to declare you've begun a trilogy? I've always wondered. When did you know you wanted to write one? What are your favorite trilogies, and do they have continuous characters and situations, or only thematic similarities? How will yours operate—do you know yet?

LM: The trilogies I know are mostly genre, though I have a friend who's writing what she calls a *roman fleuve*, a "stream" novel—Kate Bernheimer, who's doing this lovely three-part fairy-tale series on the Gold sisters, three fictional sisters whose lives she depicts in terms of fairy-tale myths, symbols, and structure. Of course there are other literary examples. I remember in college reading Durrell's *Alexandria Quartet*, for instance. But when it comes to serial novels I think more of children's lit I liked, or sci-fi—say Lloyd Alexander in fantasy, which I liked growing up, or C. S. Lewis or Edward Eager, or more recently Philip Pullman, and people like Jack Vance. But I decided impulsively on the trilogy idea, as I do on almost everything. In this instance, I knew I wanted to write about the same characters for a while and also that I didn't want to write a long book again because it's more difficult to sustain tone in a long book. Also, with a newborn and a three-year-old, I have the practical equivalent of a short attention span. Anyway, the second book is done and the thematic similarities it has are pretty embedded and obscure. Except for aloneness and dogs. Those are obvious. But it deals with the same characters as the first from a different point of view—the father of Casey, a character in the first book, who works devotedly for the IRS.

JL: Oh, now I'm excited. I wanted to know more about several of the characters in your book. Now it makes perfect sense. And this is a kind of trilogy-writing that stirs my imagination, like Durrell's, which you mention: the multiple-sides-of-same-story. I suppose in a way I wanted to write that kind of trilogy with *The Fortress of Solitude*, only I wanted it all to be inside one cover. When people object to that book, it's always the disjunctive strategy-and-viewpoint switches—which were, of course, for me, the whole point of writing it, to build a structure capacious enough to hold those kinds of disparate realities. In fact, I'm sort of doing it again in the new one, but in a way I think is likely to seem more agreeable, because I won't ask the reader to begin completely again. Instead, I'm weaving the contradictions into a single narrative, so that by the time you've agreeably finished reading my agreeable tale I hope your head will have exploded. That's always what I'm really hoping most to do, by the way. Explode heads.

LM: What writer doesn't want to do a little head-exploding? My husband always accuses me of fetishizing the poignant—he says I married him for the same reason I got a pug dog. And it's true that there's a particular combination of desire and failure that explodes my own head—the state of wanting-passionately-and-being-incapable-of-getting. Something about frustrated desire breaks my heart and compels me at the same time. And I basically interpret literature as one great frustrated gesture. In fact, I interpret most art that way: a grand moment of desire for union, for understanding, for everything. A moment that, to most people living on earth, passes unnoticed.

JL: I'm so pleased by this definition that I'm going to suggest it should be the end of our talk. Except perhaps for this wisecrack: it's a good thing you decided to be a novelist, because in the alternate universe where you didn't, you would have obviously been doomed to a career in Lacanian psychoanalytic theory. We're all better off in this universe.

"If Dean Street Could Talk":
Jonathan Lethem

Brian Berger/2009

This interview originally ran in *Stop Smiling*, Issue 38 (2009), the third annual "20 Interviews" edition.

Jonathan Lethem isn't just any Brooklyn writer—he grew up there, on Dean Street, between Bond and Nevins specifically. This is well known, of course, and this geographical fact defined the forty-five-year-old's most celebrated work, the Tourettec tour-Detective-force *Motherless Brooklyn* (1999), and its follow-up, which can be briefly described as the autobiography of a place, *The Fortress of Solitude* (2003). That place is so-called Boerum Hill, a sixties real estate fiction primarily designed to obscure the area's race- and class-riven history. That this history—and, indeed, even in an era of hyper-gentrification, its multilayered, multiethnic residential and industrial reality—remains little known despite Lethem's testimony is puzzling. It makes you wonder what people like about the guy anyway.

In many cases, even in Lethem's hometown, it's *Motherless*' funk-loving hero, Lionel Essrog, they love, which is fair enough. The freighted life and times of Lionel's creator is his business. Likewise, if some believe that *Motherless* made its author an "overnight" success, Lethem is an uncomplaining beneficiary, albeit a self-aware one disinclined to heed public expectations. *Motherless* was in fact Lethem's fifth novel, with a short story collection in tow, and its author hardly the first Brooklynite to assay either Dean Street or Boerum Hill. He was preceded by, among others: bank robber and two-time memoirist Willie Sutton; Diggers non-leader and *Ringolevio* (1972) author Emmett Grogan; Spike Lee, who filmed his 1994 adaptation of Richard Price's *Clockers* in the nearby Gowanus Houses, the same projects Mos Def shouts-out in his *Black on Both Sides* anthem, "Brooklyn" (1999). Even Lionel Essrog has a popular precedent in Popeye Doyle, Gene Hackman's bond-age-loving, Gravesend-residing character in *The French Connection* (1971); that Lionel is a private detective and Popeye a cop matters not.

Or maybe it does, a little bit. William Friedkin's *The French Connection* was based on actual events, the film an adaptation—sometimes faithful, sometimes dramatically heightened—of journalist Robin Moore's 1969 book of the same title. It's a process—the assessment and expression of overlapping realities—Lethem is very familiar with, both in his own work and that of the numerous artists he is a generous admirer of. First in a writing studio overlooking the Gowanus Canal, then in the apartment Lethem shares with his wife, writer and filmmaker Amy Barrett, their young son Everett and a Jack Russell terrier, Maisey, we discussed some of those influences.

Stop Smiling: I see you have Nathanael West on your desk—what's going on there?

Jonathan Lethem: That's my work right now, I'm going to write a new introduction to West's *Miss Lonelyhearts & The Day of the Locust*. So that's a pretty exciting assignment. I devoured West when I was a teenager, so it's a good way to reacquaint myself with what feels like a very strong influence. But in fact, the details, I barely remember them—that paradox of things I ingested at a very early point become hugely formative but by now are totally unfamiliar.

SS: I wouldn't compare you to *Day of the Locust* protagonist Tod Hackett, but it seems some people were rooting for your last novel, *You Don't Love Me Yet* (2007), to fail. Did you sense that also?

JL: Yes. As of *Fortress of Solitude*, I was a traditionally grandiose, emotionally sincere American novelist; with *You Don't Love Me Yet* it appears I'm writing a thin, frothy romantic novel set in the wrong city. That was something I willed into being—I was ready to throw off any sense that I was going to write sprawling social novels set in Brooklyn and become the Brooklyn Faulkner. Neither *Motherless* nor *Fortress* exactly fits that description, but the accumulated image of the two books seemed to project that.

I don't know if it would have been easy or hard for someone else to follow through with it, but it was totally out of the question for me. And really, for anyone who had even glanced at the earlier work that'd be obvious. But there were a lot of people—and an important critical framework—which had never glanced at the earlier work. *You Don't Love Me Yet* was a way to shrug that off with a degree of self-destructive glee, to say I'm going to disappoint people on a number of different levels so we can start over again about expectations. Coming out of four or five years of writing responsibly with *Fortress* and the biographical essays of *The Disappointment Artist* (2005), I wanted to rediscover a sense of capriciousness.

SS: So there are no further adventures of Lionel Essrog forthcoming? Maybe he can quit the private eye racket and become a Brooklyn boutique hotel detective.

JL: Oh, you don't know how many people are hoping I'll change my mind. It evokes a lot of sweetness for me that people adore that character, and I adore him. He's nicer than I am, so it's great that people fell in love with Lionel. But I couldn't do it again in any way that'd be meaningful.

SS: *You Don't Love Me Yet* is set in Los Angeles. Did you feel Raymond Chandler and Ross Macdonald looking over your shoulder at all?

JL: Setting it in LA was my way of trashing the idea of expertise. If all my authority as a writer comes from Brooklyn, then what happens to that writer when he writes about a place where he has zero credibility?

Taking on Macdonald and Chandler as prose models is how I taught myself to write—*Gun, with Occasional Music* (1994) comes out of going to school on those guys, but I didn't think of them consciously at all until halfway through *You Don't Love Me Yet*. The models I had in mind—and they're ones nobody is expected to realize—were Muriel Spark and Iris Murdoch. I was thinking, "What if I set one of these slightly plastic, mordant social comedies in American hipster culture? What would Iris Murdoch do?"

SS: I don't want to characterize it as a failure because Daniel Fuchs had a hard time well before you came along, but you wrote the introduction to the latest edition of Fuchs's Brooklyn novels from the thirties, which are not widely read, whereas your Library of America work as the editor of their Philip K. Dick collection has been surprisingly successful. Is it correct to say Fuchs wasn't quite welcomed back, even here in Brooklyn?

JL: That was a total publishing failure and distinguished as such not just by comparison to Dick but Fuchs' John Updike–introduced *Hollywood Stories*, which did get some play. *The Brooklyn Novels* collection is immense (927 pages), and that's a problem, but Fuchs has been unsuccessfully republished a few different times. Somehow they're books the world has been inoculated against. But I'll also say I love them so much, but I'm not sure I hit the biggest home run with my introduction. I didn't delve as deeply as I could have.

SS: One of your lesser-known Brooklyn influences is Ralph Bakshi, the Brownsville-raised animator who did *Heavy Traffic* (1973)—based in part on his inability to get a film version of Hubert Selby's *Last Exit to Brooklyn* made—and the brilliant blaxploitation satire *Coonskin* (1975).

JL: *Heavy Traffic* in particular was a signal example of combining New York vernacular texture—that feeling of being a kid encountering the city in that kind of way, bridging the world of a dreamy, artistic, imaginative weirdness—with the life of the neighborhood. Bakshi's style is so inclusive, so rapturous and incisive, so fantastical and has so much grit in it. And all those things helped mark the landscape that I could write *Fortress* into.

SS: Some people felt *Fortress of Solitude* was obsessively long, but I didn't feel it sag. If anything, some episodes could have been further elongated. It's like you hear there was once a four-hour cut of Peckinpah's *Pat Garrett and Billy the Kid* (1973) and think, "Wow, that would be amazing."

JL: I love immensity in films specifically and I like my immense novels—I've read all twelve volumes of Anthony Powell's *A Dance to the Music of Time* and I loved Samuel Delany's *Dhalgren* (1975). I wanted to write a book that had that total saturation that, when you're excited, feels like it's infinite. It doesn't mean *Fortress* is unedited. It was about a hundred pages longer than it is now, and I reduced it not by block cuts as they say in film but by concentration: stripping sentences, clauses, by tightening and making sure that even in a capacious, fulsome voice there wasn't any flab. Or at least less flab.

SS: Did anyone compare *Fortress* to its antecedents as a Brooklyn street novel, Gilbert Sorrentino's *Steelwork* (1970) and Wallace Markfield's *Teitlebaum's Window* (1971)? Sorrentino is a Catholic in Bay Ridge, Markfield is a Jew in Brighton Beach, but your acuities are similar.

JL: No, people didn't even take my bait—and in some ways my principal model among New York novels—James Baldwin's *Another Country*. *Steelwork* meant a lot to me, as did glimpses of Joseph McElroy's first novel, *A Smuggler's Bible*—not the entirety of the book but where he talks about excavating the ancient school days and pavement games. Strangely enough, even Don DeLillo's *Libra*. The first forty pages with Oswald as a boy on the subway trains, smashing through the tunnels, standing in the front window, looking at the station come in and the track pulls under his feet and Oswald basically getting yoked in the playground in the Bronx. They're not even chapters but paragraphs, where I tasted a writer going to that sensation of boyhood in New York City.

SS: There's a curious paradox with *Fortress*: People are glad to accept you as the Virgil of Gowanus, but your local renown seems to refuse or at least skim over those intensities—affluence and poverty, white, black, Latino and Arab. It's like Ralph Ellison's *Invisible Man* in a way.
JL: It's the *Invisible Man* and no matter how much I thrust it at people, I failed totally. What I wanted to say is the past is present, there's no change in a sense. And everybody decided to award me the role of the person who remembered this stuff—they didn't want to contend with it themselves, the contradictions weren't manifest in our lives presently.

I've been contacted by journalists who wanted to write about *Fortress* and I'd invite them to meet me where I was living, on Bergen Street near Court. We'd go for a walk around the neighborhood and they'd be like, "So you really got mugged on these streets?" After a while I started walking the journalists through the projects to see how they felt about it, because nearly everyone in NYC has these boundaries and their denial is so strong they don't know they have them. People live in this neighborhood and it allows them to think crime or poverty or crack is in the past, and it's because they don't walk on certain blocks.

It's an incredible thing to walk the block of Warren Street from Smith to Hoyt and let yourself feel the changes that are coming on incrementally with every footstep. The crack den that I portray in the end of *Fortress*—it's not gone.

SS: When did you learn to drive?
JL: Not until I got to California. My first wife, Shelley Jackson, taught me to drive in a beaten-up Peugeot we'd bought together. I lived in the Bay Area for a couple years without knowing how to drive: I just imposed my New Yorker's paradigm on the place and took buses, subways and did things within walking distance.

SS: Was your relocation there related to your love for Philip K. Dick?
JL: In many ways getting out to California was a reflex because I'd been vowing all through my high school years that I was going to go make a pilgrimage and meet him. He died just before I might have pulled off the trip, but I still had this image of myself as enacting my destiny by going to Berkeley to meet Dick. Of course, I was off by many hundreds of miles, he was living in

Orange County at that point—I was a little confused. When I first lived in Berkeley, I got an apartment, by dumb luck, that was two blocks from Francisco Street, where Dick had written a preponderance of his early work; lots and lots of novels that I loved were written just a couple blocks from where I set up shop to write *Gun, with Occasional Music* and *Amnesia Moon*, my overtly Dickian homages.

SS: Did you already know Paul Williams, the early rock criticism pioneer, creator of *Crawdaddy* and executor of Dick's literary estate?

JL: Yes. I moved to Berkeley and immediately fell in with Paul Williams, who was a Dylan critic and palled around with Brian Wilson during the Smile era. Paul had just been given the task of sorting out the posthumous papers—the posthumous career—of Dick, which didn't seem like a going concern. The guy's work had had its moment and failed in the world at large. There was this cult of seven hundred to eight hundred people who subscribed to the Philip K. Dick Society Newsletter, which Paul published. We were like the last line of defense for this guy being forgotten or not. Us and a lot of academics like Fredric Jameson—that was the secret weapon. They were also digesting his accomplishments and starting to write about them. But the idea of Vintage having every novel Dick had ever written in a shiny paperback edition would have seemed totally farcical.

SS: Farcical and dangerous, if somebody accidentally grabs, say, *Dr. Futurity* instead of *Ubik.* This is a related shot in the dark but, being in the Bay Area, were you a Residents fan at all?

JL: Oh yeah, I was a crazy Ralph Records guy in Brooklyn! Two of my coolest friends growing up in Park Slope turned me on to Fred Frith, Renaldo and the Loaf and, above all, the Residents. I saw my first and only Residents show when I got out to San Francisco—it felt like I'd gone to heaven.

The other fateful thing about my interest in the Residents—and this ran smack into PKD—is Gary Panter, who later became a friend of mine. Panter was doing the album covers for a lot of those Ralph records. I looked at the artwork on those records and recognized it as having a kinship with comic and surrealist art I liked, and the punk posters that defined my experience in high school. Without putting a name to it, those drawings felt right to me. The bizarre thing is the way I first learned of Gary Panter: In the second or third issue of the PKD Society Newsletter was a photograph of Dick near the end of his life being visited by Gary Panter and Gary's then-wife Nicole, with Dick wearing a Ralph Records T-shirt that said "Rozz-Tox" on it. It was like having my brain twisted into a pretzel seeing Dick wearing a drawing that I associated with the Residents—it was like a total Pynchon moment: Everything does nest together in one place.

SS: When you moved back to Brooklyn at the end of 1995, did you bring a car with you? I ask because *Motherless* requires a driver's knowledge of the city that some people never attain.

JL: Oh, that's a good story. I left behind a little Corolla. It was the first car I ever owned solo that was just my car and it was a hand-me-down. I got the vanity license plate I'd been fantasizing about, SQUALOR, so it said California SQUALOR. This license plate was slightly famous locally and when I met Daniel Clowes, the person who introduced us said, "Jonathan used to drive a car called SQUALOR around Berkeley." And Dan said, "Oh my God, I love that car! I used to see it all the time." This Corolla wasn't going to make it across the country, so when I left for Brooklyn I gave it to my sister, who was also living in Berkeley. When she came to New York, she gave SQUA-LOR to a friend of hers who eventually let another friend borrow it and SQUALOR was used in an armed robbery of a Carl's Jr. and apprehended. So SQUALOR went into police custody. I think it's a pretty poor idea to commit armed robbery of a hamburger joint if your getaway car has a vanity license plate.

The Rumpus Long Interview
with Jonathan Lethem

Ronnie Scott/2010

From *The Rumpus*, January 19, 2010. Reprinted by permission of Ronnie Scott.

Jonathan Lethem's new book, *Chronic City*, is so damn big it's overstuffed; or that's what Michiko Kakutani says. Fair enough: It's at different times to different strengths concerned by technology, space, local government, war; there is then a fear of the false, a fear of the real, the fear of all components of the simulacra, basically, and then above all, of the city. As often as it feels like it's a present-day story, *Chronic City* seems to me as though it lives down somewhere deeper in the past. And if it does need overstuffing just to fit all that it does, it demonstrates well that in the novel, lives live well alongside others.

It's the story of Chase Insteadman, a minor Upper East Side celebrity. He is a former child star, lately better-known as the male half of the universe's longest-distance relationship. His fiancée is Janice Trumbull, an astronaut trapped in a decaying satellite, which is blocked from re-entering our atmosphere by an orbiting bank of Chinese space-mines. Himself trapped between his twin peripheral celebrities, Chase falls in with Perkus Tooth, a hyper-literate nuisance-critic of the Lester Bangs variety (though Perkus Tooth denies the type). The rest, again, is stuffed: it's bright and hyper, but Lethem's noir-brain still dabs up a little dimness at the edges; it's a buddy book, but always cannibalized by that vagued-out, stoner paranoia. As stuffed as it is, it's a fun book to talk about, so we did.

It was 4 a.m. here in Australia. We discussed the book, the city, Skype, what he's working on, his basic tools, his experience of starting projects, the Upper East Side specifically, place in general, genre in general, *McSweeney's* specifically, how he is not magic realism, and why there is a book-within-a-book in *Chronic City* which he chose to title *Obstinate Dust*.

165

The Rumpus: Wow. Can you see me?
Jonathan Lethem: Right now I see only myself.

Rumpus: Okay. Wonderful. I don't think I have camera capacity. But I can see you.
Lethem: You were not expecting that.

Rumpus: No, I was not. I've barely used Skype in my life.
Lethem: Anytime anyone suggests Skype to me I think they're the old hands. But you're using it because it can record directly onto your computer.

Rumpus: Yes I am. But I don't think the video. But that's okay, I don't need it. Yeah! How are you?
Lethem: Uh, fine, fine. It's midday here, very cold, and already been to my office and done a little work, so, yeah.

Rumpus: Is your office near your house?
Lethem: About six blocks away.

Rumpus: Cool. Is that Brooklyn?
Lethem: Yes, exactly.

Rumpus: Cool. What are you working on?
Lethem: Right now I am trying to get going on a very short book about a movie. I'm writing about Jonathan Carpenter's *They Live.*

Rumpus: Okay, this is the guy who did *Halloween.*
Lethem: Yes. *Halloween, Dark Star, The Thing, Assault on Precinct 13*—the original *Assault on Precinct 13.* And, what else would you know?

Rumpus: He did the *Halloween* score as well, right?
Lethem: Yes, he always does the music for his own films.

Rumpus: That's exciting. Why are you writing about that?
Lethem: It's a film I sort of love, although it's problematic. It's a deliberate B-movie and it has all sorts of slippages in it. It's a weirdly shoddy, great film. But I like writing about film and I haven't done that kind of cultural studies stuff since I finished *The Disappointment Artist.* And then I've got

a friend who's editing this series of short books on films. Do you know the *33⅓* series?

Rumpus: I was just thinking that it sounds similar.

Lethem: It's very much in that mode, and I'm actually gonna be doing one of those as well. So I'll be doing one little book about a film, and then one little book about an album. I'm gonna write about Talking Heads' *Fear of Music*.

Rumpus: That's really exciting. After *Chronic City*—well, it's quite early in the day here, so I'll read directly from my notes. I wanted to ask you: "What other cultural shit do you want to write authoritatively about?" Because *Chronic City* seems just completely stuffed with information, and you do seem just to be really interested in, uh, in a whole lot of stuff.

Lethem: Well, there's things that loom very large for me for which I haven't found a way. I've often thought that if I ever was to write a real, full-length book about a cultural subject, it would probably be Alfred Hitchcock. And he's so important to me and I've read so much about him—there is a tremendous number of books already about Hitchcock—that I've never managed to put very much about him into words. He's the largest unacknowledged presence in my own range of influences. I've written about other figures like Cassavetes or Philip K. Dick or [Bob] Dylan a number of times, so that's one, for sure.

Rumpus: How much does something like Hitchcock or John Carpenter influence your fiction?

Lethem: Film in general is very nourishing to my writing. The form is such a close narrative cousin to the novel in the twentieth century, and I write in a dialogue with film very often. Hitchcock is particularly influential, just in the way he structures narrative and the way that, under his consciousness of the charged quality of certain settings and certain objects, parts of the world take on this metaphysical quality.

Rumpus: It's funny to think about *Chronic City* filmically, but it does make sense. There are those few scenes where your narrator slips into this free indirect third-person style, which I love that you use not as the standard mode of telling the story, because it's a first-person story, but as just another device.

Lethem: When he becomes the narrator of other people's chapters of course

I was thinking of it as the Philip Roth trick, the Zuckerman trick, where in a book like *The Human Stain* or *American Pastoral* Roth allows Zuckerman to know more than he can possibly really be authorized to know about the lives of other people. But I don't think that trick probably originates with Roth. In fact I was just rereading a Norman Mailer novel called *The Deer Park*, and it's there too. Mailer uses it very unselfconsciously. His first-person narrator suddenly becomes a third-person storyteller. So I'd actually be interested in tracing what the common denominator for that is.

I don't know where it comes from, but more and more I've looked for models of total freedom in narrative style. When you say the free indirect style—which is to use subjective and objective sentences, to use stream of consciousness sentences, in the middle of third-person narration—that's one kind of freedom. But I guess I'm in a way interested in even more radical notions of that, like you encounter in—well, you encounter them in places like Dickens, where no one had made up any rules yet, so there were no kind of craft rules. No one had named the free indirect style, and first and third person and past and present tense were not as restricted as they are now.

Rumpus: There's *The Art of the Novel* by Milan Kundera where he's talking about *Don Quixote* and at the time that it was written, that and a whole bunch of other books indicate all the alternate paths that the European novel could have taken but didn't. I think it's interesting how these things just do become modes that you can slip in and out of, so long as readers are receptive to what you can do.

Lethem: Well, it's always voice. Voice is the great persuader. When something's working, it's because the implicit narrator, the fictional writer who's writing everything, slips into a mode of authority and persuasiveness that can put over whatever it likes. And you see that in Bolaño now, and people have been very inspired to radical strategies by Bolaño's freedom to authorize himself to use all sorts of different modes simultaneously. But fundamentally it's just his persuasiveness and brilliance and charm that make that work.

Rumpus: How often do you try out a voice that ends up being completely not persuasive at all?

Lethem: I don't really have that experience. I don't write stuff that isn't working past a few sentences, I don't make those kind of—I don't go down wrong paths, I'd rather stare at the screen and delete until I've put something down that is working. So, I don't discard material; I don't have a lot of false starts or unfinished stories or novels lying around. I kind of hammer at stuff and make it work.

Rumpus: Cool, so something like *Chronic City*, is that—I guess this is the wrong question, but is there then an idea that you have fully-formed before you write it?

Lethem: I know a lot, but there's vastly more that I haven't discovered yet. A novel is enormous, and especially a longer book. I mean, *Chronic City*'s not the longest. But it's pretty encompassing and various, and so I have the characters, at the outset; I have the primary characters and a few key set pieces in mind, and usually some very strong sense of an ending, an image or a situation that I want to end at. A feeling of resolution that I'm writing toward, and I may have scraps of other things, descriptions of sequences or transitions that I'm interested in. But most of it? You can't plan a novel entirely, or the plan is as long as the novel. So there's vast areas of darkness and improvisation where you're just discovering what's necessary as you work.

Rumpus: So there's something like the story of Janice Trumbull in the space station, which I figure might be something that you could have in mind before you write it. But then something like how there are so many "un" and "in" and "irr" words in it, relationships between things and their negatives; is that then something that emerges as you write?

Lethem: Yeah, that kind of theme begins as a matter of character and voice. The Perkus Tooth character has that obsession with things that are opposite, with deceptions and disguises and unmasking things. And so the more he began to be interested in that stuff—the more he talked about it as a character—the more I realized it was revealing to me some of the thematic structure of the book. But you know, you try not to worry about this stuff as you go along; it's more important to commit to the more tangible things, the characters, the situations, and the places, and the scenes. The deeper thematic schemes tend to trickle in and take care of themselves.

Rumpus: It's interesting, as an Australian, that your book is an incredibly New York novel, which, you know—we kinda eat that stuff up. But we get strange impressions of New York here. Mine come from *Gossip Girl*. Have you seen *Gossip Girl*?

Lethem: I never have.

Rumpus: Okay, it makes for a strange authority on the Upper East Side, and everything looks very glamorous and awful all at once. What would you tell Australians about the Upper East Side?

Lethem: The reason I was drawn to use it is this doubleness it has. I don't know where *Gossip Girl* is set, but there's this quarter of power, Park Avenue and Madison Avenue, and Fifth, along the edge of the park, that is rightly resented and envied and treated as a kind of palace of fantasy, and Madison Avenue is literally, or is synonymous with, the advertising industry. And yet the trick to the Upper East Side is you go a bit further east, past Lexington Avenue and onto Third and Second Avenue and beyond that, and you're in a kind of Podunk zone of Manhattan, very drab and unfashionable and sometimes quite affordable; there are a lot of rent-controlled apartments there and the shops never change. There's a lot of really dull-looking businesses that have been there forever. It's one of the parts of the city that is a kind of backwater. It reminds me the most of Manhattan as I was growing up. And so these two things are side-by-side, and that's what attracted me to it as a subject for *Chronic City*, because that fact that the city is both so real and so unreal at the same time—the two things never resolve, they just interpenetrate, endlessly. That was what struck me as being useful about it.

Rumpus: You've said elsewhere that you wanted the book to have a floating feel, temporally, and it reminds me of these eighties New York movies that I've seen, *Teenage Mutant Ninja Turtles* or something. They're not dystopic, but they're sort of dark, all the dark colors are accelerated and all of that. Does your book feel contemporary to you? Does it feel like the New York that you see around you?

Lethem: It's a reality-shifted version of the middle of this past decade. The book was conceived in 2004, and I think it sort of centers in-between the two disasters, 9/11 and then the economic collapse, that defined the beginning and the end of this decade. And it's about being lost somewhere in-between those two. So, yeah, I think it's a pretty contemporary description. But New York was a virtual reality for a long time before there even was that description or that idea. It's always been a place made up by some degree of projection and fantasy. And aspiration. And so I think I'm also describing something quite eternal that's embedded in the life of the city.

Rumpus: Do you ever consider living somewhere else again?

Lethem: Well sure, I do all the time. I've kind of thrived on running away from this place as an adult. I went to California for so long and then came back, but even after that. We have a farmhouse in Maine that we go to and

I'm constantly badgering my wife to consider living up there full-time. And very few people know that I was living in Toronto for a couple of years. Most of *Fortress of Solitude* was written sitting in coffee shops in Canada. And so I like to run away from this place and then dream my way back to it in the work.

Rumpus: Is it easier to write about a place when you have some kind of immediate distance from it, or is it easier to write about a place when you're in just the milieu and the midst of it?

Lethem: I like both. While I was writing the Brooklyn books I was always sort of running back and forth to the neighborhoods and walking the streets again but then going off to an artists' colony or to Canada or wherever to write. And it's true also that with *Chronic City* I had to make these periodic forays to the Upper East Side, but I certainly wasn't sitting up there writing it.

Rumpus: Peering into some kind of upper-class apartment from the fire escape.

Lethem: Or lower-class. I've got plenty of friends who live there and they're not on Park Avenue. But my windows into the milieu of wealth come from a variety of places, accidental encounters that have come out of serving on the boards of art organizations or attending stupid benefits or gala functions. A little bit of that goes a very long way.

Rumpus: Okay. Once again, I probably won't ask the correct question, but maybe this is interesting to talk about. How culturally aware are you of your novel's positioning? It seems like people can't really review your stuff without making some cultural or contextual comment that never feels completely right, but which has something to do with hipsterism and Michael Chabon and genre and *McSweeney's*. Do you think about that?

Lethem: Yeah, I only notice what you noticed, that it never seems right. But I don't try to anticipate or control it. It seems like a very hopeless way to focus my own energy. First of all, I wouldn't get a result that I liked anyway by trying to control these things. And, it's not my job. I just write the things. But for me, for instance, *McSweeney's*: I published four or five novels before *McSweeney's* ever existed, so when I see myself called a *McSweeney's* writer I feel that particularly impoverished framework really represents someone not only with very, very little cultural perspective—for whom I guess a very new magazine has caught their fancy and it looms so, so large that it seems to define any writer who's ever appeared there—but also someone who's not even got the ability to, like, look up the dates of my publications. But in general, even when it's not quite as exaggerated or thin as that kind of remark, I'm always conscious of a much more traditional and usually much older set of frameworks that are being ascribed to me.

The simplest thing to point out—it seems almost silly to point it out—is that I didn't grow up reading Michael Chabon because he didn't exist. And we can't have influenced each other the way I was influenced, and always will be, by reading the mid-century writers who loomed so large for me, Joseph Heller and Nabokov and Barthelme and Philip K. Dick and for that matter Jack Kerouac. And then even later, as I was coming of age, I was never a very eager reader of brand new books. I lurked in used bookstores, so I didn't even know of the existence of my so-called cohort or contemporaries until very recently, and I was quite far along with what I was doing by that point. So it tends to be much more revealing of a projection on the part of the person offering up these descriptions. But I've done what I can to sort of say: Well, actually, I'm always thinking about Lewis Carroll and Charles Dickens and Graham Greene and Kafka pretty much anytime I do anything, because they were so original in forming my view of things. And then also Borges and Julio Cortazar and writers I fell in love with just shortly after that. And yet, I'll always, of course, for very understandable reasons, be talked about as if I'm kind of engaged in a permanent alliance, a project, in tandem with Jeff Eugenides, or Michael. Whose books I love, by the way. I mean, it's very honoring to be put with Michael Chabon or any number of other people whom I get compared to. But it usually does strike me as a real misunderstanding of where the energy in my own process comes from.

Rumpus: Yeah, cool. I can never even tell if it's meant to be negative or if it's meant to be congratulatory. Just what kind of comment it is. So, in another instance, it didn't hit me until I saw a number of reviews that something like the tiger is actually this trope of magic realism.

Lethem: Well, the tiger is a lot of things for me, and I can't really clear it up, or . . . Magic realism, you heard me sort of sigh, I've never identified very readily with that phrase. It describes a very particular South American movement. And the word magic, even if you just separate that bit, doesn't seem to me like what I'm doing. I do like to put dreamlike, non-interpretable, allegorical elements into my work, to draw it into a charged, strange relationship to reality. But I don't think of it as either magic or realism. I just don't think that name fits. You know. The tiger connects to me to a number of things, and is also William Blake's tiger, and Kafka has a parable about leopards breaking into a temple, and then I borrowed it, as I mention in the book, very directly from a writer named Charles Finney. He wrote a book called *The Unholy City*, and other places it came from may not even be completely conscious. It struck me afterwards that I was maybe teasing a little bit about *Life of Pi*, which is another book with a borrowed tiger. But I don't put things in in a programmatic way. I don't have like a—"Oh, I've got this book and now I'll put this tiger in and it will be such and such a thing."

Rumpus: Very exotic!

Lethem: It was native to the book. It arrived when this version of New York City arrived. So I don't have the best tools for picking it apart afterwards.

Rumpus: What's *Obstinate Dust* all about? Why did you include it, and include it the way you did?

Lethem: Well, uh. There's a gesture in this book and in my work in general. I have a tremendous interest in the impossible artworks. And you have *Obstinate Dust* in this book, but also the fjord, Noteless's sculptures. And in *Fortress of Solitude* Abraham's film is another one of these. And I really am drawn to endlessness and inapproachability in art in general. I guess I haven't really committed anything that risks making that kind of total statement, but I like to watch thirteen-hour movies and read books that don't have endings and so on. And so I'm thinking about that as a kind of gesture, in this sleepwalker's world of *Chronic City*—obviously that book, along with Noteless's sculptures, are attempts to startle people into awakeness, to do something that would actually break through. Then it's also a joke about the way unread books can become cultural tokens, or objects of fascination and energy, and I'm thinking about obviously David Foster Wallace there. But also Samuel Delany's *Dhalgren* is sort of enfolded in that, and *The Man Without Qualities* is another one. But the reference to Wallace became strange, because he died while I was finishing this book. I'd already put the reference in and then it felt disturbing to me, but it didn't seem right to take it out. It was as though I'd be erasing him in some way. So what I ended up doing was strengthening that reference. I put it in again at the end of the book to make it mean a little more, and then I felt that it would be okay. I hope it is okay.

Rumpus: I think it is. Has anybody said anything bad about it to you?

Lethem: No. But people—as much as you might imagine from the violence of Internet conversation that people will say the bad things they're thinking—people in person never do. They might hide them on some blog, but in person they never confront you. So I don't know.

It seems possible to think I'm dishonoring *Infinite Jest*, but I don't have that in mind at all. My characters are often caustic about a lot of things, the city itself for instance, and one another, and all sorts of cultural objects; for instance just to give a silly example, the way that Chase is very harsh about *Dead Men Don't Wear Plaid*, the Steve Martin movie. But if anything gets into my books at all, as an overt reference or slightly disguised the way that David Foster Wallace is slightly disguised, it's almost invariably because the thing has meaning to me, tremendous value and interest. I don't really bother putting in anything that I dislike. So people are often thinking I'm attacking stuff that I'm actually terrifically interested in. It's just that in conversation they sometimes get some scuff marks on them. That's where the pleasure of handling things is. You can't help but scuff them up a little bit.

An Interview with Jonathan Lethem

Michael Silverblatt/2010

From *Bookworm*, KCRW-FM, January 28, 2010. Copyright © 2010 by KCRW-FM. Reprinted by permission.

Silverblatt: I'm Michael Silverblatt and this is *Bookworm*. Today I'm happy to have as my guest Jonathan Lethem, whose newest book, *Chronic City*, has recently been published by Doubleday. He's the author as well of, among other things, oh, *Fortress of Solitude, Motherless Brooklyn, You Don't Know Me Yet, Girl in Landscape, As She Climbed Across the Table*, a raft of novels, essays. And he has edited, I think, the three volumes in the Library of American collections of Philip K. Dick and done an introduction recently for the New Directions edition of *Miss Lonelyhearts*, a recent essay about his father recently appeared in *Granta*, and a book by L. J. Davis was given an introduction by him in the *New York Review of Books* series. Now this book seems to be a collision between the kinds of books you've written recently and the books you started out with. Where did it begin?

Lethem: I like that description. I think it is a collision and a recapitulation of in some ways everything I feel I can do. Well, one source you mentioned was I reencountered Philip K. Dick reading the books to edit them for the Library of America. I had been relying on, you know, twenty-five- and thirty-year-old memories of his books. And it didn't ever keep me from speaking of them [laughter] with great confidence, because I read them so closely and repeatedly when I was a teenager. But I mostly hadn't revisited them. And when I did in order to put together those collections, I guess I found a new usefulness, a new relevance to my own work in Dick. And I thought I can do something with this. I can make a little more of what I know from reading him now and there were things that in fact had escaped me because I wasn't already a novelist when I read them.

So now I looked at them and I thought about how they were put together and I realized that I could absorb their lessons differently. So the reality inversions specifically, the paradoxes and the ground kind of falling away under the characters' feet, which is Dick's characteristic move, real characters in an unreal world, suddenly seemed very urgent to me. And I guess it was a lucky piece of timing because I was also experiencing a feeling that New York City had become unreal. This was in 2004. And I wanted to write about this sensation, which I guess verges on a kind of paranoid insight. But I didn't feel that it was paranoid, because I felt it was an experience of sensibility, the city's consciousness, not a belief that it was a literal, virtual reality or unreality, but that it might as well be one. And that if I could find a way to say this, I'd have a subject that felt very, very urgent to me. And Dick gave me the methods, reminded me of the methods that might be useful.

Silverblatt: That disappearance of a feeling of reality or a feeling of groundedness, it's easily achieved in the novel, but how did it come to be easily achieved in life?

Lethem: Well, I think easily might not be the word. I think the cost was very high, the cost of the present unreality in New York City, if what I'm diagnosing is meaningful, if it's true outside my own experience. I mean, I associate the start of the start of this book, the point of origin for *Chronic City*, was the fact of the re-election of George Bush three years after 9/11. And I didn't want either of those public facts to be explicit subjects in the book, but I don't mind saying afterwards that the sense of despair and the way bringing him back into office and therefore ratifying, you know, being complicit with everything that happened in the first four years, made New York City feel to me a place of great despair and great irrelevance. It was as though the emotions that attached to 9/11 had been stolen for a greater crime. And we were all culpable in a way with letting them be stolen.

Silverblatt: Well, isn't it possible that it's not New York City in particular, that wherever we've been, we've been commentators on the growing unreality or dreamlike quality of life after it was usurped?

Lethem: I'm sure that's true. And I don't imagine that any of this is a strictly local condition or necessarily as exactly historical as I'm suggesting. But as a storyteller, I had to find a home for the sensation and it had a very obvious [laughter], very native home for me. And that was the island of Manhattan, which is a kind of virtual reality. It's always been susceptible to so much projection, so much transference that the real lives that are being lived there are always under the shadow of an enormous cloud of these projections of money and power and fantasy.

Silverblatt: What I noticed about the unreality of this book, there are many prototypes that might be named for characters in this book, particularly Perkus Tooth, who is a kind of, I don't even know how to put it, culture theorist—
Lethem: Yeah.

Silverblatt: —I guess.
Lethem: Cultural obsessive.

Silverblatt: But the people I knew who were in that role, a woman in this book describes him as being a crash between Pauline Kael and Hunter Thompson. And for five minutes. But those people it seemed had a lot to say. What was interesting about Perkus to me is that he never reaches the conclusion of any of his statements.
Lethem: Yeah.

Silverblatt: He's not, strangely, a brilliant figure. He seems more like someone who's brazening it out.
Lethem: Yeah.

Silverblatt: He's lost and the dots he's found kind of can't be connected.
Lethem: Right.

Silverblatt: And so he's found an unusually featherweight friend who wouldn't know the difference between talking to Seymour Krim or Pauline Kael or many of the other resident—
Lethem: George Trow.

Silverblatt: George Trow, Leslie Fiedler.
Lethem: Yeah.

Silverblatt: The people who became geniuses of American pop culture analysis.
Lethem: Yeah.

Silverblatt: You're not even sure that these people are heroes of Perkus Tooth. He seems like many things nowadays to be a phenomenon without the reality behind him.

Lethem: I think you're dead right. It's funny, I was asked a question that disconcerted me a couple of days ago. Someone said, do you think Perkus Tooth is a good writer? And I thought about it for a second and I said I think he's no writer at all. He's kind of the raw nerve, a symptom, more than he is a critic in command of his materials. But what he stands for, and it's almost infinitely poignant to me, you know, it's not something I'm condescending to, is this sensation of the inexpressible wrongness of everyday life. He's being driven crazy by what he can't put across, but he suspects, but he can't, not only can't he put it into any kind of fully culminated essay or even broadside, because he likes to write his thoughts down on broadsides and poster them around the world. But he can't even get it across in the space of a conversation. And I think that's what's so stirring about so many people that we might meet who are in effect stuck on a paranoid theory. And Perkus doesn't have one—he has a hundred. But their spirit of inquiry can be meaningful, even when their conclusion is hopeless.

Silverblatt: Now he becomes friends with, befriends, is befriended by Chase—
Lethem: Insteadman. Chase Insteadman.

Silverblatt: And Chase was a child star in which he has been put down on a television show, berated by a crusty lawyer—
Lethem: [laughter]

Silverblatt: —type.
Lethem: Yeah.

Silverblatt: And now it's almost as if he's stepped down with Perkus because he's largely berated by someone with even less power.
Lethem: Right.

Silverblatt: Who makes him feel that he is without context. And that's what I felt that this book ultimately became about, the fact that as George W. S. Trow called it around fifteen, twenty years ago, he said in the context of no context. That that condition, contextlessness, not knowing how to put the pieces together or even where the pieces came from, has become a part of American culture so that rather than conspiracy theory, we now have creepy facts or coups that lead to no consistent theory.
Lethem: Um-hm. Yeah. Well, right. Chase is the ultimate blank slate, but

he's also, I think you're very canny to point out that his role was to be berated on television, which, you know, he was sort of a reverse Michael J. Fox. He was a fresh-faced teenage kid who took it instead of dishing it out. [laughter] But what he's gone on to do is, continued to be a minor public shock absorber. His pleasantness and his willingness to accept minor indignities and still remain charming makes him a useful token to move around. And he's very, very acquiescent. So in a way his relationship with Perkus and Perkus's ferocity towards him isn't so different from what he's already been doing. And I was very interested in thinking about the condition of an actor, someone who's learned to operate within scripts that are handed to them, whether the scripts are worth anything or not. Because it seemed to me that in a way stood for the problem of a lot of us in our, as we get through our days, that the scripts right now aren't very good. But we don't know how to step outside them very readily or at all.

Silverblatt: I'm Michael Silverblatt. This is *Bookworm*. And I'm talking with Jonathan Lethem about his new novel, *Chronic City*. In my reading of these books, I mean, once upon a time you could ask Samuel Beckett, who are your influences? And well, you couldn't exactly ask because he wouldn't answer.
Lethem: Yeah.

Silverblatt: But his influences were everything.
Lethem: Right.

Silverblatt: Now you've got Jonathan Lethem and you can fairly well look at the books and say who the influences are. It's as if the time you're writing about, but also the books you're writing are confessions of a sort that go like there were heroes once. Or we thought there were heroes once. It's hard to imagine a culture in which writers and filmmakers and artists were major heroes, but to some extent, we are smaller. The big paranoic theories of *Gravity's Rainbow* aren't going to be connectable here. That they're more shambling, benign, hypothetical, sometimes just goofy and wacky, as if the parts of Pynchon that were historical or drew fear from huge historic sources now, in the absence of context, only the wackiness is left.
Lethem: Well, your description is very seductive, Michael. I mean, I can't completely agree, but I understand that that feeling is evoked in a way. But I don't see the conclusions of my project exactly as you describe. Either the aesthetics, I guess what you'd call the magpie aesthetics or the transparency

of influence, something I've always been very eager to describe, seemed important to me to describe. Nor the fates of the characters. I think in each of the apocalyptic books I've written, that's most specifically *Amnesia Moon* and *Chronic City* and then, in another sense, a realistic apocalyptic book is *Fortress of Solitude.* The characters are bereft of large historical, theoretical devices by the end. But they're turning just at the end to extremely intimate operations of empathy and connection. Which isn't to say they renounce those theories that helped crack the façade open. It's just that once it's been cracked open, it's not replaced with a new regime. [laughter] It's replaced with intimate action, with behavior, I mean, this is going to sound awfully Norman Rockwellish, but it becomes a matter of neighborliness. To whom are you immediately adjacent when the veneer is stripped away? And what do you say to them? And where do you go from there? And I think Chase is a fairly hopeful figure at the end of this quite sad series of unveilings at the end of *Chronic City.*

Silverblatt: This is a huge subject right now and it's very confusing to me, to be honest. Because it used to be as an intellectual, one's indifference to mere people was prized. Now when people, for instance, write about *Bookworm,* they say that what they like about it is that it wants to present the figure of the intellectual as an empathetic figure. And empathy seems to be both the new path and the buzzword. And it's not quite clear yet where it will take us. A good ten or twelve years ago when someone like Susan Sontag would have said empathy is a mug's game.
Lethem: Yeah.

Silverblatt: Empathy is the thing resorted to by people who don't know anything. But now empathy may be the last chance we have to rekindle a human connective spirit that is the spirit of literature however, whatever literature is to become.
Lethem: Well, you know, I don't always think of the enterprise on such apocalyptic terms, despite [laughter] the fact that I write, sometimes write apocalyptic books. I'm pretty interested in what's going on right now, even if the results are inconclusive. I think people are actually really looking for the nourishment of intellectual experience. And very, very excited to connect with books when they do. But they're not sure what it means. I think you're right to say that people aren't sure where it's going to get them right now.

Silverblatt: So let's go back to *Chronic City.* Because I see this again as using oblique or interesting strategies that we end up with a hotel for dogs put together by rich people who've got concerns for animal rights and into this hotel homeless people have managed occasionally to crawl. Now on the one hand, this would seem like the most basic kind of social satire. That we're taking care of our dogs better than of our humans. And yet the book keeps dodging the attempts to make that kind of easy point. It seems to me that the book really wants to keep shifting to the side and say, yes, yes that is inhuman, but couldn't we just take this as a comic foible of our last years and move past it? Yeah, it's horrible, but somehow we've got to find a way to sneak the homeless into the dog hotels if that's—

Lethem: Right. [overlapping voices] I like that description a lot, Michael. I think that in a way what you say is true that, I mean, a writer, a social satirist looking for ways to exemplify the hypocrisies of contemporary, economic disparities, the unacknowledged class system, it's almost impossible not to find easy targets. It's so near at hand that you only have to turn your hand and it falls into your grasp. And so I couldn't be terribly interested with looking for those kinds of symbols. Instead I wanted to talk about what happens when you and I and everyone we know lives with them right in front of our face, two inches from our face, and yet they're not spoken of. It's the denial, it's the fact that symbols of this kind of reality proliferate wildly in books and in life. Every day you open the newspaper and you find another allegory that would have made Karl Marx's or Roland Barthes's jaw drop. [laughter] And yet we all go on reading that newspaper, we all go on moving through our days, and this is the subject of the book is what we do instead, what we think about and how we behave in the absence of that conversation. When everything is as exaggerated and hysterically out of whack, and yet somehow the machine tumbles forward, day to day, and we wake up and take our positions inside it. Well, that's an interesting subject and an elusive one. The social satire is not elusive at all. All you have to do is take it to the ultimate degree and then you've got John Carpenter's *They Live* or *Idiocracy*. And then you've said it as stridently as you possibly can. You've made the cartoon of reality into a cartoon and then it can be shrugged off again. I was trying not to shrug it off. I was trying to inhabit it with these characters. It's the fact that we all live in a situation that is patently absurd in many ways, and yet we have no opportunity to take it lightly. We're living real lives. It's tragic.

Silverblatt: So in other words, it's life within a cartoon, but the cartoon is horrible, and so we have to find a solution to the problems that have turned the horrible into a cartoon. The out-of-whack became the wacky. And now we have to cope with wackiness somehow and the solution to that or part of it is empathy?

Lethem: Well, I think it's negotiated in. I don't mean to fall into the trap of saying there can be a kind of a non-ideological space. But you do the best you can. You meet what's before you. You try to solve the cartoon conundrums that come your way with as much real sincerity as you can bring to them.

Index

Wood, Natalie, 55
Woods, Tiger, 59
Woolrich, Cornell, 13, 35
Wyoming, 3

Yaddo, 81, 92
Yates, Richard, 44, 110
You Don't Love Me Yet, xi, 133, 135,
    138–39, 141–44, 146, 147, 148, 149,
    155, 159–60
Young, Neil, 56
Youngman, Henny, 58

9 781604 739725